A History of an Ordinary Man

Colin Potter

Published by New Generation Publishing in 2023

Copyright © Colin Potter 2023

The author asserts the moral right under the Copyright, Designs and Patents Act 1988 to be identified as the author of this work.

All Rights reserved. No part of this publication may be reproduced, stored in a retrieval system or transmitted, in any form or by any means without the prior consent of the author, nor be otherwise circulated in any form of binding or cover other than that which it is published and without a similar condition being imposed on the subsequent purchaser.

ISBN: 978-1-80369-793-2

You can follow the author on Twitter: @ColinPo66924747

www.newgeneration-publishing.com

New Generation Publishing

This book is dedicated to

Wendy for always being by my side giving me love and support

And to my Mam & Dad for giving me life and love

Contents

Introduction 1
Chapter 1: The Journey Begins 3
Chapter 2: Infant and Junior School Years 16
Chapter 3: Learning to Labour 22
Chapter 4: "Jack's got more say over yer now than yer fatha" 29
Chapter 5: Late Teenage Years and a New Job 40
Chapter 6: My Old Man 57
Chapter 7: Wouldn't It Be Nice? 67
Chapter 8: Talking about Mam 85
Chapter 9: Life Goes On 88
Chapter 10: What About Loyalty? 99
Chapter 11: Hoping for a Change of Luck 122
Chapter 12: Being a Full-time Student 149
Chapter 13: From Blue to White-Collar Work 159
Chapter 14: The 'White-Collar' Blues – from the Frying Pan into the Fire 169
Chapter 15: Time to Dig Deep 174
Chapter 16: 'Give a dog a bad name' 180
Chapter 17: A New Chapter Begins 189
Chapter 18: A Period of Establishment 201
Chapter 19: As One Door Opens, Another Slams in your Face! ... 218
Chapter 20: 'From me to you, to you to me' 230
Chapter 21: Explaining Another Crisis of Capital 239
Chapter 22: Attempts at Leading a 'Normal' Life 249
Chapter 23: Me and Old Age 263

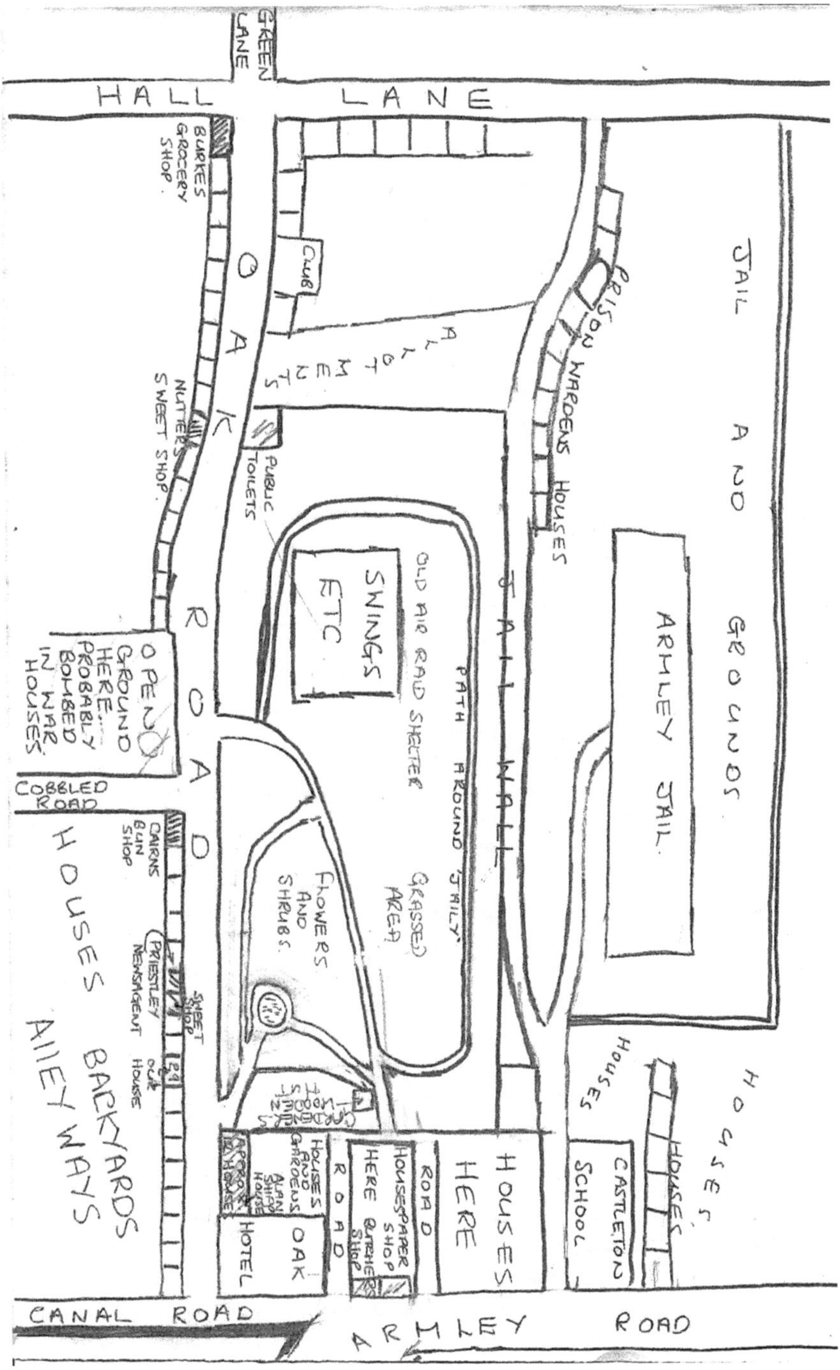
GREEN LANE
HALL LANE
BURKES GROCERY SHOP.
CLUB
OAK ROAD
ALLOTMENTS
NUTTERS SWEET SHOP.
PUBLIC TOILETS
PRISON WARDENS HOUSES
JAIL AND GROUNDS
OLD AIR RAID SHELTER
SWINGS ETC
PATH AROUND 'JAIL'
JAIL WALL
ARMLEY JAIL.
OPEN GROUND HERE. PROBABLY BOMBED IN WAR HOUSES.
COBBLED ROAD
CAIRNS BUN SHOP
HOUSES
FLOWERS AND SHRUBS.
GRASSED AREA
PRIESTLEY NEWSAGENT
SWEET SHOP
OUR HOUSE
BACKYARDS
ALLEYWAYS
HOUSES AND GARDENS
ROAD
HOUSES PAPER SHOP HERE
BUTCHERS SHOP
OAK HOTEL
HOUSES HERE
CASTLETON SCHOOL
HOUSES
HOUSES.
CANAL ROAD
ARMLEY ROAD

(28/11/1979)

I travel back and forth through life
Seeing good, bad, joy and strife
Things I see are clear as glass
And even though the years may pass
Each one to keep alongside the other
To take out at any time
But until then they are under cover
Out of sight but not of mind

A sort of time traveller I am
Pleasing where I go and when I can
Doing no harm when I sit in a chair
Just close my eyes and go anywhere
Off to a time in years gone by
As if when my eyes are closed I fly
Alas I land it's my minds eye

(30/4/1981)

He's a man, he's a child
He's so meek and so mild
And so easy going as butter
But stood on the corner
Just like young Jack Horner
Mi'self I think he's a nutter

(30/4/1981)

Oh to be a boy again
And doing this and that
We'd be out then be in
To see what's on the telly
Don't put your head near Dad's feet
Just in case they're smelly

(26/5/1981)

I see the faces, as I know I always will
But is it fair that only I can see?
And, if they say it does not matter
Then my time and writing is all for me

I would like to think it is of interest
As anyone's life should be
To people who are close to them
But then it's only me

Your faces will stay with you
As mine will stay with me
And will yours really matter
As mine have done to me?

Introduction

I must have been around the age of twenty-two or three when, having gone through a period of reflection, I decided that I would write about my life thus far. Having bought an A4 hard-backed writing book, I began to set out the memories that I had of my early childhood, along with those of my first home.

However, after writing no more than several pages, that initial urge – with all the thoughts and reflections that fed into it – lost its momentum and fizzled out. At the time this was probably due to the day-to-day matters of simply living one's life, but the idea remained in my head, just like a seed that was waiting to one day germinate and grow.

In late 1979, I had recently become an adult orphan and that must have stimulated another period of reflection because, over two to three years, I began yet again to 'play' at writing about my life and background history. I had kept the old hardback book and began to transfer this initial writing onto loose-leaf paper that I kept in a ring binder. I added to this, but not greatly, and with that record by my side now, I have to confess that I wrote no more than ten pages over this period. I would never have earned a living as an author.

However, added to the above, I drew three separate sketches, with the first showing the fireplace within Oak Road, my first home, along with sketches of a 'flat iron', a 'peggy tub', a 'scrubbing board' and the old tin bath. The second offered a bird's eye view of Oak Road and the immediate places of interest that are mentioned in the following pages. The final one was merely a plan of the room layout at Oak Road. The sketches were an attempt to capture on paper things that are now consigned to history, yet they are still memories in my mind's eye. To illustrate further that I was a little more productive at this second biographical attempt, I have also retained original copies of four poems, along with the dates that I wrote them.

This second attempt at a biographical history proved more sustained though, yet again, after a relatively weak attempt, the seed was once more pushed back further inside my mind. In retrospect, this was fortuitous because to conclude my biography then would, I feel, have offered nothing more than a simple descriptive account of significant and relevant matters that had occurred in my life. By this, I mean things began to change for me around the above date of 1981, in that I slowly began to consider how my life and the lives of others in society were being shaped by things that were to some extent beyond our control.

I became the proverbial 'sponge', in that the more I read, the more I wanted to read. The driving force behind all of this was the need to know the truth about matters and, in an attempt to get at this truth, I kept asking 'why'? At the time of writing, I am aged sixty-nine and two years ago, with that biographical germ beginning to grow once more inside my head, I sat down and began in earnest to reflect upon and write my life story.

One of the reasons for writing this book is for my immediate family, because it will hopefully serve them as a legacy of how I lived my life, why I held certain opinions about particular matters and what has impacted on my life to shape these opinions and the exercising of certain choices. One theme throughout the following pages is that all of our lives are inevitably shaped by social forces, factors and influences, and many of these that shape our lives also impact upon other people and as a consequence they are mutually shared across both communities and society as a whole, though this is not always – indeed if at all – recognised.

With many of us not aware of such forces, factors and influences, and their interconnectedness to other people, we tend to wander through our days as if they will never end. Perhaps, at some later stage in life, some people might vaguely ask themselves, "What is life all about?" as if they are about to come to the end of what, for them, has been some kind of mystery tour. And so, in the following pages, there are certain junctures when I try to elucidate on certain social issues and events simply because we don't live our lives in a social vacuum. Though there are times throughout the book that I may seem critical about the lack of understanding from people, I hold complete faith and optimism in the power of human agency.

The book inevitably begins with my early life and, as much as possible, continues in a chronological form, chronicling what I have chosen as being key matters and events. Even for my early years I have, at times, attempted a retrospective look, trying to place my own history into that time period with comments about the politics and socio-economic circumstances of the day. Throughout the book, the experiences and events that I have personal awareness of are often juxtaposed with these external social forces, factors and influences, so as to place my life into a much clearer perspective and, at the same time, offer a more thorough and analytical contextual view. In order to carry this out, I have drawn on my experience as a blue and white-collar worker, an academic and forty years as an autodidact. It is my clear and unambiguous conviction that, to understand the life of any individual, you have to have an understanding of the social history in which they lived.

Chapter 1

The Journey Begins

The former historic township of Armley is now a district in the west of Leeds and, like much of the rest of the city, it grew in the period of the Industrial Revolution. Built in 1788 Armley Mills, now the Leeds Industrial Museum, was then the world's largest woollen mill and, along with the later development of other mills, Armley was then a major contributor to the economy of Leeds.

To accommodate the influx of the new industrial working class in the late 18th century and onwards, there took place the building of many thousands of back-to-back houses. These were built in the cheapest way possible, so their construction was usually substandard and their configuration did not allow for adequate ventilation or sanitation. Around the mid-19th century, this form of housing was deemed unsatisfactory and a health hazard and the passage of the Public Health Act 1875 permitted municipal authorities to ban the building of new back-to-backs. However, Leeds City Council opted not to enforce the ban, due to their popularity with builders and residents, and continued to construct them until the 1930s. My first home was a back-to-back house located on Oak Road and one of the prominent features, as one stood looking out of the front door, was Leeds Prison.

Built in 1847, the façade of Leeds Prison, with its black stone structure, was an imposing sight as it looked towards Oak Road. Armley Jail, as it was locally known, was still a place of execution right up until the 1960s. In between Oak Road and the jail was a small park which incorporated sections devoted to tarmac paths and flower beds, some small lawned areas, a playground and a large open playing field leading up to the high perimeter jail wall. This is what we called the jail field or *'jailey'*. It offered local kids somewhere to play in contrast to the rows and rows of back-to-back houses that stood behind Oak Road, with their cramped cobbled streets.

Oak Road itself ran from Armley Road for about seven hundred yards until it merged with the bottom of Hall Lane and the start of Green Lane. It had only been a few years since the end of the Second World War and the surrounding streets were interspersed with several spaces where houses had been demolished. As a child it was my understanding that these houses had fallen victim to the bombing raids during the Second World War.

In effect, in 1941 Leeds was heavily bombed as part of the overall blitz faced by the country. Just a few hundred yards away on Armley Road were two local engineering companies, Wilson & Matheson and Greenwood & Batley's. Both operated as munitions factories during the war and were no doubt targets for enemy planes on that night in 1941.

Just as many women had done during the war, my mam had worked in the former factory as part of her war effort. Looking again from the front door of the house, over at the very top left-hand side of the '*jailey*' behind the playground, was a section of raised ground that was now grassed over and this marked the place of the now obsolete air raid shelters.

On 23 November 1950, 29 Oak Road became my first home, shared with Mam and Dad and my older sister Gillian. I was born at St. Mary's Hospital, Greenhill Road, Wortley, a building that had been built in 1871 as a site for the Bramley Union Workhouse accommodating 220 inmates, but in 1948 it became known as St. Mary's Hospital. Over the years Gill has always maintained that there was another child born before her, but it either died at birth or shortly thereafter; I was never able to confirm this with either Mam or Dad.

We lived in Oak Road until approximately 1961, when I would have been about ten or eleven years old. The house itself was a typical 'two up and two down' back-to-back, with a very small garden to the rear that also incorporated the brick-built outside lavatory. We were lucky in some respects because, as I recall, unlike other back-to-back houses of this time, we didn't have to share the '*lav*' with any of our neighbours.

Entered from the front door, the kitchen/dining area was for us the main living area of the house. It had a Belfast pot sink in the corner with a cold water tap screwed to the wall above. At the side of it was a two-ring gas stove with no grill or oven and alongside this was the coal fire situated in a '*black lead*' fireplace, which also had a traditional oven that was used for cooking and baking. Such fires incorporated a 'damper', which allowed you, when baking, to move it in order to transfer the bulk of the heat across and under the oven before going up the chimney.

The coal bucket sat on the hearth plate at the side of the fireplace along with the poker. The metal hearth plate measured about four feet long and twenty inches wide and was made out of metal that was perhaps a couple of millimetres thick. There was a coloured enamel pattern on one side and, along with the fender surround, their main purpose was to prevent any coal or spark from the fire causing damage. At times, with the coals burning red, we would make toast by holding a slice of bread over the fire with a bread knife. Care had to be taken not to drop the bread into the fire or burn your hand by holding the knife too close to it. The fire was also used to boil the kettle if we had no money for the gas meter.

More often than not, the table that we ate at had newspaper over it, acting as a proxy tablecloth. When this was dirty then a new 'tablecloth' would, in due course, appear to take the place of the previous one. The floor covering was what we commonly referred to as *oil cloth* or *lino* (linoleum being the proper name), and in front of the fire hearth was a *clip rug*. Such rugs were simply small clippings of old clothes prepared and sorted into rough colour groups and punched singly through a piece of harding (sacking), which in effect was the backing of the carpet.

There were two bedrooms and, as I recall, the one at the front of the house (i.e. over the kitchen/ dining room) was hardly used, due to it being severely damp. When it was used it would have been our Gill who slept there. I recall that most of the time we had a double and a single bed in the main bedroom, where we all slept, me with Mam, and Dad with Gill in the single bed. On cold winter nights Mam and Dad's 'big' coats would be used as extra bedding and laid on top of each bed and such cold and frosty nights would see us waking up in the morning with ice on the inside of the windows.

The living room had an upright piano, harking back to the days when families made their own entertainment, though I don't believe either Mam or Dad could play. There was also a three-piece suite and a bookcase. It was the custom among working-class folk that the living room, or 'best room', was used very little. And on only one occasion do I remember my dad being in there talking to one of his mates. Most of the family living was done in the kitchen-cum-dining area.

Whilst a working-class family's meals might have varied throughout the week, Sunday tea was quite a common affair, with folk having some kind of tinned meat sandwiches, such as spam, crab or salmon, followed by tinned fruit and cream. Following Sunday lunch, if there were any leftovers (e.g. potatoes, meat and veg), then it would be heated up in the frying pan and served up for Monday's meal. This was commonly known as having a *fry up* or *bubble and squeak*. Daily breakfast was just as it is today, with possibly porridge, cereal or toast.

It was a longstanding custom in working-class families that the main breadwinner – still in this period usually the man – should be kept well-nourished and hence Dad would have something like bread and butter with some offal, such as tripe (cow's stomach), chitlings (pig derivative) or pig's trotters. The fact that it was offal is something that I learned much later in life.

That wasn't to say that the rest of us went without; I guess it was perhaps unaffordable for us all to have the same as Dad. Like most if not all of the folk in our community we were poor, and as a young boy I remember that, at one stage, we only had three chairs to seat us around the kitchen table. Being the youngest, I was left to stand and eat my meal whilst the others sat. At times, if I offered to complain about this, Mam or Dad would simply say "stand and grow", a constant comment that for a long time perplexed me. Only years later did I realise that it was just another way in which folk would make light of a situation that was not ideal.

Given our house had no bathroom, another common feature of this period was the use of the tin bath. Water would be boiled in pans and put into the bath, which would be in front of the kitchen fireplace so that especially in winter we didn't get cold. Unlike the plethora of soaps, shampoos and deodorants that adorn bathrooms today, quite often we simply used a big block of Fairy household soap for washing our hair and bodies and, at times, I would see Mam use this in order to get the collars on Dad's work shirts clean. When bathing was finished, the bath was sometimes emptied with a jug and poured down the sink, or on other occasions either Mam or Dad would drag it to the front door and simply empty it into the street.

Washing clothes was done with the 'peggy tub' and wash board. This was a real chore and so, in the midst of every mother's week, there was a preferred designated 'wash day'. The washed clothes were ironed with the flat iron that was place on a 'clean' grate by the coal fire until it reached a reasonable temperature for ironing the clothes. Of course, the trick was also to keep the flat of the iron clean so as not to dirty the clothes. Certainly by the late 1950s and early 60s the development of consumer goods saw the widespread use of electric irons and twin-tub washing machines – it was still too early for automatic ones. I remember all too well touching an electric plug on the skirting board in the kitchen and getting an electric shock, which looking back went some way to illustrating the poor state of repair in many of these houses.

Coal was delivered once a week and all houses like ours had an external coal grate (approximately 400mm square) in the pavement by the house wall. They were often secured to the cellar by a chain to prevent them from being stolen or getting lost. The *'coal man'* would simply lift the grate out and empty the specified number of sacks down into the cellar. Once the coal man had gone, people would come out of their homes and sweep the bits of coal and dust down into the cellar and then replace the coal grate.

On one occasion when Mam and Dad were out, my older sister, Gill, persuaded me to go into the cellar to fill the coal bucket. I was reluctant due to the fact that there was no electric light in the cellar and, once down there in the pitch black, she shouted something scary down the cellar steps, which frightened the living daylights out of me and caused me to scurry up the steps to safety.

The coin-operated gas meter was also down in the cellar and this needed the periodic insertion of what was commonly known as a 'bob', or a shilling piece (ten pence in today's money), in order for gas to be released for us to use. Mam and Dad often recited an amusing little ditty which went like this... *"If tha Bob doesn't give ar Bob that bob that tha Bob owes ar Bob then ar Bob's gonna give tha Bob a bob on't nose."*

Also, at times when it was felt that the metre was about to 'run out', a shilling was inserted to keep the gas flowing and they would say *"glad you dropped in bob, I was just going out"*. Strange what one remembers as a child, but the frequent utterance of such comments means there are some things you don't forget too easily. Such meters were not dissimilar to the token meters of today, although one difference then was that around each quarter the *'gas man'* would call to empty the meter and, following a calculation of cost for usage, if the monetary content in the meter was over the usage cost then a money rebate was given. This was always very well received.

Our house was of course rented, and I remember one particular day when the *'rent man'* was due to call. Mam had me hide with her in absolute silence behind the door as we ignored his knocking. At the same time if, as people would do, he peered through the window to see if anyone was in, he would be unable to see us. I realised much later that she hadn't got the rent and wanted to avoid seeing him and perhaps getting a load of grief.

In retrospect, I guess that like most other people in our community, we were relatively poor and the quality of our housing was even poorer. Yet life was very happy and, just like all children as a young boy, I accepted both my immediate and wider surroundings as normal and merely 'just the way things are'. This was the extent of my world and, generally speaking at the time, I had no reason to doubt that this was indeed the way that everyone lived.

Mam and Dad were married on 22 December 1934. I'm not sure if Oak Road was their first home or not, but when Dad enlisted in the Army on 24 April 1940, the address on his enlistment papers was 29 Oak Road. As I now look back at our material surroundings years later, although they were grim people would actively cling on to them and, in times of adversity, Mam and Dad would always say that no matter how bad things get the main thing is to *"always keep a roof over yer head"*. For communities like ours, the home might not have much to offer in a material sense, but it was better than being homeless.

Upon his discharge from the Royal Artillery, Dad resumed his pre-war employment with Walkers on Kirkstall Road. I am not too sure about the date when he left Walkers, but my first recollection of him working was at Dixon's Mill towards the bottom of Armley Road (later to become Simpson & Solk). Here he worked as a boiler-man, often starting early (5.00am – 5.30am) as he was responsible for operating the coal-fired boilers that heated the factory.

When I was aged about eight, during the school holidays he would allow me to spend some time with him in and around the factory. The rear of the factory backed on to the Leeds and Liverpool Canal, just below a set of locks, and when the mill was quiet, usually on Saturday mornings, Dad and I would spend an hour or so on the canal bank fishing. It was here where I was taught how to fish and I recall these early ventures saw us using very basic tackle, such as straight canes with no fishing reels but some fine thread from the mill tied to the end of each canes with a bent pin on the end. Nevertheless, we still caught fish, much to my delight and, for many years to come, I continued to enjoy fresh water fishing.

One particular day, me and another mate had gone to the barber's situated by the bridge over the canal, opposite where the Armley Industrial Museum stands today. After coming out of the barber's, we ventured onto the canal towpath and were peering over into the water looking for fish when I lost my balance and went into the water feet first.

I got out okay and, when I got home in my soaking clothes, I sneaked into the living room and changed into clean clothing. Being young and naïve, I thought it would be okay to leave my wet things behind one of the sitting room chairs. Now, as I said earlier, the living room was hardly used, but either the same day or the next Dad had one of his mates visit and, of course, he took him into the 'best room' for their natter. He somehow found my wet clothing and I had to explain what had happened. Dad very rarely lost his temper and, despite him no doubt thinking what might have happened, he was forgiving without imposing any sanctions on me. In fact, Dad was a very mild-mannered man and seemed to get on with almost anyone.

I remember him becoming quite friendly with the lock keeper who lived in the house by the canal locks opposite the factory gate, where we sometimes fished. The role of the keeper was to operate the locks for the barges that went up and down the canal. I didn't realise it then, but this was a job that was in the final throes of its existence. On at least one occasion, the keeper gave Dad some vegetables out of his allotment.

One of the chaps that also worked in the mill was a young man called Fred Tasker. Now, at this point in my life, whilst I had occasionally travelled on a train, bus and a tram, I had never been in a car or on a motorbike. Fred owned a BSA 650cc Golden Flash motorbike and sidecar and occasionally, much to my delight, he would give me and Dad a lift home. Fred also lived in a back-to-back house (Eleventh Avenue?) just off Green Lane, close to Wellington Road and the Crown Cinema.

Friday was Dad's payday and apparently at some point there was some entrepreneurial person at the mill gates selling sweets to the workers as they 'clocked out' and headed off for home, so Dad would often bring some home for me and Gill. Although I probably wasn't ten years old at the time, I recall that one of the downsides of his job was that, every so often, his role as boiler-man meant that, on a weekend when no one was working and the boilers were cold, he would have to go in to work and, in turn, clean each of the boilers out. This is a memory that stayed in my mind and I always remember him complaining to Mam about this dusty, dirty and very onerous task.

Years later, I became aware that industrial pipework of this period was insulated with asbestos cement and in the 1980s I remember reading an article about the long-known hazards of asbestos. For example, a Factory Inspector's report in the 1890s spoke about the potential hazards of working with asbestos. All this pre-dated The Health & Safety at Work Act, 1974, so I very much doubt that even a basic face mask to prevent the inhalation of asbestos dust would have been available to Dad. Probably, at the very best, he would have had a handkerchief over his mouth and nose, amounting to no protection at all.

Pubs and working men's clubs were still the focal point for meeting friends and socialising. Mam and dad tended to use the Albion pub, which was just above Dixon's on Armley Road. They came home one night and, from what I gather, Dad had been involved in an altercation with someone else in there. He was never a loud-mouth or a brawler and, as a consequence, they started using The Oak Hotel pub, which was at the bottom of Oak Road opposite the railway bridge on Armley Road.

Dad was a good singer and would often get up in the pub, as others did, and sing with the traditional pub piano for accompaniment. His favourite song by far was Danny Boy, which probably stemmed from his army days in Ireland.

At one point in time, Mam took up a part-time job as a cleaner at what was then the Shell Mex offices, Leeds city centre adjacent to the old West Yorkshire bus station. She would start work quite early in the morning but be home in time for Gill and I to go to school. On occasion, when old diaries were thrown away, she would bring them home for me and our Gill to draw in. Next door to us was an old lady called Mrs. Lindley and Mam kept an eye on her, offering practical help such as giving her a cooked meal.

I suppose Mam would not accept any payment for her help so every Sunday Mrs. Lindley would give me and our Gill one penny each. If on a Sunday I was *lakin'* out somewhere on the 'jailey', I often heard Mam shout from our front door, and at the top of her voice, "Colin, your Sunday penny!" I would drop whatever I was doing and run home for my penny. This way of summoning children was the norm. For example, the Oxley family used to live two or three streets behind us and I often heard Mrs. Oxley shouting at the top of her voice for Michael, Tony or Peter, who would be out playing somewhere. She had a right pair of lungs on her!

However, back to the penny, which in those days was worth something to children. Further up Oak Road towards Green Lane, there was a shop commonly known as Nutters. Besides the usual *'penny tray'*, offering a dazzling array of sweets, you could also buy a glass of pop, such as Tizer, Jusoda, Dandelion & Burdock and Shandy. There were several glass sizes, depending on how much you had to spend. You could also take back empty glass pop bottles and get a penny or two as the refund.

When I look back, the community had a wide range of shops that, overall, reduced the need to go into 'town' (i.e. Leeds city centre) to shop. Within easy walking distance were two fish shops, butchers, a Co-operative store, Cairn's bakers, a couple of newsagents, a barber's and Burke's Grocery Shop. This shop was on the junction with Oak Road, Hall Lane and Green Lane and Saturday morning Mam would go to Burke's for the bulk of the shopping. Sometimes, through the week, if we ran out of something and had no money, we would go to Burke's for it and *'tick up'* until the following Saturday, when Mam would then not only get the groceries for the following week, but at the same time pay for what we had *'ticked up'* during that time.

At times, we would also venture onto Wellington Road, which offered a bigger range of shops. I recall a clothes shop that Mam always referred to as *'the murder shop'*. I always felt a tinge of fear going in because it was my fearful belief that someone had been murdered in there when, in effect, years later I realised it got its name due to *'murdering'* the prices.

Not all clothes were shop bought as we often had jumpers to wear that mam had knitted for us. On occasion, when we had outgrown these, Mam would unpick the jumper and get us to unravel all of the wool and roll it up into one or more balls, all depending on the amount of reclaimed wool. She would then re-use the wool by incorporating it into the knitting of some new item of clothing. I had a school friend who wore socks that had been knitted by his Mam.

Mam and Dad also used to buy clothes through a club or check trade and I recall a lengthy period whereby each Friday evening (that being pay day) an agent called Mr. Ramsden would call to collect a payment and take the opportunity to ask if we needed any further items of clothing so as to perpetuate the debt. There was a shop for this business, which was on the fringe of the city centre, and at times we would call in there to get certain items.

This was a period when there were many other families in our community doing the same thing, utilizing the practice of such clothing clubs and check trading, which often became a habit. This was reinforced by the house-to-house agents, who were adept at persuading clients to keep their "account open continuously", so that in many cases more money is leaking away weekly in this way than can really be spared. Though clubs and check traders might have been cheaper than *'the big shops'*, and let people take items away for a small down payment, the overall quality of the materials was poor. And so it went on, with no access to significant sums of money and using a system of juggling finances, families ended up living week to week.

Though the aforementioned piano in our living room was not the focal point for our family, sing song music was heard at times in the house due to a rather large valve-type radio set that sat on a shelf on the kitchen wall. Then, at the age of about five years old, we began renting a television set, which was not uncommon around this time as many families rented items such as washing machines and television sets. Our 'telly' had a 14" screen and was set in a cube-type polished wood cabinet.

I believe we were one of the first amongst our immediate neighbours to get a telly and, on particular one summer's teatime we were watching the children's *Lone Ranger* Western series when, all of a sudden, my mam alerted us all to the fact that Keith Smith – a lad about three years older than me from a few doors up the street – was standing on the wall at the other side of the road peering in through our sash windows in order to get a glimpse of the telly which was positioned in the kitchen area.

As a family we would often group around the telly on an evening, or at the weekends, viewing whatever was on. What contributed to this family cohesion was the fact that there was just the one coal fire and, on cold evenings, to sit for any length of time in another room was simply not appealing and neither was it cost effective to light the fire in that room.

Another contributing factor was that my bedroom would have been no different to that of other kids in our community, in that it held little attraction. It simply had an *oil cloth/lino floor*, a bed, a chest of drawers and possibly a small wardrobe. Today, most homes have central heating, carpets throughout and kids have a telly in their bedrooms, quite often with numerous other electrical gadgets and toys. One downside to this is that, in some homes, there may well be the fragmentation of family life. For example, if you didn't want to watch the same programme on the telly as your Mam and Dad then that was tough. In contrast, today's child would probably go to their bedroom and watch something they prefer, or play with any one of a multiplicity of toys and electronic gadgets.

When I was old enough, I was allowed to go with my mates most Saturday afternoons and watch the matinee at the Crown Cinema on Wellington Road at the end of Green Lane. The admission was seven old pennies and for this we got to see a number of cartoons, along with a short black and white comic movie, such as Abbot and Costello or The Three Stooges. The main film would be some action movie such as a Western. The place was jam packed with kids and all inhibitions were set aside as en-mass we would laugh out loud at the comedy and then, in the main film, collectively be in uproar with alternating booing of the bad guys, and then wild cheering for the good guys. On one occasion, after seeing a Zorro movie, I came out of the cinema along with a number of other mates all fired up and enthusiastically imitating the masked hero by throwing our coats over our shoulders with only the top button fastened in a cloak-like fashion. Off we went running down Green Lane, chasing each other with pretend swords attempting to make the mark of Zorro (i.e. a 'Z' on the forehead of the 'weaker swordsman').

I honestly couldn't say how many friends I had, but much of our playing or *'lakin' out"* took place on the *'jailey'*. For some of the reasons given above, unlike kids of today, children were not 'home centred'.

There were a number of other back-to-back houses on Armley Road, just below Greenwood and Batley's, and the kids from our area would have periodic soccer matches against a group from down the road. Kids taking part were of all different ages and teams often numbered in the region of about twenty a side. Similarly, we would play a derivative of rugby, which we called 'touch and *pass'*, though I myself preferred soccer. Another regular pastime was running races. This might be short sprint races or long distance, which meant running around the large perimeter path that encompassed the big grassed area close to the wall of the prison. Once again, the *'competitors'* would be of different ages, but we gave it our all. Games of cricket were also held, which at times saw us compete once again with our peers from down Armley Road. At times, the ball would be a proper cricket one, or *'corkey'* as we called them, and when one of these was used and you had no leg pads then you learned to be adept at either hitting it or just simply getting out of the way. Other games played were 'kick out ball', hopscotch and 'stretch'.

'Stretch' was played with a either a penknife or sheath knife, which were both quite popular at the time and frequently carried. However, unlike today, such knives were not seen as potential weapons. The game of 'stretch' began with you and your opponent facing each other with both feet together. Then, with approximately a distance of a metre between you, you then took it in turns to throw the knife to the outside of your opponent's feet. Where the knife stuck in the ground meant that your opponent had to stretch his or her leg to that position. The ultimate aim was to get your opponent to stretch so much that they went off balance and the one left standing was the winner. As the reader has probably guessed by now, one of the downsides of this game was the potential for your opponent to throw badly, which meant you had to be alert and move your foot pretty sharpish if need be!

One other game was called *'piggy'*. This comprised of a short piece of wood, about 4" to 6", and a longer piece about 18". The lengths of both depended on what could be found. The smaller of the two would have both ends shaved with a knife so that they were spindle-like. Taking it in turns with the large stick, we would hit the smaller one on either end, thus flipping it in the air and, before it hit the ground, it had to be hit again, directing it to some predetermined target in the distance. The first to reach the target was the winner. I am not too sure of the origins of the name of this game, *'piggy'*, but it may date back to days gone by when pigs were driven to market using a staff or stick. Looking back, we seemed to be always *lakin'* out, playing some game or another.

At some stage, we might be playing competitively at marbles, or *'taws'* as we referred to them, and then in autumn it might be 'conkers', having first of all tried to toughen them up by placing them in the oven for a short whilst. *Whip and tops* were still quite popular along with *yo yo's*. We often played street games, such as *'kick out ball'* and *hopscotch,* where the pavement *'flags'* would be used to chalk things out. At times we would *'raid'* toilet yards in order to get cardboard and paper from out of the bins so that we could light a fire, usually in the very top right-hand corner of the *'jailey'* itself.

On other occasions, we might visit a quarry and try to catch frogs/toads and tadpoles, sometimes bringing them home in *jam jar* bottles. For a time, a number of us became interested in train spotting and, having managed to get a train spotter's book, we would go off collecting steam train numbers and, hopefully, those with names that, when seen, would prompt a shout to go up from someone: "*It's a namer!*" There were various train spotting booklets you could buy with the aim of collecting as many train numbers and names as possible. To aid us in our quest, one popular place we went to was the *'the rec'*, which crudely was and still is between Oldfield Lane and Whitehall Road. There was a railway goods yard here along with a track that also carried other trains into the city centre.

Pastimes seemed to come and go and at one stage wooden *bogeys* became hugely popular. All my mates seemed to have one and there would be races to see who could go the fastest. I am not sure whether I had asked for a bogey or had given some grumble at not having one, but one summer's evening Dad brought one home that he had made for me at work. I was over the moon and remember carving on it the name '*Hi Ho Silver'*, which was of course the name of the Lone Ranger's horse.

Bonfire night brought with it a gradual build-up of excitement several weeks prior to the event, when we would go out *'chumping'*, with the wood being stored somewhere close to where the fire was going to be. Sometimes we would go *raiding* the wood piles gathered by other community groups and, in turn, our wood was also *raided,* which all added to the fun and excitement. Bonfire night was an ideal time for some people to get rid of some worn-out household items, such as carpets, chairs etc.

Oak Road wasn't appropriate to have a bonfire and the event tended to take place in one of the many cobbled stone back-to-back streets. With the bonfire piled high on the night itself, the residents in the houses on the opposite sides of the street and adjacent to the fire would cover their sash windows with cardboard or something. This was done so that once the fire was lit the heat from the fire would not crack and break the glass. Casting my mind back, bonfire night was something of a community event, with both young and old joining in. Within several weeks of bonfire night, passing minds would turn to the next big event: Christmas.

On the run up to Christmas, I remember quite well that several of us would often go carol singing on evenings. As we went door to door, we would give it our all as we sang in their entirety four or five carols at each house. When we had finished our repertoire of carols, we would knock on the door, and with a bit of luck, receive a few *'coppers'* for our efforts.

On Christmas morning, Gill and I would have a pillowcase waiting for us either side of the fireplace. Along with whatever toys we had, there was always an apple and orange each, along with a new shilling piece (worth twelve pennies then, but in today's money 10p). I remember one year getting a six-foot x three-foot snooker table, which brought many good hours of recreation.

From a relative early age (perhaps five or six years old) we used to have a one-week caravan holiday at Filey and, though one year we went to Skipsea, there seemed to be a consensus from the four of us that Filey was better largely because the beach was sandy and not mostly pebbles. For a young boy, the holiday journey just in itself was a huge adventure. We would catch the bus into the city centre and to the train station, suit cases and all.

I remember that on at least one occasion we boarded the train at the Central Train Station, which before it was demolished stood halfway up Wellington Street. For me, there was always a real excitement as we boarded the train, and this was heightened as the steam train chugged out of the station, gathering momentum and, at times along the way, we could hear the loud tooting of its whistle. For a young boy who had never been in a car and only occasionally travelled on a tram or bus, this was a fantastic experience.

When we finally arrived at Filey station and got off the train, we were greeted by a small number of local children of about ten or twelve years old, each with a small wooden hand cart. The children would eagerly ask passengers if they could carry their bags and/or suitcases. I remember one year Dad put the cases on such a cart and the young boy walked with us, pulling it along the fifteen or twenty minute walk to the caravan site. The young boy had no set fee and relied on whatever people thought his services were worth. I believe Dad gave him a *'tanner'* (six pennies or two and a half pence in today's money), which in the mid-1950s was a reasonable amount.

The caravan was on the Collins site, which is still operating today, and my recollection is that we went there over a number of years for our holiday. The caravan was a converted railway carriage with all the wheels removed. It had a kitchen, living area and two bedrooms. Lighting and cooking was by Calor gas with the internal lights having a mantle and needing to be lit by a match. There was a chemical toilet outside which was periodically emptied by staff on the site.

On one occasion, when we were all walking down the pathway to the beach, Mam found a silver half a crown (worth thirty pennies or 12 ½ p today), much to everyone's delight as this was a decent sum of money. Thereafter, whenever we ventured down that same path, Mam would always say *"eyes down"* and as kids Gill and I would eagerly scan the path for any money.

Even today, I enjoy going to Filey and have fond memories, probably because it has changed so very little. The Star pub, where Mum and Dad liked to have a drink, still stands and so does the Brigg Cinema (though it is now a restaurant), where Gill and I once went to see the new epic Western *The Big Country*, starring Gregory Peck.

One year, when I was about eight or nine years old, we took with us to Filey a mate of mine by the name of Alan Shipp who was part of a large family who all lived at the bottom of our street. Towards the end of the week, my mam noticed that his coat pockets were bulging and she asked him what he had got in them. To everyone's surprise, they were full of all sorts of ice cream and sweet wrappers and, upon seeing this, Mam probed further, asking why he was keeping all of these used wrappers. His simple reply was that his father had told him before he left home that when Alan returned from holiday he wanted to see what he had spent his money on! Over the years, Mam and Dad would often recall this event with much hilarity.

This was a period when going on holiday meant going to some seaside resort or another. Just like kids today, we would enjoy playing various bat and ball games on the beach, building sand castles, running in and out of the sea and, if we were lucky, having a donkey ride. Today, some things are different, but still the same. These holidays were very happy occasions and it is my understanding that they were financed by Mam and Dad taking out a loan and then paying it off over the course of the year in time to take out another one the year after.

Chapter 2

Infant and junior school years

Castleton Junior and Infant School was positioned on Armley Road and was only a several hundred yard walk from our house. There were times when my school shoes had a worn-out hole in one or both soles, so Mam would make a cardboard inner piece to act as a cover. This *new insole* was cut from a breakfast cereal packet with great precision and wasn't too bad at all – until you had to walk in wet weather! I don't remember too much about my time in the infants section, but there is one thing that has stayed with me over the years.

When I was four years old, I went into hospital to have a reasonably sized fatty lump – known as a Lipoma – removed from my stomach. Following my discharge, I had to take iron tablets every day and shortly afterwards, when I started infant school, I was given a tablet at *'milk time'* by the teacher. For some reason I always found the tablets difficult to swallow and once broken they tasted absolutely awful.

On one occasion, I remember hiding one behind a radiator, but another pupil saw this and snitched on me to the teacher who promptly took me to the Headteacher's Office. Upon hearing of my misdemeanour, she gave me a toffee to chew on. Now, these toffees were for special occasions – that is, they were given out in assembly to those pupils whose birthday it was, so initially my first thoughts at being given a toffee probably were, 'Yeah, this is good'. Anyway, once I got chewing this toffee, she popped a tablet in my mouth and instructed me to chew that along with the toffee. Simply not a nice experience! My time in the infant school was rather uneventful. However, in contrast and upon reflection, it seems that in the junior school some teachers seemed to act as if teaching working-class kids was some kind of penance that had been imposed upon them.

I was probably only in the first year when I took a dislike to a teacher called Mr Zoltie. He would rant and bellow at the class and I remember going through a period at home whereby, just as I was ready to leave for school, I would feign feeling sick. Eventually, my mam realised something was wrong and must have spoken to the school because, all of a sudden, I was moved to another class.

There was one occasion when our class being taught by Mr Lyons had ended and we went straight into break, or *'playtime'* as we called it. Another lad and I realised that we had left our books in the classroom so we sneaked back into the school. As we tentatively approached the classroom door, Mr. Lyons saw us and roared out, "What do you boys want?"

I meekly replied, "Please sir, we want us books."

He bellowed loudly back, "Us books? Us books? There is no such thing as us books!"

At the time, I was completely perplexed and my immediate thought was 'Corse there is. I can see 'em.' It was years later that I realised he was correcting my poor grammar. The teachers all appeared to speak well and seemingly descended from another world on the school each day.

Much of my memories of junior school are about games and sports activities. At playtimes we would often play cricket or soccer with a small tennis ball. Sometimes, a couple of lads would link up by putting their arms around each other's shoulders and walk about singing, "All in for Cowboys an' Indians. No girls allowed!" As was usually the case, the two became three, four, five and so on until it was felt that the numbers were sufficient to have a game of Cowboys and Indians. We passed through a phase whereby a number of boys came to school with metal *segs* in the heel and sole of their shoes or boots. These metal *segs* were essentially hammered in to the heels and soles of boots and shoes in order to delay them from wearing out, but much to our delight they also proved great for us to run in and then slide for some distance on the surface of the playground.

As I passed through my years in the juniors, I became quite adept at a number of sports. As a member of the cricket team, I was a pretty useful bowler and on one occasion, as was customary after a school match, the result of the team was announced the following morning in assembly and I got a mention for taking seven wickets for five runs. The teacher who took us for sport was called Mr Jowett and he took time out once at *'playtime'* to show me how to spin the ball. This only happened on one occasion yet this, albeit small, recognition that I had some ability clearly gave me a lift and left me with lasting positive feelings. As a bowler, I was a slow-to-medium pace with a very good line and length, so he thought that I might improve further if I could develop my ability to spin the ball.

I also proved to be a pretty good sprinter. I was entered into the Leeds Schools Athletics event at Temple Newsam and won a couple of certificates and a badge. I proudly kept a programme from the event that had my name printed inside and it is still with me today. No doubt our frequent *lakin'* of games such as cricket, running and football on the *'jailey'* contributed towards some level of my sporting development.

I also played in the school soccer team and was overjoyed when one day the teacher told me that my name had been put forward to have trials for the Leeds City Boys Junior Team. The trials were held one Saturday morning at the team's ground on Oldfield Lane, Wortley. I remember so well Dad saying to me that he would give me a *'tanner'* for each goal I scored. Well, I managed to score two goals, but disappointingly never progressed any further, although being in the Castleton school football team brought some additional benefits.

The school received a regular allocation of free tickets to watch the Leeds United home games and these were given to those boys in the football team that wanted to go. Leeds played in the old Second Division then, but I eagerly received my ticket and went to the games with several mates. Don Revie had been bought from Manchester City and I remember seeing him play when he was the player/manager. It would have been during the late 1950s that I also remember seeing Brian Clough in a Middlesbro team play against Leeds. I became a firm fan and I would go to as many home games as possible.

Academically, I guess I was about average. After sports my favourite subject was history and the teaching of these lessons focused very much around famous battles and Kings and Queens. At home, as a family we had a variety of books, some of which I still have to this day. Along with a number of various novels, in particular there was an encyclopedia, *The Complete Works of William Shakespeare*, a science/technology book titled *See How It Works*, *The Bible in Pictures*, *100 Years in Pictures* and a volume of six books, each one covering the years of the Second World War. Like many people that have little materially and then worked hard for what they have got, Dad was particularly upset on one occasion when a friend of his returned the collection of Second World War books with one or more of them having being damaged.

One of my outstanding memories of junior school was my failure to pass the 11-Plus examination. This meant that a number of my school friends who had passed the exam were viewed as more academically gifted and left Castleton Junior School in order to complete their education at West Leeds Grammar School, whilst the remaining pupils, including myself, were scheduled to attend Armley Park Secondary Modern School.

Secondary schooling came about in 1944 when the government introduced a tripartite system, which also included technical and grammar schools. Depending upon the aptitude and levels of attainment in junior school, a child would be channeled into one of these schools, but the tripartite system was not without its problems and critics, chiefly because it tended to perpetuate class inequalities, with middle and upper-class parents proving more able to get their children into the schools that produced the best results. Hence these types of schools also tended to reinforce class subcultures; that is to say schools ensured that children from a certain social-class background remained within that social class and learned social behaviour suited to that class.

In response to this, it is worth pointing out that nobody expected working-class kids in communities that I grew up in to excel academically. Throughout all of my school years, I can honestly say that in the home, community or in school I never heard the word 'university'. Upon leaving school, working-class girls would traditionally go into jobs such as tailoring or retail, the boys would take up some form of blue-collar manual work that would either be unskilled, semi-skilled or skilled. Even more importantly, like so many others, I individualised my own failure regarding the 11-plus exam and to a certain extent that remains with me still today.

Around this time, that is 1960-61, things were also happening at home. Dixon's Mill, where Dad worked, had closed down and he had gone for a similar job elsewhere. However, rather than being a coal boiler system the company in question was using gas boilers. This was a sign of the times that, in the sphere of work, things were changing for him. He didn't get the job and eventually he went to work with British Rail as a *'Ganger Man'* and essentially this meant he was working with a number of other men laying new rail tracks and repairing the old. Just around the same time, our home in Oak Road and the surrounding back-to-back streets became part of a Local Authority Slum Clearance Order. In response to this, Dad made an application to British Rail and was successful in getting one of their houses across the city in the East End Park area.

I believe we moved in the summer school holidays of 1962 because I don't remember continuing to attend Castleton Primary School after moving to our new home. I had told Mam and Dad that I wanted to go to Armley Park Secondary, where I would at least be with my mates and others that I knew, rather than go to a new school in the East End Park area. My sister had already attended that school, but had left for the world of work.

Looking back, the paternalism of British Rail – in owning property and renting it to their workers – is something I find quite interesting about that period. Indeed, 2 Pontefract Place, which was at the side of the railway bridge on Long Close Lane, became my second home. As was often the case in such houses, on the day we moved in the sash windows in the main bedroom had to be removed from the frame due to the fact that the double wardrobe could not be taken up the staircase. Hence rope (probably the washing line) was put around the wardrobe and someone hung out of the bedroom window and hauled it up from the *ginnel* below and in through the opening in the frame.

The house had at some stage been a corner shop with the shop window and door on the lane itself. Similar to Oak Road, the house was a back-to-back with the front door taking you out onto a *ginnel* or passage and right in front of you was a high wall separating the front of the house from a steep railway banking.

There were approximately 8-10 houses in Pontefract Place, with only several at the other end having a very small garden as the railway wall weaved away from these houses, offering a little more space. The yard hosting the four toilets for these houses was roughly in the middle and, for us and everyone else, it was a short walk away up the passage. It wasn't uncommon to be using the loo only to have some neighbour attempting to push the door open not realising it was being used. Just like Oak Road, Pontefract Place was part of a large working-class community covering Cross Green, East End Park and Richmond Hill, all of whom were largely housed in similar back-to-back properties.

Our new home was essentially a 'two up and two down', comprising of a sizeable kitchen-cum-dining room with a door in the corner taking you down into the cellar. The kitchen had a cream enamel sink top with just a cold water tap fastened back to the wall. We had a gas cooker, which may have been left in by the previous tenants, but nevertheless the old two-ring gas stove was discarded. In this room was also the coal fire set in a '*Yorkshire Range*' wrought-iron fireplace. I remember Mam being really pleased with this extra feature as it apparently offered her improved cooking and baking facilities.

The sitting room had been the shop area with the external bottom section of the big window sporting what appeared to be a very large sheet of hardboard over it to protect the glass window from breaking. At the side of the window was what had been the shop door, which opened out on to Long Close Lane. There was no coal or gas fire in the room to afford any kind of heat.

Access to the two bedrooms was via the door in the kitchen. The top of the stairs opened into the main bedroom, which was above the kitchen area. There were two more doors in the main bedroom, one leading into a smaller bedroom above the old shop area and the second leading up into an attic space that could be used as another bedroom. Just like Oak Road, the house had no hot water, no bath and an outside toilet, still I remember Mam expressing that it was a much better house.

Once again, the main living area for us as a family was the kitchen-cum-dining room and, consequently, this was the setting for the rented television we had brought with us, still with its 14" black and white screen. Colour TVs were still a few years away – well, at least they were for us.

A couple of hundred yards down Long Close Lane, on the right-hand side of the road, was a Conservative Club and again just below this was the Hampton Public House. There were random corner shops spread about, but at the bottom of Long Close Lane was Upper Accommodation Road, with its small yet varied number of shops. At the top of Long Close Lane was Pontefract Lane and this ran from York Road at one end through to East End Park at the other. On the lane was the Princess Cinema, along with a good number and range of shops. Supermarkets were very much in their infancy and the one I recall my Mam shopping at occasionally was Willis Ludlow's in the Town Centre, close to the market.

Such things as car ownership and indeed post-war mass consumerism were still developing slowly and, therefore, many communities such as ours were definite entities, in that they still lived, worked and socialised together. Whereas families might watch the telly together at times they were not necessarily home centred. My bedroom was perhaps the norm for a child at that time, in that it had a bed, chest of drawers and *lino* floor covering. This was still a period in which there was a rigid division of labour in and around the household, with a clear distinction between what was held to be a man's and a woman's work.

Mam and Dad seemed to soon settle into their new environment and made friends, adopting the Hampton Pub as their local, whereas I on the other hand, being an eleven year old who was still reasonably shy, found it difficult to make new friends. Around this period my mam was working with a woman who lived several streets from us, and she had a couple of sons, one of whom was around my age. I was duly introduced to Alan Abbott, the lad in question, and I began knocking about with him and his mates.

Things were fine for a number of months. However, one lad that I found rather unpredictable became very aggressive towards me on one occasion, so I withdrew my friendship from them. Upon hearing of this, Mam spoke to Alan's mam and, though he subsequently called for me on several occasions, I said I wasn't playing out and instead I kept myself busy *lakin'* with my toys'. I had lots of soldiers' and would spend hours setting them all up and then act out mock battles. Drawing and painting were other interests that kept me busy. Once I started at Armley Park Secondary School I occasionally met up with mates from there at holiday times.

Chapter 3

Learning to Labour

The 1870 Education Act did not provide free or universal education, though it did allow for the establishment of school boards where there was a clear educational need. Armley Park School was erected as a Board school and opened on 27th September 1900. It initially catered for approximately 400 infants on the ground floor and 780 mixed scholars on the first. The fact that the school yard was very small makes one wonder how so many children could have been catered for.

Stanningley Road is routed right in front of the school, with Cecil Road to the right of it. Though Mam and Dad must have had some concerns about what they might have viewed as my social isolation around where we now lived, they allowed me to attend Armley Park Secondary School. They applied for a free bus pass on my behalf and each day I would travel back and forth from Cross Green, through the city centre and on to school. My first recollection of schooling here was not a happy one.

It was in the first few weeks of the new term and our class was having a French lesson. Mrs. Smith, the teacher, for some reason called me out to the front of the class. I clearly must have done something to annoy her, but with no explanation, as soon as I got within striking distance of her, she lashed out slapping me fiercely on the side of my face. I remember the tears coming to my eyes, but even more so I remember never again having any inclination to learn French. I had suffered her physical abuse, which I never had experienced from my parents.

Some children that complained to their parent's about being punished at school got the stock response, *"Well, yer must ah been doin' summat wrong to start wi."* After a time you went home and simply didn't mention that you had been on the receiving end of corporal punishment, particularly from someone whose role was to nurture your education. This wasn't to be my last experience of what was euphemistically regarded as 'corporal punishment'. Secondary Modern Schools primarily taught their pupils certain traits, such as discipline, punctuality, obedience to authority, along with other things in order to make for a placid workforce.

I don't wish to over-simplify matters, as there is clearly a degree of complexity around educational achievement. The scope of this book doesn't allow for a sociology of education, but there is some merit in exploring a number of issues. At the point of early child development, the Intelligence Quotient (IQ) does not differ across both class and ethnicity, so we have to consider other causes for inequality in educational attainment.

Having set aside nature as having a major role, there is merit in looking at some aspects that feed into the social construction of educational inequality. The starting point has to be an acknowledgement that capitalist societies are marked by an inequality of conditions. All of our teachers were middle class and some, I would argue, have different expectations of the learning capacities that children from different social classes have. In practice, with some teachers having labelled working-class kids as underachievers, they would teach them accordingly. With the gradual passage of time, children would become aware that there was little or no confidence in their abilities, fail to see the point in trying, and hence simply they wouldn't achieve their full potential and so fail to attain good grades. Thus teachers and others with similar negative views felt vindicated and such outcomes can be seen as no more that a self-fulfilling prophesy.

It was the case then, and it is still the case today, that there is a sheer inability – caused by types of poor and inadequate housing – to offer reasonable private space for children to study and do homework. Private wealth is the foundation of capitalist societies, which offers the ability for some parents to buy private education and pass wealth on to subsequent generations via inheritance or gifts. Since the first British social mobility study by David Glass in 1949, followed by subsequent studies, education has consistently been identified as a key factor in perpetuating social-class inequality and life chances.

Closely connected with upper-class education is the significant benefit brought about by the influence of 'social connections' in perpetuating inequalities from one generation to the next. Private education leads to inequality of opportunity, yet such education remains a key and legitimate factor of life and, whilst we are all encouraged to believe in equal opportunities, it is very much the case that the opposite tacitly remains not only a fact of life but a principle in law. It is indeed the case that some children from less well-off backgrounds gain access to public schools through scholarships, but those few that do 'make it' serve only to act as a 'safety valve', thus perpetuating the illusion of equality of opportunity and so, for those left behind, there is the individualisation of failure.

As eleven to thirteen year olds, part of our curriculum included swimming lessons. I'm not too sure who the teacher was, but once a week our class would troop up to the swimming baths just off Armley Town Street. My recollection of these lessons was that, for most of the time, the teacher would bellow out both his instructions and pour scorn on those he perceived as not listening or who happened to be performing badly.

On one occasion, he was teaching us all how to dive and as a class we were all told to gather around him at the side of the deep end of the pool.

In turn, he would call an individual out and, after some basic instruction, they were expected to attempt to dive into the pool. All well and good, but as the person began to jump and lift their body off the ground, the teacher used an arm to push back the person's legs at the point of the shin bones in order to propel them downwards in to the water. After a very short time of watching some of the disastrous results, we were all filled with trepidation at the prospect of it being our turn. Luckily for me and some others, he aborted matters and put us all back to swimming in the pool.

The school's Deputy Head was an elderly chap by the name of Mr Hinchcliffe. I say elderly, but I viewed him as a man in his late fifties or older. On occasion, when talking, spittle would form and this would cling desperately to both his top and bottom lip as he spoke. It was almost like a short musical string straining but never actually breaking away from either lip.

This chap taught us for technical drawing classes and had a very short and volatile temper. It wasn't uncommon for him to suddenly throw the blackboard rubber at some hapless boy who he viewed as not taking notice. On one occasion we were attempting an isometric drawing of a large nut and bolt in his class, this being perhaps five to six inches long. For some reason, someone got the giggles and the next thing we knew was Mr Hinchcliffe grabbing the bolt off the desk and ferociously throwing it in the direction of the culprit. Instinctively bodies dived out of the way as the bolt was propelled through the air and hit the back wall of the classroom with a thud, leaving a hole in the plaster.

One of the more reasonably progressive teachers was Jack Berry, the P.E./Games Teacher. Just like in junior school, I continued to enjoy my football, cricket and athletics, and I eventually played in the school Intermediate side (eleven to thirteen year olds) and later in the full senior side. Our home games were held and played on Armley Park and there were usually a very small number of parents that came to watch.

On one occasion, much to my delight and surprise, I saw that my dad had turned up and was standing on the touch line in his boiler suit and work jacket. It was a great feeling and I felt several inches taller as I played my heart out. I think it was the first and only time that he was able to be there. On reflection, I now realise how difficult it must have been for him to leave work early and make the journey to the ground by bus.

At one time, the school must have had a rugby team as the shirts we played in were thick rugby ones with black and orange hoops and large white collars. Jack Berry was also in a pop group called the Four Statesmen, so I was suitably impressed. Being a young adolescent, I was gradually getting into pop music and the sub-culture that was emerging with it. At one stage, Jack Berry taught our class for music lessons.

One day, much to our delight, he brought his electric guitar in and, at one stage in the lesson, he proceeded to play out the extended intro of the latest Number One hit single by the Beatles: 'I Feel Fine'. Whilst this in itself was interesting to listen to, overall in fairness I don't recall learning much at all about music.

Although I had failed my 11 Plus examination, Secondary school kids were able to take the 13 Plus examination, which meant that if you passed this you could go into a GCE stream within the school and work towards your General Certificate of Education exams. If you failed that then you would do the lesser Certificate of Secondary Education exams. I ended up passing my 13 Plus and was duly placed into a first-year GCE class.

Initially, I was quite pleased with myself – and who wouldn't be? At times we all like to feel a sense of achievement and, anyway, I enjoyed most of the subject areas at school, apart from maths, which I found rather dry and boring. Oh, and of course not forgetting French! One of the things prevalent at school – clearly mirroring society – but not noticed by us as pupils or indeed possibly by our parents was gender inequality.

In particular, the clear divide here was that the girls would have cookery and needlework classes further on down Armley Road, at what was locally referred to as the 'Clock School'. In turn, the boys would troop up past the library on Armley Town Street to some buildings where we were taught metal craft and woodwork. Towards the end of my first year in the GCE class, I remember being told by a teacher that, though my class work was okay, I needed to improve in relation to the homework that was being set.

Given I had no mates in the East End Park area, I really had no excuses. I remember saying that I simply couldn't be bothered to either do work or revise at home and, consequently, for the following year I was placed in a CSE class. As I reflect on this moment in time, now I can only think that I was beginning to resent school and see it as having little value.

By this stage, I had been subject to the cane on a number of occasions and even had the slipper – the preferred form of corporal punishment – from Jack Berry. I have a clear memory of being caned on two separate occasions by different teachers, Mr. Pearson, our history teacher, and Mr. Hinchcliffe. Both instances stand out because, after the initial verbal rebuke from them as they raised the cane above their heads and then delivered it, I could see the clear and evident temper and loss of control in their faces. Mr. Hinchcliffe failed to strike me across my fingers and hit me instead across the palm of my hand, which subsequently became bruised.

I came from a loving home where physical violence was so rare that, in fact, I can't remember ever being struck by my mam or dad. The reader can be forgiven in thinking that I was some kind of tearaway. I wasn't a fighter, so I don't recall being punished for that. Being unable to remember any reason behind my being punished, I can only conclude it was for minor disruption within the classroom, but on each occasion, I believe that within me there was increasing resentment.

Many years later as a parent myself, at one particular school Governors' meeting, one parent member spoke actively in favour of corporal punishment, in that as far as he was concerned it had certainly stopped him from misbehaving therefore it should also stop others too. In turn, I said that it had only made me feel resentment to those physically punishing me and hence it had a negative impact on my educational achievement. Being a young teenager, I started to become interested in youth culture instead.

I remember asking my mam and dad if I could have a studded leather jacket only to be told no. Near the school bus stop at the bottom of Armley Town Street there was a shop known simply as the Overall Shop and they sold *'drain pipe'* jeans in a range of colours and with different colour piping down the side of the legs and around the pockets. I used to gaze in the window and think they were really cool, though I never got a pair until several years later. The best I achieved was a 'donkey jacket', which at that time were worn by workmen and these were an all-black industrial material with a plastic waterproof covering over the shoulders. I was able to sneak about half a dozen studs in the back above the bottom seam, presumably without Mam and Dad noticing. Along with this, at one stage I also sported a pair of black leather Tuf boots, another item of men's work-wear and to some onlookers I must have looked like a young manual worker.

I was simply marking time until I was able to leave school. However, though my academic achievements had dipped, there was one after school event I looked forward to that was organised by Jack Berry and the girls games teacher every Friday between 4.00pm – 5.00pm, and this was an informal gathering where pop records were played on the school's large record player and, in turn, the sound was emitted through the school's huge music speakers. Our youthful inhibitions were temporarily suspended as we did the 'Twist' to songs such as 'The Locomotion' (Little Eva), 'Let's Dance' (Chris Montez) and 'The Twist' by Chubby Checker.

Being at this time about fifteen years old, I still enjoyed sports and especially football when one day Jack Berry the games teacher approached me saying that he had put my name forward regarding trials for the Leeds City Boys Senior Team. The words had just been uttered by him when he promptly followed up by saying, "But you won't get anywhere." My face changed from one that was beaming to a look of sheer confusion. He quickly explained that it wasn't that I might not be good enough, but simply that the selectors presiding over the trials would be more inclined to pick lads from their own schools.

I eventually passed through several trial stages and the highlight for me was, one evening after school, when the remaining trialists all met at

Elland Road football ground. I was ecstatic because I was still watching Leeds United when I could. We used the same dressing room as the United First Team and then had a session in the club gym, followed by a kick about in the empty car park. At the end, the selectors called out the names of the boys going forward to the next trial, but disappointingly I wasn't one of them. I remembered what Jack Berry had said to me, though in reality I acknowledged that I probably just wasn't good enough after all.

Perhaps my favourite academic topic was history and, as a fifteen year old, one of my last memories of school came from a history lesson. Mr. Pearson was our usual teacher, but on this particular day we were being taught by a male student. It was either in this class or it had been on another occasion that the student teacher broke out in a fit of temper declaring to the whole class something to the effect of "this is the worst school I could have been given as a student placement!" I have never forgotten that and his damning declaration to pupils and I wonder what kind of a teacher this particular student became.

Well, I might have annoyed him somehow that day as, for some reason, he walked up between the desks to where I was sitting and slapped me across my face. Clearly I was deeply upset and I yelled out something to the effect that I was going to get him. A day or so later we had a games lesson on Armley Park, which in effect was a game of football. Whilst Jack Berry the games teacher was there, I was surprised to see the student and Mr Stoker, a young teacher that took us for wood and metalwork. As the game got going, the reason for the latter two's presence became evident. Jack Berry refereed the game and the two teachers went on to the opposing team and proceeded to 'sandwich' me and dish out excessive physical treatment as and when they could throughout the game, which I took without any form of retaliation.

As the time to leave school for the world of work grew closer, Mr Stoker took a number of us to a smallish engineering company near Whingate junction. As we were being shown around, I remember that the sheer clatter and noise of the place quite simply put me off. One thing for certain was that no one wanted to work at Blakey's, a factory close to the school that made metal *segs* for nailing into the soles and heels of boots and shoes, which had a very bad reputation.

A careers officer visited the school and the impression was something like… 'Well, what job do you want to do?' Looking back as an extremely naïve potential young worker about to leave school and search for a job, the UK economy was in a pretty good shape. The employment market was buoyant and youth unemployment just didn't appear to be an issue. At the time, I recall my dad suggesting that I might want to go into printing, but in essence I don't remember having any clear idea about the type of work I wanted to do. This said, for some reason I applied to work for British Gas, which was then a nationalised utility.

When I attended the exam for prospective applicants at their offices on North Street in Leeds, the hall was filled with many other would-be hopefuls too, but in reality I struggled with the psychometric test and, in due course, I was notified that I had failed the test. Then for some reason I applied for the job of apprentice plumber at a firm called H. Gahan & Son, Nowell Lane, a street on the right at the top of Lupton Avenue, Harehills.

I remember attending on my own and being interviewed by the owner, Jack Gahan, and a chap from his offices called George Holleran. Following the interview, I was told that I had been successful, but as I was leaving Jack Gahan made a comment about me getting my hair cut before I started work for him. My hair was probably just over my collar, quite short compared to many lads who were mimicking the members of pop bands with their very long hair. Getting my hair cut was no issue at all because, for me, I was entering the world of work and as such I harboured no thoughts of disappointing my new boss.

When I broke the news to Mam and Dad about my success, they said, "You've done the right thing, luv, getting a trade behind yer." I have often reflected on their response and understood that, in essence, what they meant was that the types of work on offer for working-class lads was some form of blue-collar work, so unskilled, semi-skilled or skilled. I am sure they felt a degree of pride and relief as I was about to embark on a five year apprenticeship for the latter. And so, at the age of fifteen years old, I left Armley Park Secondary School in the summer of 1966. Some twelve years later, it finally closed as an 'educational' institution and became business premises.

Chapter 4

"Jack's got more say over yer now than yer fatha"

Being three years older than me, my sister, Gill, had left Armley Park School the year prior to me starting. Her first job was in a city centre shoe shop as a sales assistant. In February 1964 she married Bernard Poole, a lad from Middleton. Their first home was a small flat, 5 Hill Street at the end of Tempest Lane, Beeston. Their first child, Michael, was born later that year in April. Around this time in1965, Dad left the railway and went to work at Clark's Dyers, Kirkstall Road. Before being demolished some years later, Clarke's was situated on a site that gave way to a new Charlie Brown's auto centre and behind there was the RSPCA.

I recall on one occasion Dad bringing home from work some old stationary, primarily because of the old postage stamps that were attached. I was still collecting stamps and moreover, yes, I was still using our Gill's nail varnish when I ran out of stencils to stick the stamps in my album!

Dad was a grafter and once he came home limping badly. He explained to Mam that whilst busy working he had felt something give in the back of his leg. I remember that for days and possibly longer he limped badly to and from work, rather than spend time on sick. On another somewhat humorous occasion he arrived home late one evening explaining that he had fallen asleep on the bus and, instead of getting off at his normal stop, some several miles later he woke up when the bus had reached the terminus point at Cross Gates. So, he had to get the bus back from there.

Mam also had a change of work when she left her cleaning job at Shell Mex on Eastgate and got a similar job at Sumrie Clothes on York Road opposite the White Horse Pub and about two hundred yards up from what is now a probation office at the bottom of Lupton Avenue. Due in part to the decline in clothing manufacture, Sumrie was taken over by Executex in the late 1980s.

It was time for me to begin my working life too. Mam and Dad had bought me a Swiss army knife, which I ended up keeping for many years. This type of knife, complete with the multi-purpose blades, was widely seen as a starting point for my tool kit as a young apprentice.

Jack Gahan had inherited the plumbing firm from his father, and I was informed along the way that at that time it was the second biggest plumbing firm in Leeds. It was an ideal firm for a budding young apprentice plumber as it undertook a diverse range of work, including small repairs, domestic central heating (that was really taking off at the time in middle-class homes), and also new work.

Steve Sunderland, another lad, had also been taken on along with me. Indeed, the firm had a good spread of apprentices across the age range of fifteen to twenty years old. My apprenticeship was to be five years and I was told that, after a suitable time period, I would become what was officially regarded as indentured (So a formal Deed of Apprenticeship would be drawn up). The firm had a number of office staff, with Eddie Richardson (who had previously *'served on the tools'*) being the general manager, Wilf the van driver, Frank the Storeman, and a couple of clerical workers.

Steve and I were told that we would each spend a week in turn working in the stores with Frank. First thing on a morning was often busy, with plumbers producing lists, wanting all types of different fittings from the stores, and both Steve and I were told that we needed to familiarise ourselves with the range and types of fittings commonly being used so that we could *'talk the talk'*. We were both given a Yorkshire Copper Works catalogue of fittings and told that we must learn it both thoroughly, and from front to back, so as to be aware of not only the range of fittings but how they were referred to. I still remember to this day, for example, an ½" 12 is a elbow, a ½" 63 is a bent tap connector, a ¾" 64 is a bent cylinder union, and so on.

Our wages were a *'week in hand'* and payday was to be each Thursday, with my first wage being around £3.16 shillings. The abolition of The Truck Acts didn't occur until the early 1980s, so all workers would have been paid in cash. On my first pay day, Eddie and Frank came walking towards me and I looked expectantly at the brown pay packet in Eddie's hand, and they too noticed the hint of excitement from me.

Eddie said something like, "Yer know it's custom, don't yer, that yer give yer first pay packet back t'lad's so that they can have a drink on yer?" I froze, not knowing what to say, but dutifully nodded in agreement whilst at the same time thinking, 'What will my mam say when I go home with no wage?' After a few seconds, they put me out of my misery and both broke out in laughter, with Eddie thrusting the pay packet into my much relieved hands.

Another resident in the *'shop'* was Jim Ingle, a plumber by trade, but he spent the majority of his time welding in the 'shop'. Jim would bend, shape and weld a lot of radiators specifically for the bay windows on certain heating jobs. He was probably in his forties and had a really dry character, besides also working part time as a bar man in the Dog and Gun pub on York Road.

It was the lads' job to go to the shop for the plumbers at *snap time,* so I was often sent over the road to the corner shop for sandwiches. On one occasion Jim said he wanted a fried egg sandwich and, in a serious manner, instructed me to tell the lady in the shop that he wanted the egg so runny that when he bit into it the yolk would run all over his chin! This was a wind up, of course, akin to other wind ups, such as "Go t'shop, lad, and git mi a bubble for mi spirit level."

I was quite deferential at work, acknowledging that I was merely an apprentice and keen to learn from the tradesmen around me. I now had the status of being a young worker who at times reveled in the fact that I came home with dirty clothes in the same way that my dad did. Starting times were 8.00am and I was always punctual, even if I had to get a bus to a particular job. When working with other plumbers I was keen to learn and enhance my understanding of the trade. However, as with life in general, things don't always run smoothly.

There were two old plumbers at the firm in their early sixties and they carried out the small repair jobs. Albert Lindley was a short bow-legged be-spectacled and inoffensive plumber, but Wilf Pennel constantly went on about how things were better years ago. One day he was telling me that, when he was a lad, if there were any blocked toilets, the plumbers used to instruct him to take his coat off, roll his sleeve up and shove his arm down the pan to unblock it. "We dint have plungers like now. That's how we did it then."

Sod's law came into play when, some time after Wilf had been bleating on about this, we were down amongst the back-to-back houses behind Compton Road doing small repairs when one of the jobs we came across was a blocked outside toilet. I could see the delight in Wilf's face as he looked firstly down at the blockage and then at me, gleefully instructing me to "Tek yer coat off, get tha sleeve rolled up and stick yer arm down't pot and git that cleared."

I tried to reason with him as much as I could that we had the toilet plunger with us, so why not use that? In the end, Wilf gave me an ultimatum. "Either git yer arm down't pot or go back t'shop and tell em why I sent yer back!"

Quietly, I left him and made my way back to the shop, thinking that "well, that's it. I've refused to do as I'm told so they'll sack me". With trepidation I walked into the shop and looked into the office. Inside were a couple of clerical workers, Frank the Storeman and Eddie Richardson. Eddie saw me and said, "Where's Wilf?"

Fearing the worst, I related my sorry story and, dreading the response from Eddie, I had no sooner finished when I was greeted by a loud outburst of spontaneous laughter by everyone in the office. Eddie said something to the effect of "I don't blame yer, kid. We don't do things like that anymore – that's what the plunger's for."

Crisis averted, and with great relief, I got on with things just as before. Some time later, I found myself working again with Wilf in the Roundhay area doing guttering. It was a large house and we were using a triple wooden extension ladder, no longer used today for health and safety reasons. At one stage, Wilf was at the top and I was at the bottom, *footing* the ladder to prevent it slipping.

I must have lost concentration for, all of a sudden, I heard Wilf yell down "what the bloody hell are yer doin'?" I must have had a pop song going round my head and, more so, I was part dancing on the bottom rung of the ladder. Upon hearing Wilf yell, I looked up and the triple extension ladder (due to its sheer length) was *whipping* quite severely with Wilf holding on for dear life at the top!

As a young apprentice, my role was to observe what plumbers were doing and the processes related to various jobs. As this knowledge progressed, you would be expected to pre-empt certain processes by passing the plumber the right tool or fitting, thus enabling continuity of the job itself. Over time, you would be given a small task to do and, at around seventeen or eighteen years old, these tasks would be more substantial and you would be loosely referred to as an 'Improver'. In the first instance, I didn't mind the fetching and carrying and being sent to the sandwich shop, as for me it was all part of the job, which allowed me – for the first time in my life – to travel in a car or (to be precise) the firm's van.

Overall, the firm's transport comprised of two or three vans along with a hand cart. The latter was a relic of bygone days, but still used for *jobbing repair* purposes, such as carrying cast-iron gutters, fall pipes and, of course, the plumber's tools. The cart was literally dragged along the roads and streets from job to job.

Jack was clearly keen to develop the business and, around 1966-67, he took over a plumbing firm in Bradford that had gone bust. Upon reflection, he made the wrong decision in giving the previous owner the job of managing it. This chap eventually ran the business into the ground, but before that happened, we played a couple of football matches against them and, as the first game approached, Eddie wrote the names of our team on the board in the office, along with the colours we were playing in (i.e. *'plumbers black'* and *'boss white'*), which reflected a couple of plumbing materials.

In the autumn, we all met at the Leeds City train station for the annual firm's trip to the Blackpool illuminations and two or three carriages were reserved so that we could collectively travel as a group. The obligatory crates of beer and pies were loaded aboard and off we went.

Upon reaching our destination, we broke off in small groups and those who had previously attended these trips advised others to make sure to go in the Wintergarden in the evening, as Jack was always in and would buy the beer. The word was true and later that evening he did indeed buy the beer.

As we made our way back to the railway station, I remember seeing some of our lads very drunk on another platform. As we boarded the Leeds train these lads shouted across that we were all on the wrong train, so a few got off believing this to be the case. Unfortunately, it was us that were on the correct train all along and the next day we were told the lads that had erroneously changed trains ended up not in Leeds but Bradford!

Our journey back to Leeds saw bodies slumped over seats and tables with people hanging out of windows trying to get some fresh air to avoid illness, though for one lad this had the opposite effect. Not a pretty sight, seeing vomit splashed on the outside of the adjacent window! I can still see Frank the Storeman in the guard's carriage, sat down and slumped over a wheel like a young boy pretending to drive the train.

Things were going well for me at Gahan's and, in September of 1966, I began my studies at college. I was made fully aware from the outset that, as part of my apprenticeship, I would have to attend one full day and two evenings at the building college. Initially, the full day was at the old Cross Green School (close to the Black Dog pub) and two evenings at Roseville Road College.

Within a few months of attending college, I struck up a friendship with a lad called Dougie, who was from the Halton area. I began meeting up with him and his mates on evenings at the top of Halton Hill, just by the shops on the left-hand side, opposite where the Lidl store is standing today. Along with a group of Dougie's mates, we just used to hang about, both watching and commenting on the frequent passing of motorbikes apparently on their way to and from the village of Sherburn in Elmete, which the lads informed me was a popular meeting place for motorcyclists.

There was a lad called Chris Bogg, who was several years older than me, who owned a Honda 90cc. On occasion, Chris would take me so far home on the back of his bike, dropping me off at the bottom of Pontefract Lane, leaving me to take the short walk the rest of the way home. At this point in the 1960s, there were no laws regarding the compulsory wearing of crash helmets. I really got a kick out of these rides home and slowly became interested in motorbikes. Around this time Steve Sunderland was learning to ride a motorbike and used to arrive at work on a Honda 50cc. This only served to increase my interest.

Eventually, our plumbing studies were moved to the new Leeds College of Building, North Street. More importantly, I also had a date for the signing of my Deed of Apprenticeship.

On the evening of 5th May 1967, my dad and I attended Gahan's Offices after work in the evening to be given an overview of the Deed, which then resulted in the formality of the document being signed. A day or so later, upon hearing of the meeting, Jim Ingle made the comment that, "Jack's got more say over yer now than yer father." To this day I still have that Deed of Apprenticeship and an indication of the degree of formality of the formal covenant between my employer and I was...

> "That the Apprentice shall faithfully and honestly serve the employer as his Apprentice and be diligent to learn the trade or business aforesaid and shall at all times willingly obey and perform the lawful and reasonable commands and requirements of the Employer and/or of his authorized representatives and keep the secrets of his trade and shall not otherwise be gainfully employed in the said trade or business."

Over the years, there have been occasions that I have felt dismay when I have heard belittling and disparaging comments about certain trade persons. Plumbing then and now requires a lot of learning and skill as the recurring examples of poor DIY serve to testify.

Back then, both sheet lead and lead pipe were still being quite widely used, though the latter was beginning to decline in favour of copper pipe. And so, to join lead pipe to lead or even to copper pipe, one had carry out what was known as *wiping* a plumbing joint. I won't labour the whole process, but both ends of the pipe had to be prepared, cleaned, fluxed and with the blowlamp you had to gradually melt a partial stick of solder on to the joint and, at the same time, use a moleskin cloth to gradually form a joint before completing it. You had to maintain the right temperature, otherwise the solder would be too hard to manipulate and 'wipe', or it would be too hot and simply drop off the joint. If you were jointing two pieces of pipe, then the finished product looked like the shape of an egg, though this varied when you were wiping a branch or tee joint.

One had to use specific tools, such as a shave hook, tan pin, bent pin and pipe clamps, with the joint that was being worked upon, potentially at any angle, vertically, diagonally or horizontally. Of course, the true test was if it held water without leaking!

This was only a small part of the skill of being a plumber and, after being at Gahan's for a while, other apprentice's at college and plumbers would ask inquisitively if you could wipe a plumbing joint. If you answered 'yes', then the usual retort back was "but can yer also wipe a branch joint?" This was seen as more difficult to do and it was something of a badge of honour to be able to reply that you could do both types of joint. Sheet lead was widely in use then and, to some extent, it still is today.

External chimney stacks on a roof are weathered at the back by a sheet lead *gutter back* and the front by a lead *apron*. Then it was customary for both to be formed from a piece of sheet lead and, to create these two items, one had initially to form the two corners, noting the required distance so that it fitted around the chimney, and then work or *dress* the sheet lead slowly and deliberately until both corners had been formed. This is a time-consuming process and the trick is not to tear the lead in the *dressing process,* thus rendering it useless as a waterproof item. The specific wooden tools used were made from hickory and would be a *dresser, bossing or bending stick* and *mallet.*

Some ten years ago, I had reason to put these traditional skills to good use when our elderly next-door neighbour had the lead *apron* stolen from the front of her chimney. This was due to somebody climbing on her bungalow fence and ripping it off, no doubt for the lowly scrap value. Luckily, I had some sheet lead in the garage and was able to make the new item for her.

Glazing also had a certain amount of skill to it because the rebate on the wooden frames needed a bead of putty to be applied to bed the glass window into the frame. Once the glass was in and *sprigged* with several panel pins, then another bead of putty was applied around the rebate again and it was then *pointed off* with a putty *pointing* knife. Rather than just apply putty in a random manner, one would have a ball of putty in the hand and apply or *'run'* it constantly and evenly around the rebate. It followed then that a usual comment between plumbers and apprentices would be "can yer *run* putty yet"? If the answer was "yes", then the follow up questions would be "okay, but can yer *run* putty both up as well as down the frame? And can yer *run* putty with both hands?" It was all light-hearted banter yet attached was a feeling of pride if you were able to answer 'yes' to such questions, and this all served to remind you that you were training to become a skilled tradesman.

Away from work, I was still hanging around with the lads up Halton watching motorbikes pass and at times trying to guess the make and model from the sound of the exhaust before the bike came into view.

It would be around this time that one of the Halton lads, Eddie, and I decided to hitchhike to Scarborough. I believe it was a Bank Holiday weekend, and I don't remember if I told Mam and Dad what my plans were or not. I am sure I did because there was nowhere else that I would be staying and there were no 'sleep-overs' in those days. This being the 1960s, we were in the midst of a real explosion of youth culture (a term coined in 1943 by the American Sociologist Talcott Parsons). Lads had very long hair and generally young people consumed popular music, clothes made primarily for young people, and all manner of material goods, if they were able to afford them. Added to this, there simply seemed to be more freedom to do things than our parents had ever experienced.

I am sure I had been up front with Mam and Dad because a year or so later they were on a week's caravan holiday at Filey with our Gill's son, Michael, and I remember hitchhiking on my own over to see them. Looking back, I like to think that Mam and Dad were, to a certain degree, in tune with the freedoms that were on offer to teenagers in the 1960s and so decided to trust me to be responsible.

It was around 1967 that Dad moved jobs due to the imminent closure of Clarks Dyers and moved to Hudswell Clarke engineering in Hunslet. This company had been in existence since 1861, initially making locomotive engines, first steam and then diesel, but in the 1960s they diversified into non-railway products, such as civil engineering machinery. In fact, our Gill's husband, Bernard, had left Clarks Dyers earlier and it was him who got Dad the start at Hunslet.

Dad was still working twelve-hour days and would make his *'mashings'* up on a morning to take with him for when he was able to have a 'brew' at work. Often, I would watch him neatly tearing perhaps three or four strips of newspaper and then putting a teaspoonful of tea on each piece, followed by perhaps two teaspoons of sugar, before meticulously folding each *mashing* and then placing them in his khaki shoulder bag along with his *sarnies*. Depending on where I was working, me and Mam would still share the walk to work on a morning before we went our separate ways at the bottom of Lupton Avenue, with her then walking the short distance to Sumries as I myself took the short walk to Gahan's *shop*.

It would have been around this time that I recall being at home one day, along with Mam and Dad, and I got up out of the chair and simply said that I was "going for a pee." My dad instinctively in his usual inoffensive tone of voice rebuked me for using crude language such as the word "pee". In fact, Mam and Dad might use the curse word 'bloody', but would never use the 'f' word, like so many seem to do today. No doubt men and women will perhaps swear at work, and indeed that is something I have done myself, but I have adopted the same values as my parents and never used such coarse swear words within the family home.

Recently, I was having a conversation with a teenage member of the family about this and, in a matter of fact way, she said that not only her parents, but her friend's parents swore freely in their own home. When I expressed my dismay at this, she remarked that perhaps today it is now more acceptable than when I was young. I didn't respond further, but instead thought 'why would you want the bastardisation of family conversation to become more acceptable?'

Back in the mid-1960s, our Gill and Bernard were now living up Middleton and close to Bernard's parents. I had also started hanging around with Steve Sunderland in my spare time. Steve lived with his mum and dad in the Ambertons, on the Gipton council estate. Gipton then was a good place to live and didn't appear to have any of the social problems that were to be found a number of years later. They lived only a stone's throw from the Amberton Sports Centre, whose events and activities attracted many people from outside the immediate area. I confess to being a little envious of Steve's council house semi, with the nice gardens and inside bathroom and toilet, as opposed to our back-to-back.

Steve was friendly with the Towns family who lived nearby and Dave Towns was interested in motor bikes too, and at the time had a Francis Barnet. Steve heard of a lad on the estate selling a BSA C15 250cc bike for £15 and, though I knew relatively nothing about mechanics, I duly bought it. Mam and Dad allowed me to keep it in the living room with a waterproof canvas sheet under it so that the carpet didn't get marked.

The kitchen/dining room was still the main room that was ever used and, in fact, I don't recall Mam or Dad ever sitting in the living room. Together with Steve and Dave, we would take the bike down Black Road, Cross Green, because there was a lot of wasteland that we were able to use for off road riding. This enabled me to get used to riding it, but it soon proved to be a '*dog*' of a bike with a number of things wrong with it.

One evening, Steve called at our house and, upon entering the living room where it was kept, he became horrified when he saw a number of mechanical bits on the waterproof sheet where the bike stood. "What do yer think yer doing?" he exclaimed.

"Well, you and Dave said tuther day that there was summat wrong wit' clutch," I replied.

"Yeah, that's right wi did, but that's gearbox yer messin' wi'!"

This was certainly my first serious lesson in motorcycle mechanics, but luckily we both managed to fit the various pieces back into the gear box. Since then, I have always bought a manual to go along with the various bikes and cars that I have bought.

It wasn't too long before I traded the bike in for a 1965 BSA C15 250cc, bought on hire purchase from Walter Wraggs Motorcycles, who were then situated opposite the Central Bus Station. Motorcycles and music became my two main passions. Since the age of about fourteen I have been very interested in pop music and, upon starting work, I was regularly buying vinyl singles, extended plays (EPs) and long-playing albums (LPs).

Work was going really well, and I was enjoying a spectrum of jobs ranging from small repair, central heating and new work, such as housing and some plumbing on the new Pudsey Crawshaw School that was being built. Hence it was something of a shock when in 1968 the news broke that H. Gahan's was about to go bankrupt. Being an Indentured Apprentice in such events as this, it was the employer's responsibility to try and find you an alternative position with a plumbing company, but with everyone seemingly focused on their own situation, I looked around myself and eventually got a job with Leonard Atkinson, whose yard was situated in The Calls near to the city centre and Leeds Parish Church.

Atkinson was an elderly man, possibly sixty years old, though being only sixteen years old myself anyone over fifty looked elderly to me back then. The firm itself was much smaller than Gahan's and I soon found myself working alongside an older plumber on some new-build several-storey flats in Headingley.

I found it very difficult to settle following the demise of Gahan's, but I was lucky that Harold, the plumber I was working with, was very supportive. He was a bespectacled chap who was small in stature and sported a moustache and, in fact, can't have been too far off retirement. He hadn't been working with Atkinson's for too long and one particular day we were both outside working in a trench laying a 15mm copper water main from the pavement and into the building. Harold was using a junior hacksaw to cut the pipe, but the blade appeared rather blunt. Without uttering a word, he quickly turned his back on me then turned back in a flash and began attacking the pipe with his false teeth! Who says that older people don't have a sense of humour?

Harold acknowledged that perhaps Atkinson's were not the best firm for me to serve the remainder of my apprenticeship with. I had only been with my new firm a matter of months when Harold came in one day with a cutting from the *Yorkshire Evening Post*. It was an advert for an apprentice plumber with a company named L.S. Rhodes, Beeston. Harold and I discussed the job, which from the advert sounded okay, but my main concern was the potential poor impression I would give to any prospective new employer due to being only a few months with Atkinson's and now wanting to leave. Harold thought momentarily on the issue and then said to me that, if the question arose, I was to say that "I think I'll better mi-self by coming to work for you."

I was using my motorbike for work so off I went up to Beeston to enquire about the job. On the journey there, I kept repeating over and over in my head what Harold said that I should say if the need arises.

L.S Rhodes's shop was then located at the bottom of Beeston Hill. I got off my motorbike, dressed in my leather jacket decorated with lots of bike badges and leather fringe hanging from the front, back and arms and with my crash helmet similarly sporting a host of bike related badges, and I headed for the front door.

There were a number of other small shops in the vicinity and in the shop window, belonging to what was hopefully going to be my new employer, I could see a display with, on the one side a white bathroom suite and on the other a kitchen sink cabinet, sink top and taps. I entered the shop to be greeted by a smartly dressed chap, perhaps aged mid-50s.

His *dead-pan* face peered curiously at me over his gold-rim half-moon glasses before asking if he could be of assistance. His demeanour put me more on edge as I nervously explained my interest in the post being advertised for an apprentice plumber and, in response, he asked who it was that I was currently working for.

When I replied that it was Atkinson's, he came back commenting that he knew Leonard Atkinson well and pointedly asked me why I wanted to leave in order to come and work for him. I instinctively remembered

Harold's words verbatim and I replied, "I think I'll better mi-self by coming to work for you."

At this he paused, still with a dead-pan look and, with head slightly bowed as he looked intently over his half-moon gold-rimmed spectacles at this young leather-clad motorcyclist cum apprentice plumber. Then he bluntly said, "Well, you'll certainly do that."

Following some further conversation, he said that he would let me know and that was that. I got on my bike and journeyed back to work, explaining to Harold what had transpired. When I went home later that day after finishing work, I also explained the events to Mam and Dad, not really knowing what was going to happen, if indeed anything at all. I didn't have to wait too long because later that evening there was a knock on the door.

When I opened it, standing there in the dark was Mr. Rhodes who, without any formalities, simply looked at me and said, "Well, do you want that job or not?"

I simply replied "yes" and that was that.

Chapter 5

Late Teenage Years and a New Job

Stan Rhodes had not been a plumber himself and I never took the trouble to enquire how it was that both he and his wife, Mary, had come to run the business. They lived in a large semi-detached house just above Cross Flatts Park and had never had any children. The plumbing shop was then situated at the bottom of Beeston Hill, with several other small shops surrounding it.

On the other side of the road, a little further on down was the Malvern Road School and below that was a children's nursery, though historically the building had been a former Workhouse. Almost opposite this was Shaftesbury House Hostel for homeless persons. The hostel was officially opened in 1938, offering temporary accommodation for 516 persons and at the time it was divided into male and female sections, with their separate entrances, common rooms and dining rooms. Shared kitchen and laundry facilities were also provided.

When Shaftesbury House opened, all of the rooms were fully furnished with a different colour scheme for each floor. Built in the period of the Depression it would often offer accommodation to persons that were '*on the tramp*' or, in other words, people looking for work and often drawn from other parts of the country *tramping* around on foot in the hope of finding a job.

As a local authority homeless person's hostel, the building finally closed its doors in the late 1990s. A short walk away took one into Holbeck and, at this period in time, the old public wash-house was still standing, though it was no longer being used. Forming part of South Leeds, Beeston and Holbeck, like other parts of the city, still had many back-to-back houses with poor amenities.

Historically, and with the onset of the Industrial Revolution, it quickly became acknowledged that the new factories, mills and engineering buildings – due to the prevailing winds – belched and spewed out their filthy and foul-smelling fumes persistently to the south of the city. Therefore, many factory and mill owners had their homes built to the north in places such as Chapeltown, which is situated on the fringe of the city centre. During the mid-19th century many working men's clubs were being founded in working-class communities around the country. In 1871 the formation of the Holbeck Working Men's came about and today it is viewed as the oldest continuous surviving club in the country.

For L.S. Rhodes, one of the main areas of work was what was known as a *conversion*. In the 1960s much of the Leeds back-to-back housing stock, with no bathrooms and outside toilets, was being upgraded. Such properties were essentially two up and two down, so new dormer windows were fitted in the attic space, thus creating another bedroom. If they had an existing bath at all it was often fitted in the small scullery kitchen and would have a wooden cover over the top so that it could be used as an additional worktop and perhaps storage underneath. The small second bedroom was converted into a bathroom. New kitchen sink units were also fitted, along with new plumbing pipework and electric rewiring.

Besides 'conversions' and local 'jobbing' work, the firm had a city council contract to carry out repair work on the Seacroft North and South Council Housing Estates. This just about summed up the work undertaken at the firm. The men that were employed roughly comprised of about six plumbers, with Alan Garnet (or AG) the foreman, two brothers (Jim and Sam Ford) who did a range of building jobbing work (i.e. roofing, plastering, bricklaying and tiling). Jim Ford was the second foreman. There were also two labourers (one being Bernard Walsh and the other John Dukes), two joiners (Keith and Eric Jenkins), and Jack Bundy, a painter and decorator. Though range and quality of work fell way short of the plumbing work undertaken by Gahans, I decided to settle down and get on with things.

An integral part of the working week included Saturday mornings, but for single time only. No one, including myself, was impressed with this arrangement, essentially for two reasons, because firstly the work completed on Saturday mornings was widely regarded as overtime and, secondly, given this it should have been paid at time and a half. However, more importantly for me, Stan Rhodes took over the Deed of Apprenticeship and allowed my college work to continue as before.

The paternalism of Stan and Mary Rhodes manifested itself in countless ways. As workmen we were not allowed to use the front shop door, but instead had to enter through the door from the yard at the back of the building. Depending upon instructions, we all met at 8.00am, either at 'the shop' or up in the detached garage of his home. This was to complete our *day books,* concerning the work and time spent on our particular job the day before and to give Stan an update on work progress.

I discovered that Bernard Walsh lived at East End Park and knew my mam and dad. Bernard presented himself as a quiet and thoughtful chap and one day he asked me if I had ever noticed the dynamics that often occurred with these early-morning events, when Stan was querying with individuals how their jobs were progressing. Seeing my vague look, Bernard explained further that, no matter how well individuals might offer good feedback on their progress with certain jobs, Stan never offered praise. In fact, he would often moan that he thought this or that would have been completed by now, leaving the hapless worker in question to feel deflated and somewhat demoralised in front of the rest of the lads. This, as Bernard pointed out, was Stan's active use of psychology to keep us all on our toes.

I also learned that both foremen, Alan and Jim, had informally been told that, when Stan and Mary retired the firm, it would be left to them. This I am sure contributed to their petty jealousy of each other and so, in turn, they would creep and crawl around Stan and Mary, trying to outdo one another. For example, there had been a longstanding situation where Jim would collect and pay for the Rhodes's morning and evening papers, along with Mary's weekly magazines. Apparently, this was something he had begun of his own volition. However, on one occasion, he complained to me and another chap that the Rhodeses owed him over £10 for unpaid papers and magazines. This was quite a significant amount of money back then and the other guy rebuked him for getting himself into such an invidious situation. Jim instinctively became defensive, saying something to the effect that he wasn't really bothered because, when he did finally get paid, the lump sum in itself would be very nice. Given the location of the Rhodeses' home, both Jim and Alan themselves lived quite close, with the former being on the end of Old Lane and the latter close to Elland Road football ground. This being the case, the petty rivalry between Alan and Jim revealed itself in other ways too. For example, on one occasion, the ever-observant Bernard asked if I noticed the common exchange of words between Alan and Jim on a Monday mornings. I said "no" and Bernard explained that it often went like so...

"Did you see owt o' Stan over the weekend, Alan?"

"No, we went past their house Saturday afternoon. The garage doors were open and Stan's car was in the drive, but I didn't see either Stan or Mary. What about you, Jim?"

"Well, we went past on Sunday night. The bedroom light was on and the curtains were open, the garage doors were shut and Stan's car was in the drive, but I didn't see either of them."

With Bernard drawing this to my attention, I would often be amused when such future verbal exchanges occurred between them. Their rivalry was constant, with each one worried that the other may be getting looked upon more favourably than they were. Everyone felt that the Rhodeses were very much aware of this petty rivalry and manipulated matters at times to suit their own ends. When they went on holiday (even abroad), at some stage they would ring the office to ask if everything was okay. On such occasions some of the lads would remark that that just about summed up the amount of trust they had in Alan and Jim to run things, even for a short period.

At Christmas the function room in the Beeston Conservative Club was hired and a party was held a week or so before the festive holidays. For a number of weeks prior to *'the bash'*, we all had to pay something like a sixpence per week as a contribution towards it. Although nothing was ever said there was a tacit acknowledgement amongst us that any failure to attend, without good reason, would place you in the Rhodeses' *bad books*. Indeed it seemed always the case that, for some reason or another, one of the workers would find themselves in the *bad books*.

Our attendance at *'the bash'* meant that as workers we could invite wives and/or girlfriends, or simply friends. I was still in regular touch with my old apprentice mate Steve Sunderland, so the first *'bash'* I attended he came along with me. Upon entering the large room, one was immediately struck by the rigid layout of the seating arrangements. On the left-hand side of the dance floor were seated Stan, Mary and all of *the great and the good* friends. On the right-hand side sat the workers and whoever they might have brought with them. It was social-class apartheid with everyone tacitly knowing their place in the proceedings.

A string quartet played music and those who wished would get up and dance, perhaps a waltz or something appropriate for whatever tune was being played. Now I honestly don't recall things, but the next day I was informed by some lads that I was apparently *'in the bad books'* because Stan Rhodes said my mate Steve had kicked a bottle onto the dance floor. Although I stressed to him that I was completely unaware of this, it was to no avail.

Poor old Keith the joiner was also in trouble because he was found lying in the gents' urinal. Keith liked his drink as well as a regular bet on the horses and, though he was married with children, it wasn't unknown for him to get paid on Friday and then come in on Saturday morning asking Stan for a *'sub'*.

To be fair to the Rhodeses their paternalism wasn't always too overbearing, and this was especially the case at Christmas. For example, several weeks beforehand, staff were asked if they preferred a choice of either two fresh chickens or a turkey to enjoy with their family on Christmas Day. They also gave each member of staff a bonus, supposedly based on how long you had worked there.

One particular year, Keith the joiner had left to be replaced by another chap, who was called Eric. Those chaps, who used a car for work purposes – driving to various jobs and often carrying others – were given around thirty shillings (£1.50) per week for petrol money. On occasion, Mary Rhodes, who made out both the wages and expenses, forgot to pay certain individuals the latter, but it was usually paid in a subsequent week or weeks.

This being the final payday and the giving of bonuses prior to Christmas, as each of the workmen completed their day's work and arrived at the shop, they were told to wait across the backyard in the joiners' shop. Then, one by one, we were called across to be given both our wages and a

Christmas bonus and, upon receipt of the latter, each one was expressly told not say anything to anyone else.

There were a number of us across the yard waiting to be called and Eric was gradually winding himself up and becoming annoyed because he was owed a certain number of weeks for his car expenses. He was duly called, and after a short while, he returned ashen faced. Asked if he had received his expenses, he commented that, after Stan had given him his wages and Christmas bonus, he had asked about his outstanding car expenses.

Stan's response had been something like, "It's Christmas, Eric. It's give and take."

Eric had frostily replied, "Yeah, but you're all take."

Stan then said, "Okay Eric, I'll give you something: your cards. Don't bother coming back after Christmas."

We were all shocked, but we could do nothing, only offer the poor man our sympathetic comments. We were all grateful for receiving a Christmas bonus, but even this was divisive. For example, some chaps disregarded what they had expressly been told by the Rhodeses and secretly revealed to others what they had been given. Not surprisingly, some became upset because others had been given more than them for no apparent reason. Following some analysis, some could only conclude that perhaps they may have been 'in the bad books' a few weeks or months previous.

The only two people never to discuss what they had been given, even to each other, was Alan and Jim. Though at times each would ask one of the lads if they knew how much the other had been given. The Rhodeses seemingly had an adult nephew called Harry and, for those that had been at the firm longer than me, it appeared that all of a sudden Harry was being talked about and visited by Stan and Mary.

Harry had learning difficulties and lived at what was then openly known as Meanwood Colony. Meanwood Park was rented in 1919 by the Leeds Corporation to provide what was then both crudely and unfortunately termed as a 'mental deficiency colony' and in 1996 it finally closed. It appeared that Stan, Mary or both became members of an internal committee and seemed to be involved with fundraising.

At one stage we were all expected to participate in a weekly raffle that offered the prize of a cushion. There was an overarching tacit expectation for everyone to buy a weekly ticket and, though we all grumbled to each other from time to time about this, we all knew that any dissenters would find themselves temporarily in the *bad books* and receiving some brusque treatment.

At times, Stan Rhodes would refer to me as having a *'dog in a manger'* attitude. I had no idea what it meant, or why I was referred to in this way, but looking back I can only think that it was related to my motorcycle. Stan seemed to be a little miffed at times because I would not use my motorcycle for work. He appeared unable to accept my explanation that it was solely for pleasure.

On a number of occasions he referred to me as *'having a chip on my shoulder'*. Such comments were not always made directly to me, but instead he expressed such remarks about me to others. Again, I honestly didn't know why, and others would laugh because I guess it meant they were not a target at that moment in time.

On one particular evening, when we had packed up on a job and were ready to go, I picked my coat up only to find that the joiner Eric had put a nail through a small piece of wood (or chip) and fastened it to the shoulder of my jacket! One of the plumbers, Rodney, who was in his mid-twenties, also used to refer to me as *'Confucious Potter'*, presumably because of my crude attempts to philosophise on certain matters.

After several months of starting at the firm it became apparent that, for some reason, the foreman, Jim, didn't like me at all and, noticing this at times, the feeling became mutual. His brother Sam was also in his late forties, but although I got on okay with him, at times he was excessively deferential.

On one occasion, Sam and I were working on the same conversion down Holbeck and, for some good reason, we went back to 'the shop' for lunch. As we finished and exited from the backyard and then crossed over Beeston Road to make our way back, Sam's walking pace was almost at Olympic speed.

Eventually, I asked what was wrong and he replied something to the effect of "hang on". Within moments, we turned the corner and his pace suddenly dropped into a steady stroll. He explained that, from the shop window, Stan would have been able to see us walking down the street and he was at pains not to demonstrate that he was anything but eager to get back to the job!

This level of deference at times from individuals verged on the fearful, as evidenced by Sam, and I am sure that I too on occasions succumbed to this aspect of the workplace sub-culture. However, as with all workplaces, there were elements of fun and laughter.

The Rhodeses had a number of *'conversions'* to carry out in the Woodviews, which were rows of back-to-backs just off Kirkstall Hill, above what is now a sports centre. Another lad and I were in the cab of the pickup wagon driven by Jim and, on this particular morning, we had the very long wooden pole ladder tied to the wagon. Indeed, the front of the ladder extended some length in front of us.

We were on our way to the Woodviews and, as Jim turned into the bottom of the street, he plowed through a line of washing strung across from one side of the street to the other. He stopped further on up the street, at the house where we were working. As we all got out a woman at the bottom was shouting furiously at us. Above her head, about nine feet apart on the clothes line, were two vertical white seams still pegged in position, but nothing hanging between them. We looked up at the front of the wagon to see a white seamless sheet wrapped around the front of the ladder! This wooden pole ladder was a pain to work with, due to it being very heavy and cumbersome to move and handle.

One day on the job in the Woodviews one of the lads purposely broke two or three of the wooden rungs of the ladder, believing that when Stan was told that the rungs had accidentally broken he would discard it and get a new extension ladder that would be easier to work with. However, upon hearing the news, Stan enquired whereabouts on the ladder were the broken rungs. When he was told that they were close to the bottom of the ladder his reply was that anyone using the ladder in future could simply step over them and on to the rung above.

One day, Stan saw some empty plastic drinking cups in the back of the pickup wagon and asked where they had come from. When he was told that a certain builder's merchants had recently installed a hot drinks machine, we were instructed not to go there ever again.

Stan had initially driven a dated Wolsely car, but changed it to a Jaguar. Though, as one lad remarked, it was the cheapest Jag of the range, we were all expected to coo over it. After all, in reality none of us could afford such a car.

One day he announced to several of us that he had been reading a car magazine article concerned with prolonging the life of the exhaust system by carefully wrapping it in tin foil paper. On a Saturday morning a plumber called Derek and I were given the job of trying to get underneath the car to wrap the entire exhaust system with tin foil – though with one condition.

Stan explicitly expressed that we didn't tear the foil, otherwise the damp would get in and cause rust. He kept coming to see us in the back yard and, under his periodic supervision, we began carefully to wrap the exhaust with the tin foil without splitting the paper. However, this eventually proved an impossible task as we each tried to put the stuff around not only the pipe, but metal exhaust clips and brackets. After much cursing we completed the task in a fashion and convinced Stan it was done without any splits in the foil.

Since the demise of Gahan's, Steve Sunderland and I had become close friends. Not only did we see each other at building college, we still hung out together socially. He too now had a BSA 250cc C15 motorcycle and together we would go for rides in to Sherburn in Elmete village and the famous Squires Café/ Milk Bar.

The café/milk bar was first opened in 1954 and was then situated just off the main street that ran through the village. The car park in front of the café was usually full of motorcycles at the weekend and certain mid-week evenings, leading to an overspill parking of bikes over the road in the fish shop car park and further down the road in two of the pub car parks. We just hung about, had a natter, a few laughs, listened to the juke box and watched bikes come in and out. Much to the relief of residents in 2002, the café moved to Newport Lane, several miles away from the village.

The 1960s was a period that not only pre-dated laws on the use of crash helmets, but likewise there were no noise restrictions from bike silencers. Dave Towns would also ride with Steve and I on occasion and one day he announced that he was to buy a BSA B33 500cc bike and sidecar from a work mate and he asked whether Steve and I wanted to go with him to Headingley to collect it. Of course we said yes and one evening the three of us caught the bus from Gipton in order to see and collect the bike.

Unfortunately, the thing wouldn't start so, having planned the best route, we decided to push it back to Dave's house, which was quite a number of miles from Headingley to Gipton! Going downhill it was fine, but it was a real tow pushing it uphill. What's more, the evening was dark and the lights on the bike didn't work. At one point, we were stopped by the police, but having explained the situation we were allowed to continue our ordeal.

We finally reached Dave's house, but there was further disappointment for him. Upon looking at the log book the bike was listed as a B31, which was a 350cc and not the 500cc he was led to believe. He then looked at the log book and to offset this disappointment he happily announced to us that there had only been three previous owners.

Now, at that time, the paper log books had the capacity to record ten owners so when Steve grabbed it from his hand, looked at it and told him this was the second log book we were in fits of laughter. Nevertheless, as owners of 250s, we were still suitably impressed with his 350cc and I guess to us size mattered.

Having carried out some work to get it running several weeks later, the three of us went to the east coast on our bikes. Journeying by road to the east coast at that time pre-dated the current set of dual carriageways and bypasses. Hence traffic had to travel through the town and city centres of Tadcaster, York and Malton, so meeting congestion was par for the course. However, once on the open road Dave, with mouth wide open and sporting his pudding-type crash helmet, frequently accelerated past us indicating with his fingers which gear he was in. As we approached the steep Whitwell Hill he had accelerated past us both at the bottom, but as we climbed the hill with rapid succession his fingers indicated the dropping of gears from 4th to 1st, which served to give me some amusement. We eventually got to Scarborough, but more laughs were to come on the way home.

Between York and Tadcaster, a section of dual carriageway was affected by roadworks. One of the good points about a solo bike is that you are rarely held up by traffic congestion because you can ease your way through on the outside. However, there was a tacit understanding with Steve and I not to do this and thus leave Dave with his bike and sidecar stuck in the traffic. However, with the traffic barely moving after a frustrating period of standing still, we both decided that enough was enough and so, having glanced at each other, we began slowly passing the parked cars in the jam.

After a short while, we were both quickly drawn to something on our left-hand side. It was Dave bouncing up and down on the uneven grassed central reservation, shouting and swearing at us to the effect that there was no way we were going to leave him behind. No doubt if he had been caught he would have been in trouble, but looking back at this period in the 1960s life seemed more carefree and less 'managed' by overbearing rules and bureaucracy.

The Towns were a bit of an eccentric family and Dave confessed to us that on one occasion the council's rent collector had noticed his attempt to bury a wreck of a motorbike in the back garden and duly gave the family a warning. I was regularly attending building college with Steve and we became mates with another apprentice plumber called Kenny, who also had a motorcycle too and lived in the Victoria's behind the White Horse Pub on York Road.

In due course Kenny introduced me and Steve to his mates, who all had bikes: Peter and a lad called Greg lived at Saxon Gardens and Charlie who lived at Halton Moor. We became a group of like-minded lads sharing bike rides, going out to the pub and pictures and, on one particular Sunday afternoon, a group of us were stood by our bikes in the car park adjacent to the boathouse at Roundhay Park. There were bikes coming and going and, being enthusiasts, we would pick up on the distant exhaust note trying to identify the make of bike before it came into view.

On this occasion, we happened to look up at the approach road to the park and car park and eventually this motorbike and sidecar appeared and came down the hill. I say sidecar, but in effect in place of the 'chair' there was a long coffin-like box on the frame, much the same as how some workmen of the day would use them for tools etc. As the rider parked the bike, the elongated hinged lid slowly lifted back and the secret prostrate passenger clambered out of the *coffin,* as if it was some kind of Dracula movie, only this lad received great shouts and roars of laughter from everyone in the car park.

This was also, of course, the period of rivalry between the two youth culture groups 'Mods and Rockers' and sociologists have since said that such sub-culture groups were primarily about *resistance and rebellion* and as such it created a *moral panic* across society. The sociology of youth culture saw 'Rockers' as being archetypal working class whilst Mods were ascribed as being the aspirational class.

On reflection none of our group was 'fighters' or lads that went looking for trouble, and thankfully we were never involved in any. As young bikers we were very much aware of the 'Rocker' image and we ourselves did our best with our image and looks to shock people by at times looking *mean and moody,* like Marlon Brando did in *The Wild Ones* movie.

I remember one evening about eight of us had decided to go into Leeds city centre and see a film at the cinema. The film had just started so it was relatively dark as we were ushered to a row with vacant seats. It seemed that no sooner had we all just been seated when we were asked to leave without any kind of explanation and no refund. Outside the cinema, we all conferred about what has just happened, with each of us saying that we had done nothing wrong.

Around this time, I had passed my motorcycle test and bought a new used bike. It was a BSA 650cc Golden Flash that had previously had a sidecar attached to it, hence it had all the standard features. As individuals being inducted into motorcycling, we all had the urge to progress and eventually get a big bike. My bike was no longer in the living room, but instead I was now renting an old rickety garage just across the road.

Mam and Dad were aware that music was my other passion and surprised me on my seventeenth birthday by getting me a fantastic radiogram. They bought it from a shop called Suggs, which was on the left-hand side of Boar Lane, just before City Square. And just as many people did then, it was bought on hire purchase at a cost of a little over ninety guineas, which was quite expensive at that period in time.

Along with this, I gradually transformed my 'new' bike into something more modern, and as a contribution towards this Dad got a guy at work to paint a sporty 'Golden Flash' sign on the top of the petrol tank. In fact, through a process of making mistakes and asking friends for mechanical advice, I became adept at carrying out all the maintenance and repairs on the bike. This went as far as taking of the cylinder head and pistons and having the head re-bored with the fitting of new piston rings, valve guides and springs.

I bought and fitted an RR T2 gearbox, though originally these were only fitted to the BSA Rocket Gold Star models, many of which raced at the Isle of Man TT's. The gear box had the effect of lifting the top speed through each of the gears and, on one occasion, I ended up achieving 70mph in first gear, though in fourth gear there was only another 5mph achieved on the top speed.

One of the lads, Peter, worked as an engineer at Crabtree Vickers on Water Lane and, at one point, he made himself a pair of silencers to fit his AJS twin and these had no baffles inside so that the noise from them was not suppressed! They sounded great and, though I didn't buy any from him, he had orders from several people all wanting to buy his *'Crabtree Megas'.*

Around this time, we were introduced to the Seacroft Civic Youth Club adjacent to the shopping centre. This was a large purpose-built 1960s club that was buzzing with young people and various activities. Having said that, most of the time we would be sat in the coffee bar with other bikers we had met from the club and various friendships were struck leading to groups enjoying rides out. For young people there is value to just hanging about.

Events like the Scarborough road races were held at Oliver's Mount and each time a group of us would go camping for the weekend. We never set out to see any of the races, but rather we went for the atmosphere and, of course, a few laughs. Initially, we camped within a farmer's field adjacent to Dennis's Holiday Park, near the Flower of May Caravan Park. Dennis's wouldn't allow motorcyclists on the site and very soon the farmers stopped allowing them on too.

On one occasion, being aware of the growing bans, we approached a farmer down the road but, with a degree of reservation, he allowed us on. The next morning, he caught us all having a fight with the small bales of hay and, after he had given us all a tongue lashing, we were sent on our way and told never to return. As far as we were concerned, it was all harmless fun, but to adults our behaviour was seen as being loutish.

I must confess, though, that on one occasion things did go very wrong. Word went around the bikers at the Seacroft Youth Club that it would be a great idea to have a 'beach party' at the east coast seaside resort of Cayton Bay. On the date of the intended event, two or three groups of bikers made their own separate ways over to Cayton. The group I was with seemed to get there first so we parked the bikes and went to the pub, which was a good mile and a half away.

Much later that evening it was now dark, and worse the wear for drink, we trod the uneven grass verge at the side of the main Filey to Scarborough road, making our way back to Cayton. Billy had his jacket on back-to-front and, along with others, he kept falling down into the grass ditches running parallel with the verge. When we got to Cayton, we met up with several lads that we knew and they quickly explained that the police had been and removed some other lads because they had apparently set fire to deckchairs. We had no tents with us, so I remember several of us sleeping on the floor of the main bus shelter right outside the entrance to the Cayton caravan holiday site.

The next morning was surreal. We awoke to find a number of holidaymakers stood silently between our prostrate bodies, waiting – children with buckets and spades – for the bus into Scarborough. No one spoke as we crawled out and stole away. We made our way home the same day and there was never any mention of having future beach parties.

On another occasion, a group of us were returning home from the coast on our bikes when just after York the BSA 250cc belonging to Steve

Connors broke down. We all stopped and, after exhaustive and unsuccessful attempts to solve the problem, Steve was left with two options: leave the bike by the roadside and risk it getting stolen or vandalised; or, because someone had a rope, it might be possible to tow him home. The latter was agreed and I towed Steve and the bike back to his home at Cavalier Flats at the bottom of East Street in Leeds.

At times on the straight road I was doing speeds of around 60mph and whenever I looked behind I saw the desperate look on his face, which was clearly visible due to his open-faced crash helmet. I finally got him and his bike home. He explained that the ride had been really airy at times, due to the fact that he had little control over his bike and going around bends at fast speeds had been terrifying for him.

A little while after that, I repeated the same favour for Dave Towns when his Triumph 500cc also broke down. On each occasion there was no thought that this was somehow a reckless act to carry out. Moreover, it was simply a case that, as previously mentioned, in these less 'socially managed times' I was able to simply carry out a big favour for a couple of friends. However, not all of our leisure was related to motorcycling.

In the 1960s live bands and discos in pubs were quite commonplace and with no admission fee. Hence on a Saturday night beginning at the Prospect, Richmond Hill and running all the way up to the Melbourne near Seacroft Hospital, you would find a number of live bands playing in various pubs. Some of us would also frequent the Central Dance Hall, at the rear of Valances by the city centre Corn Exchange, as well as both the new and old Mecca dance halls. Not that we ever danced, as I recall – though, on occasions, you would see a seated Kenny Wallis moving his legs like crazy to some music that had grabbed his mood.

We had become loosely associated with a number of fellow bikers that we had met at Seacroft YC, and at times one lad called Dave Farrar used to borrow his mum's Vauxhall Viva car for his own use. We had been on our bikes a couple of times to the Hare and Hounds at Menston where a rock and roll trio called the Dave Lee Sound played there once or twice a week. On this particular evening a number of us met up in Leeds and peer pressure was collectively exerted on Dave and, although he made desperately excuses for not doing so, it resulted in him cramming about eight of us into his mum's car for a night out at Menston. It was just one of many spontaneous acts and I guess that, like many young people then and now, we never fully thought through or understood the potential implications of such actions.

Whilst we were clearly not always riding our motorcycles, they were nevertheless at the centre of our lives. Motorcycles have always been seen by a wide section of society as dangerous. Correspondingly, some of the negative stereotypes and attitudes towards those who ride motorcycles are linked to this view. Clearly, though, not all accidents are due to the reckless and irresponsible actions of the rider, and other road users are often at fault. I came off my motorbike on several occasions. The first was when I had ridden by myself one evening to Sherburn.

I was on my BSA 250cc leaving the coffee bar and, as I approached the sweeping right-hand bend exiting the village, my position on the bike was all wrong and I dropped it and came off. I wasn't going fast and the damage to both me and the bike was superficial.

On the second occasion it was again in the evening around 9.30pm and I was on the BSA, with Steve Sunderland behind me on his bike as we came down York Road in Leeds. We were not speeding, but as we approached the Irish Centre a car pulled out of a left-hand junction in front of me. Luckily, I was able to swerve, missing the car, but as I was pulling up I came off the bike. Once again damage was negligible.

On another occasion I was on the Gold Flash with Dave Towns on the back. It was a Sunday afternoon and we were travelling down the A1 from Wetherby and on our way to Sherburn in Elmet. We were travelling at approximately 60mph when the bike began pulling to one side. For a brief moment, I thought Dave was messing about, but the bike became worse and I instinctively began to slow as quickly and safely as I could. I am not too sure at what speed the bike went over, but along with the bike we luckily escaped once more with only superficial damage. Having got up and collected ourselves we discovered that the cause for the accident was a puncture in the front tyre.

The worst accident by far was still ahead of me. It was in May 1969 and a Saturday afternoon when I had been in the city centre with Steve Sunderland and it was agreed that I would give him a lift home on the back of my bike. Steve had no crash helmet and Harehills was busy as usual with shoppers. As we went through the traffic lights at the road junction with Compton Road and Harehills Lane everything suddenly went black. The next I remember was feeling shook up and badly dazed on a hospital trolley.

Steve and I were subsequently admitted on to the same Ward at Leeds General Infirmary. He had suffered a broken jaw and some superficial cuts and bruises. Due to the open-face helmets worn back then, I had very bad gravel burns to my face, followed by my discovery shortly afterwards that I was unable to lift my left arm unaided. In other words, I could raise it with my right arm, but it would not stay up by itself.

My mam and dad came to visit but at that point I still had no idea what the cause of the accident had been. It was when Steve's parents and his older sister came by that the latter, from the foot of my bed and in a raised voice, said that I had killed a man. I had no recollection of matters surrounding the accident and Mam and Dad remained calm, refraining from badgering me for explanations. I am sure they were just glad that I was safe and relatively unharmed.

After several days we were both discharged. I was told that the injury to my arm was due to having a severed nerve in my shoulder, probably caused by the fact that in the accident the tumbling about had caused my shoulder to dislocate and, though it had re-inserted itself, the nerve had been severed in the process. My arm was put in a sling and I was told to expect an outpatient's appointment in due course so that further investigations could be made.

They wanted me to go home in an ambulance, due to the severe gravel burns on my face, but I ended up making my own way home travelling by bus. Once home, and having settled in, I remember Mam and Dad asking me if I was going to stop motorcycling.

In response, I simply said that all my mates had bikes, so what would I do if I gave it up? I clearly recall that they didn't make a big deal out of the matter and they perhaps realised my point and I don't remember any further pressure being brought to bear on me, though of course they always urged me to take care.

After a few days of being at home, I set about repairing the damage to my bike. Once this was done, I was able to ride once again. I succeeded in doing this by lifting my left arm onto the handle bars with my right arm and then, when getting off the bike, my right arm was used again to lift the left one from the handle bars. Once I had both hands on the handle bars, then I had full control of the bike's handling.

The time came when both Steve and I attended the Coroner's Inquest, carried out to establish the cause of the man's death. Witnesses confirmed that I was not speeding. The Coroner was informed that earlier that afternoon the man had been drinking and had been travelling on an on-coming bus waiting at the traffic lights on the opposite side of the crossroads. Buses then had no automatic doors and, whilst it was stationery, he decided to get off at the rear and walk around the back of the bus, which presented as a blind side in order to cross the road.

He never stopped to consider that there might be any on-coming traffic and simply stepped right into the path of my bike. It was a fatal error of judgement on his part and it wasn't until a long time after the inquest that someone said to me that his actions could have led to the deaths of either Steve or I or even both of us. Nevertheless, it is a moment in my life I have never forgotten. Several months later, I was involved in another incident that to a lesser degree also had an impact on my life.

A number of us decided to travel down to Lincolnshire to watch the motorcycle races at Cadwell Park and so, having rode down on the Saturday, we stayed at Louth with the intention of riding to the race circuit the following day. Later that evening, we had been drinking in a town centre pub and, as we all left considerably the worse for wear, within minutes a shop window was put through and I vaguely remember running in for my crash helmet. I woke up the next morning in a police cell, and apparently Charlie had been arrested too, but he was in a separate cell.

On the Monday morning we were put before the Louth Magistrates Court and were each fined £50. I arrived home later that day. I was of course still working at Rhodes's and I believe it was Mam who had contacted the firm with some excuse for my absence. Charlie and his girlfriend had a baby and several weeks later I was told that he was appealing against his conviction. The reasoning for his appeal, which everyone supported including me, was that due to his domestic commitments he could not afford to pay the fine. I went along with this and said I would support his appeal by accepting sole responsibility for the incident.

A short time later, whilst on a night out at the Hare and Hounds, I was shown a copy of the testimony that my friends had collectively drawn up in collaboration with Charlie's solicitor. Reading it left me both shocked and numb at the damning things they had not only said about me, but had allowed to be put on paper. Even then, because it seemed to be the 'right thing to do' to help Charlie, I said nothing and remained willing to accept full responsibility for the incident.

In the ensuing days I simply couldn't help but become consumed with deep emotion about what my so-called friends thought of me. When it came to the day of the hearing, we all travelled down to Lincoln by train and by now I was completely hurt and stressed out and couldn't stop thinking about their damning testimonies and, as a consequence, I hardly spoke at all on the journey there. I honestly could not remember throwing my crash helmet at the shop window, only a vague recollection of running in to retrieve it.

Charlie was in court with his solicitor whilst the rest of us were sat outside the court waiting to be called in to give evidence when two of the policemen from Louth called over to me. I went across to speak with them and one commented how silly I was to be singularly taking the blame. He reiterated that I had only been seen running into the shop for my helmet and not throwing it. His comments only served to intensify my feelings.

I retook my seat alongside Steve Sunderland, who immediately and in a brusque manner asked what they had wanted. I simply said that when this day was over, I would not be hanging around with them anymore. He retorted back, though I am not too sure what his reply was, but the next thing I had jumped to my feet and was punching him. The police pulled me off and restrained me.

Word must have been passed to Charlie's solicitor because the next thing I knew was being told that I was no longer required as a witness and that I should make my way home immediately. I kept to my word and never did hang about with them again. Every now and then I happened to bump into someone, but I would only say "hello". I couldn't comprehend how my *friends* could have treated me so badly.

Many years later I was having a general discussion with an older plumber about the notion of friends and friendship and he commented that as we pass through life, though we will have many associates, we only have very few friends. For me it was a simple but profound comment. Dave Towns hadn't been involved in the court debacle, so I began hanging around with him more. I began frequenting the Hare and Hounds at Menston more regularly and, when Dave started courting, I began to go out with his older brother Gerald.

Gerald didn't own a motorcycle, but he loved rock and roll music. I too became greatly interested in the music and before too long we both had Teddy Boy suits. We began following the Dave Lee Sound to other pub and club venues and, not too surprisingly, became mates with other like-minded lads.

Late one Saturday afternoon, Gerald and I were contemplating what to do that evening and I spontaneously suggested a ride over to Scarborough so we could spend the evening there. We got there on the bike in good time and made our way to The Silver Grid up in the town centre. The pub was used by bikers and, at the end of the evening, with fish and chips tucked inside our jackets, we got onto the bike and went to Cayton Bay.

I parked the bike by a path that led on to the cliffs. I remember it was a lovely summer's evening as we ate our fish and chips and, though neither of us had a sleeping bag, it was warm and dry. I awoke the next morning to a fantastic vista of a beautiful blue sea and the emerging blue sky. I had recently bought the Van Morrison Moon Dance album and a track called Brand New Day immediately sprang into my mind as I laid there and watched the sun rise over the sea.

We travelled home late that day, having had a really good time. On one particular evening, we were in the Gate pub at Seacroft, listening to the DJ, when towards the end of the night we met a lad that I knew called Pete Waters and he introduced us to his friend who had an old Ford Popular, the type with only the three gears.

Another act of spontaneity led us on a journey that was miles away to Harry Ramsden's fish shop at Menston for late night fish and chips. On the way back the driver of the old Ford 'Pop' became rather crazy and was really caning it down Kirkstall Road from the Horsforth Ring Road and, as we approached the double 'S' bends by Kirkstall Forge, the car skidded and turned over.

Unbelievably, none of us was hurt and we all clambered out and pushed the car the right way up. Not surprisingly, the car wouldn't start so, being concerned that the accident may have been seen by someone who had then called the police, we hastily made our separate ways home on the bus.

Pete Waters later told me that his friend who had been driving that night was actually a city council bus driver! Looking back these were just events that I took in my stride. I guess life was pretty good: my job was okay, college was going well, and I now had some new mates to go out with. I simply accepted most things and tried to enjoy my life as I am sure young people have always done.

Chapter 6

My Old Man

As a young boy, I was of course oblivious to the fact that my parents and their families had lived through the mass unemployment and privations of the 1920s and 30s and, following this, their generation were also plunged into the horrors and uncertainties of the Second World War. Like many couples during the war, my parents were separated from each other, with Dad away serving in the Army whilst Mam worked in the munitions factory. I groan today when I hear people talk about how stressful modern-day life is.

My dad, George Potter, had been born on 9 March 1913 and was the youngest son of Tom and Sarah Ellen Potter, who at the time lived at 16 Sykes Street, Holbeck, Leeds. My grandad Potter was an engineer by trade who died before I ever met him, as did my grandma. Though I have no knowledge about the birth or death of my grandad Potter, I do know that my grandma was born in 1875 and passed away on 17th February 1936.

My dad was their youngest son, and he was about thirty minutes older than his twin sister, Gladys. Other children were Tom, the eldest boy; Albert; and then Ellen, the eldest girl. They all went to the Pottery Fields School and, having completed their elementary education, they left for the world of work when they were aged fourteen. The level of educational requirement for pupils always broadly mirrors the level of skills required in a developing economy.

Dad initially went to work in a mill, but then left to go and work for William Walkers on Kirkstall Road as a dyer's labourer and, being a good cricketer, he subsequently played for the work's team. In fact, including his five years' service in the war, Dad worked at Walkers for twenty-two years in total.

With the onset of the Second World War, and at the age of 27, he enlisted in the Royal Artillery on 24 April 1940. His Regiment was the 56 Medium and he served in the 122 Medium Battery. Whilst in the Army, he received a Grade 1 in relation to the operations and maintenance of wireless sets. He also trained to drive a 15cwt truck and had the rank of Gunner. He was stationed in Ireland throughout the war, due to the potential threat of German invasion. On 13 December 1945 he was released from the Army and his testimonial stated that he was…

> *"A first rate man of pleasant personality. Clean, smart, cheerful, honest and trustworthy. He is a good worker and can be recommended to work and earn his pay on any job he is given."*

I vividly remember one dark autumn evening in 1969, and with the rain just so relentless Mam explained to me that Dad was having to work over and would be home late. Not only that, but by the time he did finish work the circular bus service would have stopped running for the evening, leaving him to walk the two to three miles home from Hunslet in the pouring rain. With this, I donned my bike gear and went to get the bike out of the garage, and then I rode down to Hudswell Clarke's to pick him up.

It was only a small gesture, but I could see that he was pleased to see me and that I had thought about him. And for me I was chuffed because it was the very first time he had been on the back of my bike, but little did either of us know that it would also be the last. Strange how we remember what are sometimes such small things so vividly. For example, whenever Mam and Dad came back from a night out at the pub, he would pull his money out of his trouser pocket, count the loose change and put it on the mantle shelf above the fireplace.

He went through a period of collecting both wrist and pocket watches and would proudly show them off to me. Also, being a smoker, it was the same with any new petrol lighter that he acquired, showing off their different emblems and patterns. They had a friend who was also a regular in the Hampton Pub and he would occasionally go on holiday to Ireland and would bring back cigarette lighters that had symbols on them, such as a four-leaf clover. Essentially, these were small and simple aspects of working-class materialism across that generation as mass consumerism was still in its infancy and, moreover, then as now the ability to consume depends on one's disposable income.

Most nights when we were all tucked up in bed, I would often hear him repeatedly say to himself "Up at five int mornin', up at five int mornin'…" This always worked for him as, as workers go, he was always a very good timekeeper.

There were other old habits too. For example, whilst I might take a flask to work with me, every morning he still religiously made up his 'mashings' along with a small bottle (usually a cleaned-out medicine bottle) of milk and a teaspoon. Together with his sandwiches, he would put them in his small khaki shoulder bag ready for when he went out to work dressed in his boiler suit, overcoat and flat cap.

Mam and Dad had begun socialising in the Easy Road Working Men's Club, known locally as the *'Spit 'n' Slavva'*. Mam always carried some family photos in her handbag and it now became the norm that often they would return from the club with one or both telling me that a young woman who collected glasses and bottles had seen some of the photos and commented that she fancied me. This went on for some time, with them suggesting that I call into the club so that I might meet her, but I shrugged off their suggestions, never taking up the offer.

It was early in 1970 that Dad was admitted into hospital for tests due to a lingering cough. Mam and our Gill had gone to visit him one evening and I was at home watching the telly. Later that evening, Gill came bursting through the door. She was very upset and blurted out the news that Dad had got throat cancer. I was still trying to take it in when minutes later Mam followed her confirming the devastating news. At that moment in time, the three of us struggled to take the diagnosis in.

Within several days, Dad was discharged from hospital and scheduled to undergo a course of radiotherapy at the Cookridge Hospital. There was no chemotherapy then and we all naturally hoped that radiotherapy would work. I don't recall having much of a discussion with Mam about her feelings and I guess that I was reluctant to raise the subject for fear of upsetting her. In turn, she was probably of the same view and, for the best part, we kept our thoughts and anxieties to ourselves.

I knew very little of cancer, but at nineteen years old, why should I? However, I soon learned that in those days there was still a belief that it was a contagious disease and, as a consequence, something of a taboo topic amongst family and friends.

In due course, I announced the news to Stan Rhodes in his office, but he quickly dismissed my comments, saying something like, "No, you must have got it all wrong. I'm sure everything will be okay." Why would I get something like that wrong? Anyhow, I never spoke to him again about Dad's illness and, in turn, he never asked.

Dad was discharged from hospital, but he had never been told that he had cancer, and this must have been common practice within the NHS at the time. As a family, we too never broached it with him and, if he had any awareness of his condition, he never shared it with us.

He began his course of radiotherapy, but upon completion the clinical prognosis was that it had been unsuccessful in dealing with the malignancy. Still both Mam and I never broached matters with him and, in fact, for some time he seemed reasonably fine and would openly talk about his plans for when he was better and back at work.

At the beginning of the summer, he would walk down to the East Leeds Cricket Club (close to the Bridgefield pub) and enjoy watching a match. However, as the summer passed and his health began to deteriorate, such walks to see the cricket ceased. His trade union paid for him to have one-week convalescence in a home at the seaside, but after several days he came back saying that he was the only ill person there.

There was no hospice movement then, or anything akin to the cancer Macmillan nurses of today, so clearly the brunt of the caring fell on Mam. As Dad became weaker, she would have to wash and shave him, though on one occasion he did ask me to shave him. By now I do believe he had a very good idea what was happening to him, and we heard no more from him about his future plans.

It was on the Thursday evening of 12 November that I had helped Dad up the stairs and got him tucked up in bed. Having done this, I went back downstairs to sit with Mam and then, a while later, she said, "Colin, he's shouting for you."

When I got upstairs, he was lying flat, though his whole body was violently shaking. I ran downstairs to tell Mam and I am unsure of what happened next, but she must have asked a neighbour to call an ambulance, which eventually came and took him to hospital.

I don't believe I went into work on the Friday and Saturday morning, but if not then I would have contacted the firm with an explanation for fear of being in the *bad books*. That Friday evening and over the weekend, I never went to visit Dad in hospital as I knew deep down in my heart that this was the end.

On the Monday morning, I went into work as usual and don't recall mentioning Dad's situation with anyone. Along with a couple of other plumbers, I was given work to do on the Seacroft Estate. Early to mid-afternoon I was tracked down by Sam Ford who announced that Stan had sent him to find me because my dad had died. I went home immediately. The next day being Tuesday I travelled by bus to Rhodes's shop, arriving mid-morning in order to explain what was happening and discuss my return to work.

There were several lads in the back of the shop talking with Stan and Mary. After comments of sympathy, Mary asked me when the funeral was going to be held and I replied saying, "On Thursday, but I'll come into work tomorrow."

Mary replied back saying, "No, take the rest of the week off. There must be things to sort and there's your mother to look after." I left shortly afterwards.

As Thursday came the curtains at our house were still drawn as a mark of respect, which was something of a common practice back then. The funeral was held at Harehills Cemetery and Dad was buried in a plot that was big enough for two coffins, Dad today and the other would be for Mam on another sad day. This surprised me as I knew nothing about it, but it was clearly an arrangement privately discussed and undertaken by two people who loved each other.

From the cemetery, we went to the Irish Centre on York Road, where a room had been booked, along with tea and sandwiches provided for the mourners. Later, we all said our goodbyes and set off home. I don't recall crying at the funeral and, on reflection it seemed to take me a long time to really grieve.

Dad died at the age of fifty-seven on the 16 November 1970, exactly one week before my twentieth birthday. On the Monday after Dad's death, and on my birthday, I went back into work as agreed, but couldn't have foretold what was in store for me. As I went in through the back door, as was the norm, most of the lads were in, but I was met with an uneasy silence as practically no one spoke a word other than an odd muttering of "mornin'".

After a short while, Stan appeared in the doorway and called me through into his office and, once in there, in a stern voice he immediately demanded to know why I had not shown for work on Saturday morning. I was completely and utterly perplexed by his inquisitive and aggressive attitude and I began to reiterate what Mary had said to me when I had called at the office on the Tuesday, the day after Dad's death. I went on to explain that I had said that the funeral was on Thursday, but I would come in on the day before, that is, Wednesday. She had then said words to the effect of "no take the rest of the week off, there must be things to sort out and your there's your mother to look after."

Stan utterly refuted that she had said anything of the kind and, in doing so, he reached into the desk draw, took out my wage packet and threw it across the desk top towards me, saying, "There's yer wages there. Do you think yer suited ere?"

I was aghast and before I could speak he added, "You'd better watch yerself, off yer go." I was absolutely gutted and stunned, wondering if I was going mad.

As I wandered out into the yard the lads were busying about getting whatever materials for their jobs but Jim Ford, who was stood on the back of his pickup truck, aggressively shouted at me, "You're a right *so and so* messin' Stan and Mary about."

However, before I could reply, one of the lads that had been in the previous Tuesday, the day after Dad's death, retorted back to Jim saying, "Hey up, we wer' in't shop last Tuesday when he came in't day after his dad's death and we heard Mary tell 'im to have rest o't week off."

No more was said, but I had heard too much already and that particular experience I shall always remember. Though after that I must confess that I do not have a clue what work I did for the rest of that day.

Over the years, I have heard social commentators comment about the death of some sort of celebrity and say something like "Everyone knows where they were or what they were doing when John F Kennedy was shot" or "when Princess Diana died". Frankly, I don't have a clue on both accounts and the same would apply for any other deceased 'celebrity'. However, around the time of Dad's death, I remember events such as Clive Dunn having a record in the charts called 'Grandad' and the untimely death of Lillian Board, the British Olympic long jumper who also lost her battle with cancer in December 1970.

Her case was particularly poignant for me as it was being frequently reported upon in the news at the same time as Dad was dying. I also remember the Joni Mitchell single 'Big Yellow Taxi' being in the charts at that time, and especially the lyric that still resonates with me about the moment when the ambulance came to take Dad to hospital.

> *"Late last night I heard the screen door slam*
> *And a Big Yellow Taxi took away my old man*
> *Don't it always seem to go that you don't know what you've got till it's gone..."*

Dad was a thoroughly decent man and, over the years, I have often felt cheated that he died at such a young age. He never got to see me develop and grow or see my own family and, over the years, there have been many occasions that I wished he was still alive so that I could ask him about his life, the things he had seen and done. Bernard, my brother-in-law, still refers to him today as "Gentleman George".

On many occasions, I have often thought about the possible cause of his throat cancer. Yes, he was indeed a regular smoker, but I have never forgotten that when I was a young boy, he would often complain about the dirty periodic task of having to clean the coal-fired boilers at Dixon's Mill. Such industrial pipework was insulated with asbestos and it is possible that dust emissions were prevalent in the air. He was never given any protective equipment. As I pointed out in Chapter 1, the hazards of working with asbestos had been known for many decades.

As best we could, and in our own way, Mam and I both tried to pick our lives up after his untimely death, but it wasn't easy for either of us. As for me, I found that, on occasion when I was walking home after having been out drinking, I began scraping my knuckles on any adjacent brick wall until they bled and never stopping when they did, just simply walking on. There were several occasions when, after a night's drinking at *the Slip* and being under the influence, I walked over to the Irish Centre, where we had all gone following Dad's funeral, and threw a number of bricks, smashing windows in the building. Though these petty acts of vandalism quickly ceased, the self-harming, as it is called today, continued.

Mam herself clearly wasn't coping well being on her own in the home she had once shared with Dad. This being the case, she announced one evening that she would be calling into the Conservative Working Men's Club later that night to speak with a ward councillor about the possibility of moving house. The person that she spoke with clearly empathised with her position because, in a matter of weeks, we were offered another house at 18 St. Hilda's Crescent, not far from St. Hilda's Church which still stands today.

The house was another back-to-back, about five to ten minutes' walk from Pontefract Place. The St. Hilda's, and much of the surrounding houses, were of the traditional back-to-back type. However, this one differed from our existing home because, like many in the area, it had recently undergone *conversion* work. So, for the first time, we had an indoor bathroom and toilet. The old toilet yards were still standing, though they now only housed the dustbins and had no one scurrying up and down the street to the toilet. In place of the coal fire, there was a nice gas fire.

On the run up to the actual move, we borrowed a pram in order to transport many small items. At times, Mam would criticise the family GP for failing to see that the persistence of Dad's lingering cough meant that he had needed hospital intervention much sooner and therefore the GP had failed to act in accordance with Dad's best interests. On the face of it, she seemed to be settling in to her new home fairly well and, though she never said much, she would still have been grieving for Dad.

Some time before we moved house, I had my motorcycle stolen from the small garage/shed within the confines of the Conservative WMC grounds. I had an idea who may have stolen it, but the police said that it would probably have been stripped down quite quickly and took no action.

Mam bought me another second-hand bike which was a BSA 650cc Road Rocket and this was now being kept under a tarpaulin in the toilet yard by the new house. The year that Dad died his employer, Hudswell Clarkes, had set up a new employee insurance scheme. In due course, Mam received a financial payment and out of this she bought me the new bike, and also gave some monies to Gill and Bernard. Other money was used for furnishings in our new home.

In the absence of other leisure activities, like many of their generation, Mam and Dad had been social drinkers, meeting friends, workmates and acquaintances in the pub or club. They would exchange comments about work, family and whatever might be happening in the day's news, and the men might have a game of darts or dominoes in the 'tap room', and in those days many such rooms were out of bounds to women. Now on her own, she continued to take the five-minute walk up Easy Road to the '*Spit n Slavva'* Club for a drink and a natter with folk she knew and she enjoyed a game of bingo too. However, the move to St Hilda's Crescent also brought about a strange and uncanny happening.

Motorcycling was still a fundamental part of my life, along with popular music. My *Teddy Boy* mates and I had begun using the '*Slip Inn'* (New Regent) pub positioned several hundred yards directly behind the Irish Centre. They had a good DJ playing every Friday and Saturday evening, and the place was 'buzzing' with people and good music.

We hadn't been in the St Hilda's that long when one day Mam said, "Frank Brake lives in that house opposite to us and he's the treasurer of the Easy Road Club."

"Oh, right Mam," I replied, no doubt sounding rather disinterested.

"Do you remember me and your dad going on about that lass in the club who saw some of yer photos and said she fancied yer?"

"Yeah."

"Well, she's Frank Brake's daughter. They live straight opposite us at number seventeen."

"Right," said I.

I later saw the girl in question several times in the street before finally one Saturday evening she was in the *'Slip Inn'*. She was very attractive so, after a few drinks, I plucked up the courage and asked her if she wanted a drink. She recognised me as the new lad from over the road, but would later remind me on numerous occasions of the measly 10p I gave her for a drink.

Her name was Wendy and, after chatting for a while, she agreed that I could walk her home. However, after more drinks and dancing, I ended up going off with another girl. Luckily for me, Wendy didn't completely shun me for my stupidity and we finally had our first date, which was at the New Regent Cinema at the bottom of Stoney Rock Lane to see the film *Khartoum*, starring Charlton Heston.

After the film, we went for a drink in the New Prospect pub, Richmond Hill. This had been recently refurbished into a Western-theme setting with swing doors etc. At the time she said nothing about how I was dressed for the date, but thereafter I was frequently reminded that I had been wearing black drainpipe jeans and shoes that were black suede 'brothel creepers', along with my trusted leather jacket. I was twenty and she was sixteen years old, and we began seeing each other regularly.

I gradually became much more than just fond of her, though her demeanour at times left me unsure regarding her feelings about me. At the end of our date, I would always walk her over to her house and, after asking if I could meet her the following night, she would dismissively say, "Yer can if yer want." She was initially reluctant to show her feelings towards me and it took me a while to overcome my insecurity and anxiety caused by this flippant retort.

Much of our dating was in local pubs, such as the *'Slip Inn'*, The Bridgefield, The Yew Tree and the Victoria on York Road opposite the Irish Centre. One of the lads explained that there were several pubs in York where Teddy Boys gathered to listen and dance to rock 'n' roll music. We thus went over to York on quite a number of occasions and eventually became friends with some of them and, in turn, many of the York lads reciprocated and met up with us in the *'Slip Inn'* for a night out.

We still used to go and see the rock 'n' roll trio the Dave Lee Sound if they were performing within a reasonable distance. One day I was informed by my mam that The New Statesmen were to play on a Saturday evening at the *'Spit n Slavva'*. This interested me because my old secondary school teacher, Jack Berry, was a member of the band.

On the evening they were playing, Wendy and I walked up the steps to the concert room and, with the band between songs, Jack Berry spotted me straight away and shouted over the mike, "Yer late! Have yer gotta note?" People turned around to see who the comment was being directed to and I attempted to shrug off my embarrassment.

Besides the pubs and clubs, we enjoyed rides out on the bike together. It was probably the first occasion that we went to the coast on the bike that she confessed that, other than club members' family day trips, it was the first time she had been to the seaside. Though Wendy's dad owned a car, amongst working-class folk, car ownership was still in its infancy. Thus, for working-class kids, motorcycling offered opportunity, freedom and independence.

Her dad had formerly spent approximately twenty-five years in the Army. He was originally born on the Isle of Wight, but following a marital split his father found it difficult to cope with Frank the baby and his three older sisters. They were all put into care, which in those days meant gender segregation. He remained separated from them until the early 1980s, when they were once again finally reunited following a search by Chris, one of Wendy's brothers.

Wendy's mam, Iris, was a Leeds lass and her parents at the time still lived not too far away in Dent Street. Wendy herself was born on 5 June 1954 and she was the seventh eldest of ten children. She had been working at Kays Catalogue Company, Marshall Street, in Holbeck since leaving school and, whenever possible, I would finish work early so that I could meet her at her works.

I always found it amusing that, once the factory buzzer sounded, within seconds the doors were thrown back and hordes of workers would come running out of the building as if they were in mortal danger. On such occasions, we would walk the two to three miles home together hand in hand. As the months passed and our relationship became more serious, at times I found myself reflecting on the very sad irony that had brought us together.

In my head, things began with the death of the man that walked in front of my motorbike. Within less than twelve months of this, my dad was diagnosed with cancer. Following his death, Mam and I had moved house, but not to any old house – it was opposite the home of the girl both she and Dad said fancied me after seeing the photos shown by Mam.

On numerous occasions prior to his death they had asked me to meet her by visiting the club, but at the time I had shunned their suggestions. And now here we were together and in a serious relationship. For me, it was and still is a strange mix of circumstance and events, something one could explain away quite simply as fate.

At the time part of me felt that Dad's untimely death was simply a punishment for accidentally killing a man in the motorbike crash and so I felt that these events had been pre-ordained. However, as I have gained in years and became a conscious atheist, I have come to view such happenings as a quirk of circumstances and, though I never shared these thoughts with Mam, I am sure she must have considered herself how Dad's death had led to Wendy and me finally meeting.

Whilst my mam was happy to see me and Wendy together, I felt that her own dad wasn't too pleased. He clearly knew me, but whenever I would call for Wendy, if he answered the door, he would look at me coldly and say, "Yes, what do you want?"

In reply, I would ask, "Is Wendy in?"

There were occasions when she overheard this uneasy exchange of words and would come running down the stairs saying to her dad, "You know who it is. It's Colin. Ask him in!"

I thought it was because of the clothes I wore, but later she would tell me that he was like that with everyone. One day, Wendy had occasion to tell me that I had annoyed her dad, which initially perplexed me until she explained further.

Her dad kept pigeons and, on one particular day, I was outside our house in the street cleaning my bike. The house door was open and a song by John Leyton titled 'Wild Wind' was playing loudly on my radiogram. Wendy came over to tell me that her dad was trying to get his pigeons into the coop, but the music kept frightening them away, much to her dad's growing frustration and annoyance with me. We both laughed, but I obliged and turned the sound down.

On another occasion, her young nephew, Martin, had been messing with my bike and Wendy gave chase, but fell on the cobbled street injuring her left shoulder. She was taken to hospital by her dad and came back with her arm in a sling, having suffered a dislocation and this was to cause her frequent ongoing problems.

We had now been going out for some time and, at times, I was still scraping my knuckles on walls whilst walking home after a night out drinking. I did this on more than one occasion when I was with Wendy, much to her concern. I am not too sure when, but at some point I felt able to share my feelings with her about Dad's death. This happened on a number of occasions, with her listening empathetically to what I had to say, and as a consequence, I was at last able to shed a few tears.

Chapter 7

Wouldn't It Be Nice?

Just as many couples do, Wendy and I had a song that meant something really special to us both, and that was a Beach Boys tune called 'Wouldn't It Be Nice', but this proved to be rather more prophetic than we realised at the time. It was in early 1972 and we had been going out together for around fourteen months when, one day following a visit to see the doctor, I saw her on her way back home and it was then that she explained that she was pregnant.

At the time I was aged twenty-one and she was seventeen, but we were both in no doubt that we wanted to get married. Whilst I was to break the news with my mam, Wendy was left to broach matters with her parents – and await their reaction.

Nationally, prior to the 1959 Mental Health Act, a single woman bearing a child out of wedlock could be 'Sectioned' under the previous legislation. Such archaic legislation saw such women cruelly termed as *'Moral Imbeciles'*. Therefore, in those days there was still a huge social stigma for a woman to become pregnant out of wedlock and give birth to what would be regarded as a bastard child and, in some cases, it led to family breakups, with the pregnant woman leaving the parental home and often being ostracised.

Parental pressure also resulted in babies being taken from their mothers after birth and being adopted or taken into care. Self-styled Christian groups were often at the centre and years later it was reported that many such children were sent overseas – a practice that begun in the 1930s right up until the late 1960s – to former colonies such as Australia.

The term *'shotgun wedding'* was commonly used. However, juxtaposed with the often sorry events for working-class families around this time was the position of so-called celebrities who found themselves in the same situation, but in contrast they were deemed to have had *'a love child'*.

We were swayed by none of these potential social pressures, but we still resolved that we wanted to marry. The baby was due later that year in November. Wendy recalls that when she told her parents her dad said some very nasty things to her whilst her mam just didn't speak to her at all. Upset, she ran upstairs with her dad running after her.

She turned and said, "All I want is your help." With that, he reached out and gave her a cuddle. Even when Wendy began suffering from 'morning sickness', her mam never spoke to her about being pregnant and this ghostly silence continued right up until our wedding day, when Wendy finally left home. Her mam had said to others that Wendy didn't have to get married if she didn't want to. I really don't recall how I broached the matter with my mam, but there was no backlash from her.

My mam really liked Wendy though. At the same time, I am sure that she must have felt sad that, within a little over two years after Dad's death, she was soon to be left on her own. This said, she never put any kind of pressure on me about the pending marriage and my leaving home.

Wendy and I finally set the date of 8 July 1972 for our wedding day and began making our plans for married life together. At some stage, I explained matters to my boss Stan Rhodes and, given that the firm undertook a lot of work for private landlords, he soon came up with a back-to-back rented house for us in Beeston that was available if we wanted it. Wendy and I visited the property and, following a good look around, we said yes.

The house was again typical in character, being a 'two up and two down' with the entrance door leading in off the street and into the living room, with the scullery kitchen immediately off to the left whilst the staircase to the two bedrooms was in the corner of the room. In the scullery/kitchen, we had a sink unit with just the single cold water tap, though hot water was available from a small gas geyser fitted above the sink unit. These gas hot water geysers were initially fitted into many back-to-back houses in order to remedy the problem of having no available hot water.

In the back corner of the scullery/kitchen was a door giving access to the cellar and the toilet, as was customary with back-to-back homes, was located up the street in a toilet yard. Our first home together was going to be 16 Fulham Terrace, with the weekly rent being the princely sum of 92p – at the time, my weekly wage was around £25.

Stan and Mary Rhodes helped further by letting us choose wallpaper from a couple of decorators catalogues he had loaned to us and, though they were paying when we were making our choices, we consciously steered away from the expensive ones for fear of appearing to abuse their good will. To help with the cost of furnishings etc., I managed to secure a £350 bank loan. At the same time, for the cost of £5, from Wendy's uncle Ted we purchased a cocktail cabinet and a pair of two-seater settees, with the latter in reasonable condition, though each had a piece of plywood screwed underneath due to the springs being worn.

My mam gave us her washing machine, which had the mangle on the top for rinsing the washing, and also gave us numerous small things, such as cutlery and some solid wooden coat-hangers, which we still have today, along with some stainless-steel knives. Of course, I took with me the grand radiogram bought for me by Mam and Dad several years previous, and together both Wendy and I beavered away in our new house with absolute enthusiasm on the run up to the wedding day.

Our Gill helped us with the wallpapering, and I managed to get a decent modern gas fire, which I remember well as being a Robinson Willey Super Fire-dance with a wooden surround – such opulence! Initially, we had some laughs with the main brass light switch block on the living room wall. There were about four brass switches on the block, but when you touched one you got a slight electric shock! I reported it to Stan Rhodes and, in the interim, prior to the electrician calling to fix it, I cut and placed one-inch long pieces of plastic petrol piping over each switch. The day of the wedding arrived at last. It was to be held on a Saturday morning at the registry office, Park Square, Leeds.

That morning, once I was properly dressed for my wedding, I decided to walk into town. I was wearing my green three-piece Teddy Boy suit, with its black velvet roll-collar, black velvet flaps over the pockets and sleeve cuffs. The jacket had two black velvet buttons, forming a link fastening and the waistcoat also had black velvet buttons. My shoes were bright orange suede wedges, or brothel creepers, and the white shirt had a gold-edged ruffle, together with a green bootlace tie that had a skull and crossbones logo.

I got into town rather early, probably due to nerves, so I went into the Chicken Inn Café by the Corn Exchange. From here, I walked on to the registry office and, when I saw Wendy, she looked as gorgeous as ever dressed in a lemon short-sleeved jacket, white skirt and white shoes.

The wedding was a small affair, with those present being the two witnesses, Gill and Wendy's uncle, Ted, our parents and several friends. After the ceremony, we all went back to Wendy's parents' house to enjoy a small buffet that had been prepared.

A little later, her mam announced that she was going to cut the cake and, at this point, for some reason Wendy left the house and went next door to sit with Linda, her sister-in-law. She told me later that her reason for leaving when she did was due to the fact that, on the run up to the wedding, her mam had told her that she didn't deserve a cake, so it was my mam who had stepped in and bought the wedding cake. Therefore, the cake-cutting announcement had been simply too much for her to bear.

A small number of us went to York in the evening, which is what Wendy and I wanted, and we visited a number of rock 'n' roll pubs, as we had previously done in the past, where we knew a number of York 'Teds'. The Monday came around and we were both back at work, but a couple of weeks later we loaded the bike up and went camping for a long weekend to the east coast, near Filey.

The camp site was adjacent to Dennis's holiday site and the tent that we took with us was the ex-army khaki one that I had owned for about five years, and this measured six feet by three feet wide and three feet high, with two wooden ridge poles, no sewn-in groundsheet, but with a mosquito net over the front and rear entrances – though on reflection there were no tropical temperatures and mosquitos!

We were both really happy and delighted with our first home. Our £350 bank loan had enabled us to furnish most of the house, though we still had a number of small items to buy, such as egg cups, but in the interim, when the occasion arose, I would sit my boiled eggs in the top of a washed-out milk bottle in order to eat them.

Life is fundamentally about a multiplicity of relationships and is made special by the ones that bring with it love. We had each other and nothing about our simple surroundings was offputting or onerous, and we had lots of laughs and happy times. With the toilet yard being a short walk up the street, your immediate neighbours knew when you were going to the loo and vice versa, and we laughed like crazy one day when Jessie, the neighbour opposite us, came out of the toilet yard with her skirt tucked into the back of her knickers!

There was also the time when one evening we returned home having been out for a drink and having just got into bed I decided that I needed to go to the loo. Being a little worse for wear, I lifted the bedroom sash window and urinated through it down on to the pavement below. The following day, when I returned home from work, Wendy said to me that our next-door neighbour, Pat, was asking if "I'd heard the heavy rain last night."

In reply, I said that, "It never rained at all last night, she must have heard me weeing onto the pavement from the bedroom window." This caused us both to laugh.

Wendy continued to work at Kays and, though the pregnancy progressed, we continued to enjoy rides out on the bike and still recall one particular occasion, when she was eight months pregnant. We were travelling to Sherburn, along with two other motorcyclists, when we went over and around the old Boot 'n' Shoe flyover at eighty miles per hour, with the footrests scraping on the road. Thrilling, but oh the sheer stupidity of youth!

Shortly following this she ceased working and, on the morning of 13 November, I set off for work as usual and Wendy had said that later that day she was going down to her mam's in order to have a bath. With us having no bath, we used to get 'a strip wash' by the kitchen sink, though on occasions we had baths at our parents' houses. It was some time in the afternoon that someone at work informed me that Wendy had gone into hospital and seemed ready to deliver the baby.

That evening I went to visit her at St. James Hospital and we were told that there were no imminent signs of the baby's arrival. I stayed through the visiting period, but then had to leave at 8.30pm. The next morning someone at work told me that I had a baby son. He had been born at

9.10pm the previous evening and I was informed that thankfully the birth had been straightforward, with only a short labour process. We agreed that our son was to have the forenames of Colin, after his dad, and George, after his grandad Potter. Fair play to Stan and Mary Rhodes: they supplied us with a really good second-hand Silvercross pram.

During the first few months of Colin being born, we pushed him in the pram all over the place, and it was a fairly regular occurrence for us to walk what was perhaps three to four miles with the pram from our home in Beeston to visit our parents in Cross Green. Sometimes we would take the long way round by walking through the city centre.

The following year we had our first family holiday in a caravan at Primrose Valley and it seemed that our song 'Wouldn't It Be Nice' had come to life. Around this time, we began thinking about emigrating to Canada as Wendy's sister Jenny had actually moved there, along with her husband, several years previous. However, after giving the matter much thought, I felt that it would be unfair to my mam if we did emigrate and, although she had been quite keen on the idea, Wendy accepted my reasoning quite happily and that was that. I was by now a fully-qualified plumber, indeed a tradesman with an Advanced Craft City & Guilds Certificate in plumbing theory and practical work and, given this, I felt that it was time to move on in order to get more experience and, hopefully, an increase in wages.

Later that year, in 1973, I got a job with the Leeds Public Works Department and, after a while, though the work was okay, I was advised that if I wanted to make decent money then I would be better off doing 'site work'. I managed to get a job with a guy called Peter Kelly, who employed a large number of plumbers and electricians, doing work across West Yorkshire for the house builders Barrats. Though the work was not bonus-led, the money was an improvement.

In order to increase my mobility – and have more family-friendly transport – it was not long after this that I sold my bike and bought a three-wheeler Reliant car from Fletcher's on Meadow Lane. At that time, you could drive a three-wheeler without a car driving licence, as long as you held a full motorcycle one, and so it was that, having never driven a car before, Wendy and I laughed like crazy one Friday evening as I drove out of the forecourt onto the relatively busy Meadow Lane with the car 'kangarooing' and jerking as I set off.

I was working on a site at Knaresborough and I set off for work on the Monday morning. As I dropped down the hill from the end of our street the car was sluggish, so I duly put my foot on the accelerator. As I progressed with my journey to work, I noticed that several cars seemed to flash their lights at me, which I found a little disconcerting, though the car itself seemed to be driving okay.

As I pulled up at work, the first thing I noticed was that I had driven all the way with the hand brake on, hence the downhill sluggish motion! Because a number of cars had flashed me, I took a good look around the car in case there was problem. A foreman plumber, called George, came over and, seeing me feverishly looking over the car, enquired, "Is everything okay?"

I replied back, "I'm not sure. A few cars have flashed their lights at me on the way to work."

George said, "I bet they were other Reliants." He went on to explain that "the camaraderie amongst Reliant owners is such that they either wave or flash lights to acknowledge each other."

We both had a giggle and the potential crisis was over. He was right; future driving saw other Reliant owners either waving or flashing their lights at me and it wasn't long before I too entered the friendly world of being a three-wheeler car owner. If all that wasn't enough, the car had one other little surprise in store for me.

I had bought the car on the understanding from anecdotal comments that it didn't have a functioning reverse gear, due to the fact that I only had a full motorcycle license rather than a car and, therefore, in such circumstances the reverse gear had been blanked off. A couple of months or so after its purchase, we were visiting Stephen, Wendy's brother.

"How's the car going, Colin?"

"Not bad, Steve." I commented on how we liked the car and then said, "It's a pity, though, that there is no reverse gear due to me only having the motorbike license."

Steve replied back, "Of course it's got a reverse gear! Haven't you tried finding it?"

I shook my head. We went outside to the car and Steve got in, started the engine and straight away showed me how to select reverse gear! Another quirk was the fact that, being a three-wheeler, it was nigh on impossible to miss pot holes in the road.

Half the engine sat between the driver and front seat passenger and the bulbous fibre glass casing over this had a carpet covering. On the top was an ash tray that simply pushed into the opening for it.

At times, when we unavoidably went over a pot hole, the ash tray would spring into the air, causing much hilarity. On one occasion, we went to Skegness for a weekend camping holiday with our trusty ex-army ridge tent. However, the weather for the first night was bad, with wind and rain. At around 5am in the morning, we woke to see that the front pole had collapsed, and young Colin's head was sticking out into the elements.

We frantically packed everything up into the car and set off home. We had only gone a few miles when, sod's law, the fan belt broke. Wendy suggested tying a pair of tights around the fly and pulley wheels as a temporary measure, but I declined because this was something I had never heard of and so instead we nursed the car home. From time to time over the years, we have overheard comments about the feasibility of using ladies' tights as a proxy fan belt and, consequently, I have never been able to live it down for not taking her advice.

In the previous chapter, I commented about the time when Wendy had dislocated her left shoulder chasing her nephew, Martin, and this proved to have periodic consequences for her. Indeed, the shoulder joint was now slipping out all too easily. Once it popped out when her arms were innocently raised above her head and, on another occasion, she was on the bus by herself, but with baby Colin in her arms. When the time came to get off the bus, with one arm holding Colin and the other gripping the vertical grab rail, the bus jerked and the shoulder was out yet again. She eventually had it operated on at Pinderfields Hospital, Wakefield, where a metal pin was surgically inserted to remedy the problem.

In total it had dislocated on nine occasions. Her arm was very heavily strapped, completely to her waist for six weeks, but luckily we were friendly with Pat and Andrew, the young couple next door, and throughout the day Pat looked after young Colin. Even then in that situation, Wendy simply got on with things and was never one to complain about her incapacity or any pain and discomfort.

We always wanted another addition to the family and I was overjoyed when, in early 1975, Wendy announced that she was pregnant and that we were to have our second child. The projected date of birth was again to be later that year in November.

Our little Reliant continued to serve us well and we regularly went for drives out. One evening, when young Colin was being babysat by her mam at their home, Wendy and I were on our way home when I clipped a kerb going around a corner and the car flipped over. Fortunately, we were both unharmed, though the car itself was a write-off.

We were without a car, but I was able to arrange a 'lift' each morning, so it never affected my ability to work. As the months went by and the pregnancy progressed, we continued to enjoy going out for walks.

Eight weeks before Wendy was due to give birth, she was hospitalised due to constant high blood pressure and back pain. Thankfully, we were yet again able to rely on Pat and Andrew for child-minding and a routine emerged where I would get young Colin ready on a morning and leave him with Pat whilst I went to work and then, when home from work, I would feed and get him ready for bed before returning him to Pat as I then made my way to the bus stop and journeyed on to St. Mary's Hospital in the district of Armley.

Throughout her time in hospital, Wendy was given Valium to combat the high blood pressure. On the evening of 28 November 1975 I visited as normal and, though the baby wasn't due for another two weeks, upon entering the hospital ward, I was advised that Wendy was in a 'side room'.

As I went in and began to speak to her, it quickly became apparent that she was in a somewhat dazed manner, though she was able to tell me that we had a little girl. I spoke to the hospital staff, who informed me that the baby was in 'special care' because, apparently, it had been a very difficult birth and Wendy, as yet, hadn't seen the baby herself. However, I was taken down to the special unit where the nurse pointed to an incubator and informed me that the tiny baby inside was my daughter.

I went back to see Wendy and she told me that the birth had been very difficult for both her and the baby. My response was a natural one, as I tried to reassure her that things would now be okay. As Wendy remained in hospital to recover over the next few days, it became clear that the there was no let-up with the constant high blood pressure and back pain and, upon her hospital discharge, she was advised to visit our GP, who duly referred her to hospital for tests.

Our new baby girl was named Teresa, after the Eddie Cochran song 'Hey Teresa', and we gave her the added middle name of Louise. We were now a family of four and continued to be very happy in our little back-to-back house. Over the following few months, Wendy had a number of hospital visits to investigate the reason behind her persistent high blood pressure and back pain.

She was eventually diagnosed with having polycystic kidneys, a hereditary disease effectively meaning that there were multiple cysts on her kidneys. Over a period of time, they would grow to such an extent that they would eventually destroy her kidney function. It was suggested that the two main ways to slow this degenerative disease was firstly to reduce her salt intake and secondly to maintain her blood pressure at a reasonable level.

In addition to this, she was strongly advised not to have any more children as another pregnancy would exacerbate the problem with her kidneys. As a precaution she was advised to undergo the medical procedure for sterilisation. We had a chat about this and acknowledged that, after such an operation, she would need to be in hospital for two to three days, whereas it would be better if I had a vasectomy. Having agreed between us that this was the best course of action, and having set things into motion, I received an appointment to have the said deed done.

Having reached the hospital I was directed to the appropriate department and asked to join a queue of about ten men sat down in a corridor one Friday teatime at the Leeds General Infirmary. We all sat there like lambs going to the slaughter with one lad who, in hindsight, must have wished that he hadn't foolishly brought his mate for support. I say foolishly because all he did was relate what a grim experience it had been when he had undergone his vasectomy.

I was back at work on the Monday and, given the nature of the surgical procedure, not surprisingly lads on site were asking me, "What was it like,

Col? Did it hurt much?" To which, after a while, I used to reply, "Nah, thiz nowt to it. The worst thing is when he comes towards ya wit' two bricks in his hand!"

Young Colin was now in the small second bedroom and, upon going to bed, Wendy would have Teresa in the carry cot on the floor alongside her. One day I came home from work and Wendy was steeped in amusement and revealed that this was due to events that occurred during the previous night's sleep.

When Teresa became restless during the night, Wendy would stir from her sleep, fumble around in the cot, find the dummy and place it Teresa's mouth. However, she went on to explain that, in one instance, as she fumbled around in the cot and found she was unable to find the dummy, Teresa was becoming increasingly unsettled, so she got out of bed to turn the light on. Then, turning her attention to the cot, she was unable to see the 'lost' dummy until she glanced across at me sound asleep, but with the dummy in my mouth. She had inadvertently turned the wrong way in bed and placed the thing in my mouth!

We were very happy in our home. Then in early 1976, we were notified that Fulham Terrace and the other neighbouring back-to-back houses were to be demolished under a Slum Clearance Order.

In response to this news, we went to visit what was in effect the first phase of a new council estate at Cottingley, which had recently been completed. Having looked around, we duly applied and were subsequently successful in getting a three-bedroom house at 76 Dulverton Place. Ours was the middle of a five-block of terraced houses that included an internal bathroom, warm air central heating and a garden to the rear. We were both delighted with our new family home.

By that point I had passed my driving test whilst living in Fulham Terrace, though at that moment we still had no car. In the interim, I had left Peter Kelly's to work for Ashton Homes, Roundhay Road, Leeds, but then returned back to Kelly's when the bonus work seemed to be coming to an end. I was beginning to learn that there was often a mismatch between what I was being told at the point of enquiring about a job to the actual reality once I had begun working for a company.

With a young family, I was now more than ever conscious of trying to maximise my earnings. On a number of occasions after work or on a Saturday, I would set off with my havasack full of tools carried over my shoulder to go and do a private *'guvvy job'* just to earn an extra few quid.

It was now 1976 and this was a record-breaking red-hot summer and we had a long weekend camping at Reighton Gap followed by a planned week's camping holiday at Great Yarmouth over the summer. I had bought a second-hand Vauxhall Victor car at the Rothwell Motor Auctions and we even had a different and larger ridge tent for the four of us to camp in, with Teresa sleeping in a carry cot. We were clearly coming up in the world, having put to one side the little khaki ex-army tent. Young Colin would have been about four or five years old around this time and I decided to set about making him a wooden toy fort.

I worked on my 'project' most evenings, meticulously cutting out the walls and battlements and forming four turrets at each of the four corners, along with a drawbridge. The fort was finished off with a coat of paint and, following the completion of this a little while later, I decided to make him a wooden garage. This was completed by making a visit to a city centre model shop in order to buy the required 'gun metal' petrol pumps.

Two to three years later, I made Teresa a desk and stool with the frame supporting the wooden desk being formed out of copper piping. This was duly followed up by making her a doll's house and fitting it out with furniture, purchased again from a city centre model shop. Both of them got years of enjoyment from those toys.

Wendy was never one to sit around and she eventually resumed work again at Kays Catalogue firm in Marshall Street. Wendy's sister, Pamela, was living with her partner near to the Dewsbury Road Fire Station and at that time, with having no children herself, an arrangement was made for her to each day look after the kids at our home.

One evening, I came home from work and Wendy was complaining about severe stomach pains and, later that same evening, I rang 999 and asked for an ambulance to attend. It transpired that she had appendicitis and underwent almost immediate surgery upon reaching the hospital. Pamela had no telephone so I was resigned to waiting for her to arrive as usual the next day so that I could share the news with her.

I was working on a site at Adel and could have easily gone in late without my boss knowing, but wanting to do the right thing I rang him first thing the following morning. "Hi Peter. It's Colin. I'm just letting yer know that I'll be in late this morning cos Wendy went into hospital last night wi' appendicitis and I have to wait for her sister to come and look after the kids."

Upon hearing this he bluntly replied, "Huh, yer will have kids, won't yer?"

"Yer what?" I said.

In a rather more defensive tone, he rejoined saying, "Oh, I'm just saying kids can cause problems, can't they?" His response wasn't what I expected, given the situation, but I said no more.

When I got into work, I explained to the lads what had happened and, still feeling rankled, I told them that Kelly had initially said: "Huh, you will have kids, won't yer!" Very soon that last comment of Kelly's went all around the site and beyond onto other Barratt sites.

A week or so later, when Wendy was due to be discharged from hospital, she was advised not to do any heavy lifting for approximately six months. Teresa was only a toddler and needed frequent picking up, so I decided to ask Kelly if it was okay for me to take one-week's holiday at short notice and then, after that, Pamela would be able to call and help Wendy.

"Hi Peter. It's Colin. Wendy is due to come out of hospital in a few days, so will it be okay if I take a week's holiday?"

To which his reply was: "A week's holiday? What's up wi' her? Is she immobile or summat?"

I was ready for a negative attitude so I said, "Well, she's been told not to do any heavy lifting for six months and we have two small children at home, so what do yer think?"

He was somewhat conciliatory and said, "Well, I suppose you know best."

When I went back to work, I heard the news that Kelly had suffered a heart attack on a site at Gawthrrope near Ossett. About a week or so later, I was moved to that site in order to help the plumber there.

Upon my first day there, I said to the plumber, Peter, "Isn't this where Kelly had his heart attack?"

He acknowledged this had been the case and, paraphrasing Kelly's earlier comment to me, the plumber simply said, "Well, he will have a heart, won't he?"

A rather harsh response, but the attitude of some employers (and their foremen), I was quickly learning, simply served to create an 'us an them' mentality. Fortunately, Kelly later made a good recovery from his heart attack.

It was now 1977 and I drove to Gawthorpe one morning, having heard the news that Elvis Presley had died. Later that morning, 'Faggy' the on-site ganger man for the labourers, had drawn a full-size guitar on one of the metre-square plaster boards. He had then cut it out with a stanley knife and, using a length of electric wire for a guitar strap, the guitar was flung around his neck and he proceeded to walk around the site singing Elvis songs.

Shortly into his repertoire, I witnessed two lads from the Yorkshire Electricity Board pull up on site in their van and ask a labourer which house plot it was that required an electric service putting in. The labourer pointed to 'Faggy' as the man with the answer. They looked incredulously at 'Faggy', with his plaster board guitar still around his neck and singing away! As with most workplaces there are always humorous times to be had to alleviate the day's work.

Kelly's son, Tony, was in his early thirties and, as an electrician, he was often on one site or another. He was a rather portly man who had a habit of walking about with his hands firmly in his pockets. On one particular site, it caused some hilarity with others when I coined the nickname for him of *'Tony Pockets'* and also made comments such as, "Did you see Tony on site the other day? He had his hands in his pockets, fell over and rocked himself to sleep trying to get up."

The nickname of *'Tony Pockets'* followed him around all of the sites. Now Tony and one of the plumbing foremen, *'Tommy Glasses'*, didn't get on at all and I was in the car with Tony one day when he was 'slagging' Tommy off to the extent that he was becoming quite upset with himself. At one point, he roughly declared that, "I wish I knew who it was that started calling me 'Tony Pockets'. Every site I go to now that's all I hear. I bet it was that bastard *'Tommy Glasses'!"*

I clammed up and simply said, "Hmm."

Working for Kelly left me with a number of memorable events, with some good, some not so good, and others that on reflection were humorous. No doubt to keep costs down, I found that on the vast majority of new house-building sites that I worked on there were no washing or toilet facilities. It wasn't uncommon to enter a house that was ready to have a bathroom fitted to be met with one of two things. Firstly, upon entering a bathroom one would see that where the new toilet was to be fitted – just by the four-inch soil pipe – someone would have messed on the floor. The logic of this just failed me. Secondly, over the staircase was the airing cupboard, where the hot water cylinder was to be fitted, and from the landing floor up to the bottom of the cupboard would be around one metre, yet some individuals would climb into the cupboard, squat down and mess on the floor. I could only conclude that these were the shy people.

Sometime during 1974, there was a shortage of sugar due to national industrial action and at this time I was working on a site in Morley. I myself always brought with me a flask. One particular day, it became clear that no one in the *snap cabin* had any sugar, so one lad went to the shop to buy some icing sugar to put in the cups of tea and coffee. On the same site on one winter's day with snow on the ground, the water stand-pipe was frozen so someone crammed the kettle with snow for it to melt so they could make their drinks.

On one Saturday morning, *Cockney Ronnie,* one of the plumbers at a site in Woodlesford, spoke to me saying that he had just been approached by a couple who had come to check on the progress of their new home. The woman had commented to him that the downstairs cloakroom smelt quite bad and, in his blunt response, Ronnie explained that it is often the case that men would use such areas to urinate in. Her response was staggering, but as he said to her, if you look around the site there are no toilet facilities whatsoever for the workmen.

Cockney Ronnie was an affable chap in his late thirties with a very funny sense of humour. At lunchtimes, along with four or five other plumbers, we would be sat on the floor of a room in one of the houses being entertained by his numerous stories and jokes. *Tommy Glasses,* the foreman, was especially interested in what Ronnie had to say and, one day as we dispersed from a lunch that had overrun, Ronnie commented to me that he was aware how Tommy got hooked on his stories and at times he purposely came out with one after another in order to distract him from calling an end to the lunch time.

I was eventually moved to a new Barratts site at Hunsworth, near Cleckheaton, locally known as Cleckhuddersfax due to its close proximity to the towns of Halifax and Huddersfield. Tommy had moved there some weeks prior to start the plumbing and heating work and we were soon joined by *Cockney Ronnie,* a middle-aged chap called Rex and Mick Petty, who was about six or seven years older than me and had worked at Gahan's before they went bust.

Mick was in the Territorial Army and was something of a quiet and moody man, who appeared to say nowt but took it all in. Each day, Rex used to bring with him to work his Alsatian dog, and one day when we were in the *snap cabin,* Peter Kelly arrived on site and came in to check on our progress. Kelly was a very dry man and, at some point, he turned to Rex and asked, "What do yer call yer dog?"

"Kim," the reply came back.

Kelly rejoined, "Well, it's got a better name than you. Is it a good house dog?"

Rex answered, "Oh yes, she's a very good house dog."

Kelly came back with, "Well, it can't be that good cos it's always 'ere."

None of us were certain as to whether Kelly disapproved of the dog being brought on site or not, but Rex still continued to fetch it. Several months later, Tommy was moved to Ossett to begin plumbing work on another Barratts site and, knowing how he was taken with Ronnie, he must have spoken to Kelly for he was given the role of foreman.

This surprised the rest of us because Ronnie wasn't a time-served plumber and he openly confessed that whilst living in London he had worked as a heating engineer's mate, thus picking up some rudiments of pipe-fitting. Crudely, such men were regarded in the trade as nothing more than a *jumper-in,* though in this case Ronnie's general affability made him liked by most that came into contact with him. It was widely acknowledged by the other plumbers that he worked at a slow pace and, due to his overall lack of ability, there were certain plumbing tasks that he simply wasn't given. There were occasions when it wasn't uncommon for him to arrive in his car around 9am, with this being *snap time* he would immediately come into the cabin to have his morning break with the rest of us.

Throughout my time working at Hunsworth, I had to get the bus each morning and, being driven by their timetable, I arrived at work each morning about fifteen to twenty minutes prior to the start time of 8.00am. At the end of the day, and again because of the bus timetable, Tommy had agreed with me that I could leave around fifteen minutes early to catch the bus home. On the second day of Ronnie being in charge, at around 9.00am, he came to see me where I was working and pointedly asked, "What time did you leave last night?"

I expected some kind of joke and answered saying something like, "Around ten past four."

Again, he pointedly responded saying, "Well, finishing time is 4.30pm and that is what you are paid to work until."

I was now a little perplexed and still not grasping the situation I explained about the bus timetables, that I get to work early on a morning and that, for the past several months, Tommy, being aware of these matters, had sanctioned me leaving early to catch my bus home.

"But you're not working with Tommy now. You're working with me, and I expect you to work until 4.30pm cos that's wot yer paid to do." At that, he walked out and I was left bewildered thinking about the times when he had arrived at work at 9.00am and, without thinking of starting work, he would join the rest of us, who were beginning their morning break.

During that first week, in one way or another, he succeeded in upsetting the other plumbers too. One of the pieces of work on site was to fit a sheet lead top and cap to the downstairs eight-feet-long bay windows. To do this you would have to prepare a small section of scaffolding over the rough ground at an appropriate height and fit it out with scaffold boards. The roll of sheet lead was rolled out with some initial forming of the upstand and trimming at the ends. Because of its length, two plumbers would then lift it into place and, working at either end, they would carry out the cutting and *dressing* until it became manageable for just the one plumber to complete, which also included the finishing feature of the front being decoratively scalloped.

It would be about the second week of Ronnie being foreman when Mick Petty related events when he had the task of fitting sheet lead to one such bay window. Following the erection of the scaffolding, he had seen Ronnie walking down the site and called him over in order to give him a lift onto the bay with the sheet lead. Mick went on to explain that, when this was done, Ronnie said to him "I'll go and get my lead tools, Mick."

He then retorted back, "Don't bother. I'll do it myself."

Ronnie replied back, "Yeah, but it's a two-handed job."

This left Mick to say, "Yeah it is, but you're not a plumber are yer?"

Why is it that when some folk are given an extra ten pence per hour to be foreman or chargehand, time and time again they adopt such crass attitudes? It is a very common occurrence that only serves to promote an 'us and them' approach to the job, which is wholly counterproductive. In due course, both Rex with his dog and I were moved to the site at Ossett, with Rex's dog once again receiving attention.

One day on the site, one of the plumbers, Geoff, had been asked to take the Morris van into Leeds in order to collect some fittings from the merchants. Geoff asked Rex if he could take his dog along for the ride in the passenger seat of the van and this was agreed. However, the journey wasn't what Geoff had expected. Upon his return, Geoff explained to us all that at some point of the journey the dog appeared a little restless and initially he thought that it was trying to get comfortable on the seat, but this wasn't the case at all. It decided to mess on the seat in question, leaving Geoff bringing back more from the journey than he had bargained for. Though I was reasonably happy at Kelly's, in due course I left for a job that promised good bonus opportunities and hence more money.

In fact, along with Peter, another plumber, I left and our new employer was Stan Storer, who was based at Carlton Street in Castleford. He had a number of self-employed plumbers working for him, and we were sent to a new housing site at Lindley, Huddersfield.

In the midst of explaining what was happening on the site, Stan went out of his way to warn us beforehand about Arncliffe's site agent, a chap by the name of Len saying, "Tek no notice of him, lads. His bark's worse than his bite."

When Peter and I arrived on site there was one other 'labour only' (self-employed) plumber already working there, and he quickly explained to us that there was no bonus scheme in operation and never had been. The next day we rang Stan, repeating what we had been told about no bonus and, in response, he waffled, but I said that we would be leaving at the end of the week because we were not happy. This worried him and he came down the same day to speak to us and promised that, by the end of the week, he would have a bonus scheme ready to be put in to place. Come the end of the week, Stan had kept his promise and we remained within his employment.

In the 1970s there appeared to be plenty of work around, and certainly as I recall the issue of unemployment wasn't a significant factor, hence tradesmen such as ourselves could from time to time 'flex our skilled muscles'. The method used to gain employment for folk living in and around Leeds was the *Yorkshire Evening Post* and, from a plumber's standpoint, upon seeing an advert you simply rang the employer and, following some brief discussion, recruitment was carried out in that way.

During that first week of us being on site, for no particular reason, Len the site agent made several very sarcastic comments towards Peter and I, no doubt doing so in the simple belief that he thought he could. For example, early one morning we had just arrived on site and were carrying our tools into some bungalows when Len, who was walking down the site, saw us and snapped, "When are these bungalows gonna be done?"

"When we've finished 'em," I retorted.

"Aw right," came the reply. "You can be finished just like that!"

"So what?" I said as we continued into one of the bungalows.

Perhaps I should point out that I see myself as being no different to most people in that if I don't stick up for myself then nobody will, especially when working in such a harsh environment as a building site. On this particular occasion, I took exception to the comment and his attempts at bullying so, in a subtle way, on a number of occasions, I got my own back.

It was winter time and, though the site managers had their own cabin positioned above that of the lads, for some reason Len used to put his big woolly socks above the brazier in our *snap cabin*. One day, as I was mashing my tea and having the used tea bag on a spoon, I walked over to where his socks were hanging and dropped the hot soggy tea bag inside one of them. I repeated this on several occasions, chuckling away inside.

One day a new labourer appeared, a lad of about thirty named Keith, and it was clear from his conversation during the break times that day that the lad wasn't particularly bright. The following day, he didn't show up until dinnertime, so when we saw him we asked if he was okay. Then he related a sorry tale for his reason for being late.

"I was unemployed before this job an' I had to go t' social this morning cos I've had no money for food or bus fares for work."

We sympathised with his predicament and asked him if he had spoken with Len since arriving for work.

"Yeah, I have," the reply came back.

"And what did he say then?" I enquired.

"What, him?" he bitterly replied. "He just said if I'm not 'ere tomorrow by eight o'clock then I shouldn't bother at all."

Building sites can be very cruel places to work and one day as Keith entered the *snap cabin,* somewhat late for his lunch, perhaps this was on his mind as he left the door open. It was still winter and Neil, one of the labourers sat by the door, snapped at Keith, "Shut door, wa' yer born in a barn?"

Exercising good judgement, Keith stepped back and closed the door without saying a word; Neil presented as a man not to tangle with. Standing over six feet tall, he worked as the *central mixer man* with the day-to-day duties of keeping the gangs of bricklayers going with regular supplies of mixed mortar. He wasn't a particular bright man and spoke very little, and what he did say was often akin to a grunt.

I was down at the store one day, speaking briefly to the site storeman, an older chap around retirement age. He had his back to the entrance door as he was slagging Neil off to me when the man in question appeared out of nowhere at the entrance.

I felt a degree of trepidation and, having heard his name mentioned, Neil grunted, "Huh, yer wot?"

Instinctively the storeman said in reply, "He said yer want fit to eat wi' pigs, but I said yer wa'".

At this I froze, fearing the worst, but Neil's response was simply to say "Huh awright" and walk off. I breathed a sigh of relief.

Not long after Neil had chastised Keith for leaving the *snap cabin* door open, the situation was reversed, as Keith – wanting to get his own back – snapped at Neil, "Shut door wa' yer born in a field?" in place of 'barn'.

Len's understudy was a chap aged about sixty that wore spectacles and had a very ruddy complexion. His name was Bill Milligan and he too would at times appear to go out of his way to 'have a go' at us, but out of earshot, we would gleefully refer to him as *Billigan Milligan*.

Building sites can be dangerous places and you need your wits about you. One particular morning I had just fitted some new gutter to a house plot and, as I descended the ladder, I heard someone cry out from the adjacent house being built. The brickies' labourer had been dismantling scaffolding when a large thermalite block struck him on the head, so I instinctively grabbed a mucky rag from my tools so that he could use it to stem the bleeding.

At the same time, I said that I would get my car that was parked nearby and, on doing so, I said to him, "Get in. I know where the hospital is."

Well, I didn't really, but each morning just before I turned off the main road for Lindley, I had seen a wrought-iron sign at the side of the road saying 'Hospital', so I reckoned it was further on down the road. As I got to the main road, I noticed that blood was beginning to seep through the rag and, after a short distance, to my left I saw a big sign saying: 'General Accident'.

I turned in to the opening and, before I could park, the labourer said, "It's okay. Leave me here I'll be okay, thanks." Jumping out of the car, he began running for the main entrance.

As I turned the car around and was heading back out, he came running back shouting, "That's General Accident Insurance!"

"Get in," I said.

"No thanks, I'll go on my own." I left him to walk down to the nearby hospital.

As the Lindley site started to move closer to its finish, Peter and I were moved to another Arncliffe new housing site at York. The site agent here was a chap named Norman and he was much more affable than Len had proved to be. In fact, if we happened to see him early on a morning, Peter would greet him with, *"Mornin' Norman the foreman, who has a friend called Martin Bowman who works as a doorman down at the Gaumant."*

Norman took it in good heart, though it wasn't long before his abrupt response amounted to just two words with the latter being 'off'. One day, Peter and I were working in a house and decided to make a couple of *pea shooters*. This we did by cutting two pieces of half inch copper pipe about thirty inches long and then, because we had plenty of putty as we were carrying out all of the on-site glazing, small balls of putty around the size of a pea were formed. We then targeted some of the labourers that were working outside of a house opposite, sending them scurrying in all directions as we fired at them.

This went on for some time until we heard Norman shout for the labourers and they came together to meet with him in the middle of the road directly opposite Peter and I. Even so, as he spoke with them, we kept firing with our *putty guns* and causing at least one of them to skip in an attempt to miss our shots. Unaware of what was happening, Norman glanced at the hapless lad as though he had developed some sort of affliction that was causing his erratic movements.

Meanwhile, life at Dulverton Place wasn't too bad, but one day Wendy raised the idea – once again – of us emigrating to Canada. Her older sister, Jenny, and her family were still over there and the potential prospect seemed to offer greater opportunities for us as a family. However, once again after discussing the idea over a period of time, I came to the conclusion that I would find it hard to leave my mam behind.

Given that we now had some money saved up, we decided to put it towards buying a house and, in late 1977, we moved in to 38 Broad Lane Close in the Leeds district of Bramley. This was a fairly modern terraced house, but referred to now as a town house positioned in a cul de sac. There were quite a number of young families in the street, so both Wendy and I soon made some acquaintances and friends.

With young Colin in his new school at Wyther Park Juniors, Wendy got flexible part-time work selling Avon cosmetics whilst juggling her time caring for Teresa at home and doing the housework. When Teresa eventually started the same school as Colin, Wendy became a playground assistant there and spent several years in that job. She often commented on the fact that, at times, some kids came to school poorly dressed and some of the teachers had to buy toothpaste and brushes so that, before the start of formal lessons, certain kids could be shown how to brush their teeth. Later that year, when the time came, Mam was able to join us for Christmas Day.

Chapter 8

Talking about Mam

Earlier in 1977, Mam had moved to 33 Thorpe Gardens, Middleton, to be closer to our Gill and her family. Living in St. Hildas Crescent, an older lady had moved in at the side of her house and, at times, she would cause problems for Mam. Her new home was a one-bedroom ground floor 'cottage' flat and, initially, I spent some time there at weekends carrying out some decorating.

After a short while, Gill advised me that Mam was often in the Working Men's Club at around 6pm, although she was by no means drinking heavily; in fact according to people that she had spoken to, Mam could often be seen sitting for ages with just a half pint of beer. The problem for Gill was her concern that Mam might be getting a bad name and, within that, I am sure she was concerned how this might also reflect on her.

I now find it deeply regrettable, at least on my part, that I never took the time out to, at the very least, consider that Mam was still really missing and possibly grieving for Dad and, moreover, was lonely and perhaps even depressed. We were simply too wrapped up with our own families to recognise things that might have been of concern to her. Further to that, as previously commented upon, like so many others of their generation, Mam and Dad had been social drinkers, hence her use of the Working Men's Club was simply to have some company, to be around people and have someone to talk to.

The 13 May 1978 was a Saturday and our Gill and Bernard had gone down to London to watch the Rugby League cup final. Later that morning, I received a telephone call from Wendy's dad and, in a sombre tone, he told me that my mam was dead. He went on to say that he had been contacted with the news by Bernard's mother, who also lived in Middleton, and I should ring her for more details.

I contacted Mrs. Poole immediately and she explained that she had been alerted by one of Mam's neighbours, who had explained that she had seen her through a window slumped over in an armchair and she hadn't responded to knocks on the door or window. She went on to say that the funeral director had been contacted and she asked if I could go up to let them in. I went up immediately and saw Mam slumped in the chair, seemingly sleeping, but in effect dead. After a short while, the funeral director came and took her away.

On the Monday morning, Gill and I had an appointment with Mam's GP and, following some initial comments, I asked him, "What did she die of?"

"Old age," came the reply.

"Old age?" I quickly responded, "but she was only sixty-six years old! You don't die of old age, you die of a medical condition, so what did she die of?"

Gill seemingly grasped my point and she also asked the same question of the GP, who seemed to go on the defensive before declaring, "Perhaps we should have an autopsy carried out."

Later that day, a police car pulled up at our house in Bramley and I was taken down to the city mortuary to formally identify her. On the way down, I explained to the officer what the GP had said about Mam, being just sixty-six, but nevertheless dying of "old age".

In response, he shook his head and said, "It is the law that any person who is found dead and alone must be formally identified and an autopsy carried out to establish the cause of death."

At this I felt nothing but anger towards the GP in question, a so-called professional that was quite happy to consign Mam to her grave under some sham medical explanation presumably because he couldn't be bothered organising an autopsy. The subsequent findings of the autopsy were that Mam had died of a massive heart attack and that her death would have been very sudden.

Eveline Potter was born on 29 August 1911 and was the middle daughter of Arthur Watson. Sadly, I have no record of my Grandma Watson. As Eveline Watson, my Mam had two sisters (Edna, the eldest, and Nellie) and a brother (Arthur), who was named after his father. The Watsons lived at 16 Carlton Row, Holbeck, and along with her brother and sisters, my Mam went to Bewerley Street School. She left elementary school when she was fourteen years old and, like many young women of that period, went into tailoring, which was very much a thriving industry at that time.

She married Dad on 22 December 1934 and, when the Second World War broke out, like so many women she worked at Wilson and Mathieson's (Armley Road), which had been transformed from being an engineering factory into making munitions for the war effort. This she did throughout the war, whilst Dad was away serving with the Royal Artillery. They both served and fought for the land of their birth and, with the cessation of hostilities, like millions of others, they returned to their slum housing attempting to pick up their lives again and eke out some kind of living.

Back then, I remember Dad would get up at 5.00am and, because the circular bus hadn't begun running at that time, he would walk the two to three miles or so down to Hudswell Clarks in Hunslet to start his twelve-hour shift at 6.00am. This he did in all weathers. There were very few car owners in and around our community. Also, there were no telephones or computers and certainly no opportunity to have one's groceries delivered straight to one's door.

When Mam worked as a cleaner at the city centre Shell Offices, she too would be out early in the morning and do her work before getting back in time to ensure that Gill and I were up and ready for school. When we lived at Cross Green, she would catch the bus into Leeds' city centre for the weekly shopping before bringing it back home on the bus.

There were no fridges, dishwashers or automatic washing machines and, in the 1950s, Mam would do the household washing in the 'peggy tub' and use a hand mangle to squeeze the surplus water from the clothes. Then, with the advent in the 1960s, she used a twin-tub washing machine; though the work was a little easier, it remained very labour intensive, in keeping with other aspects of housework. We had no hot water, so everything had to be boiled and the only internal plumbing appliance was the kitchen sink, with a cold water tap. Like so many people, they simply got on with things and often made the 'best out of a bad job'. Like most folk Mam and Dad didn't appear to be political, though on more than one occasion I recall her saying that she never voted Conservative because "I have nothing to conserve". They were solid people and I could not have hoped or wished for better parents.

Mam was buried in the same grave as Dad at Harehills Cemetery, an arrangement they had privately discussed and agreed upon, and in effect this was the very last act of love between them. Inevitably, I found myself struck with thoughts, both then and now, of 'if only I had done this or that'. However, as is the case, such thoughts are always too late: what's done is done and it's too late for it to be undone.

Over the years, I have quietly envied my peers that still have one or both parents alive, who were able to see their children grow – and vice versa – and perhaps grandchildren too. I know full well how my parents would have loved our two children and fussed over them as grandparents do. When I reached the age when Dad died, that is fifty-seven, I had such poignant feelings that he had died so very young and, when I reached the age of sixty-six, the same age as when Mam died, I am struck by that very same poignancy and deep feelings of regret. Whenever I look back at the way in which we lived, in damp back-to-back houses, with outside toilets and so on, my memories are all happy ones. That is because life is essentially about people and a multitude of relationships, ranging from close family, friends, acquaintances, people at school, work and so on. I had loving parents and the two people I owe so much to have not been in my life for many years, and I shall always miss them greatly.

Chapter 9

Life Goes On

I was recently listening to a radio programme and, for the first time, I heard mention of the concept of someone being an 'adult orphan', in relation to having lost both parents. That goes some way towards explaining the feelings and emotions that I have felt over the years. Parents offer support, love and guidance and there have been several occasions – especially when Wendy has been very ill, which I shall come to later in the book – when I have deeply missed not having Mam and Dad around. That year proceeded largely uneventfully, though at the back end of the year, I found myself in hospital for about one week.

Just prior to leaving Dulverton Gardens, I had been hit at relatively close range on the earlobe with an air rifle dart fired by one of our neighbour's teenage lads. It had been a complete accident, as he was stupidly shooting at birds in a nearby tree from his kitchen window. His vision to the left was obstructed by the extended entrance to the front door, hence why, as I walked past with two bags of shopping, he erroneously pulled the trigger. It felt like someone had wacked me at the side of the head as hard as they could with a house brick. On seeing what he had done, he came running out of his house very distressed and fussing around, asking if I was okay.

Feeling dazed, I stepped into our house and announced to Wendy what had taken place. After a few minutes, I was feeling okay, although Wendy told me that a very large lump had emerged on my neck at the side of my throat and she urged me to go to the hospital A&E in order to get things checked out.

I was able to drive there with Wendy by my side and, upon our arrival, there was a short wait before I was seen by a doctor who advised me that I was okay and that the lump on my neck was the result of shock and therefore it would soon subside. Any concern passed and we got back to our daily family routine, though some twelve months later and, following frequent comments from Wendy, the lump was still present and the same size on my neck, although it was not causing me any problems.

Following visits to both our GP and then Chapel Allerton Hospital, I was informed that the lump was in effect a cyst the size of a golf ball that was attached to one of my thyroid glands. The consultant said that it was most likely benign, but as a precaution, I should have it surgically removed.

My initial response was one of reluctance, because my immediate thoughts were financial ones. Admission into hospital would mean having to take time off work, which was something I never readily did, and to do so now would mean being reliant on Statutory Sick Pay. As these thoughts ran through my head I explained my reasoning to the consultant, stating that I had felt no adverse effects over the past twelve months or so, but he responded by saying that there was no way of knowing whether the cyst was malignant or not and whether it might become malignant in the future if left. I accepted his common-sense reasoning and elected for surgery.

When able to, I explained matters to my boss Stan Storer who, some time later, after giving it some thought, acknowledged that sick pay wasn't much and, if I wanted, I could come in to the shop and carry out some lead burning and make roof flashings, gutter backs and lead aprons. Lead burning is the name given to the preparation, welding and fabrication of sheet lead items, such as lead slates and roof flashings, that needed to be fitted on house chimneys and soil pipes.

I was duly admitted into hospital and, following surgery for the removal of most of my thyroid gland, I had only been discharged from hospital about a few days when Stan rang to ask if I was ready to carry out the lead burning. I didn't really feel up to work, but given the offer of extra money, I went into work a couple of days later and spent a little less than a day lead burning and fabricating a number of sheet lead items, thankfully without incurring any pain or discomfort.

A couple of days later, he rang again and asked if I could go to a new housing site at Wilberforce near York just for a day or so. Reluctantly, I agreed, though it was now winter and I was to lose the relative warmth of working in the shop. It was my first morning on site and I was asked to fit a bathroom suite. Very soon I felt pain and discomfort from the healing wound in my neck, due to lying under the bath, stretching and straining in order to fit it.

At some point the site agent came in and said that he was really pleased I was here as he had been pushing Stan for some time in order to get another permanent plumber on site. Alarm bells immediately rang in my head; given I had only been out of hospital for ten days, Stan, somehow, seemed to think I was able to return on a full-time basis. The agreed cushion of me working a day or so each week lead burning in the shop seemed to have faded.

Later that day, I called him and said that I was in a lot of discomfort and wouldn't be able to work until the doctor advised me accordingly. This he accepted. Stan was an affable sort of chap, but one of the things that caused me, and indeed other plumbers, quite a bit of irritation was the fact that he always paid everyone by cheque.

I and others had difficulty with this because he refused to write on the cheque 'pay cash'. Hence, the cheque had to be in the bank for several days in order for it to clear. At times this caused problems because, when I placed the cheque into our bank account on a Friday evening, there were insufficient funds in the account to draw out. This pedantic practice was a bone of contention for most of the plumbers too, primarily due to the same difficulties that I had with it. More often than not Stan would personally deliver each cheque to the site that a plumber was working on and, at the same time, he was able to monitor progress.

There were other times when, as the Friday afternoon rolled on, you would have to ring the office to see if he would be bringing your cheque to the site. On one occasion, I had to travel from the site at York to Castleford to collect my wages and then head home to Leeds. Another time he resisted writing 'pay cash' on the cheque, instead he told me to go to his bank in Harehills in order to cash it there. I did this only once because it was a pain having to travel to Harehills and then having to travel across Leeds in rush hour traffic in order to get home. This practice of paying by cheque pre-dated the repeal in 1983 of The Truck Acts, which amongst other things provided for the payment of wages in cash.

The cheque issue began to more than irritate me because my standpoint was that I was always punctual with my morning arrival at a site and, having worked hard all week, I took exception to being messed about with my wages. This problem with cheques was, I believe, due to Stan having cashflow problems, which we discovered one day when Peter and I had gone to the plumbers merchants to get some materials.

Having completed our order, we told the chap behind the counter that the items were to be placed on the account of Stan Storer. Upon hearing this, he simply stared at us both and then went into the office and came out with a chap who was presumably some sort of manager and he said that the company had placed a 'stop' on Stan's account. Following comments from us about our need for the materials, he went back into the office to ring Stan, who in turn must have given some assurances because the chap came back out saying things were sorted and we could have the stuff.

At home Wendy and I were never frivolous with money. Each Friday teatime, having received my wages, we would put the money to one side for household expenditure and then I would walk up to the bank and deposit what was left. Though I required a car for work, I always tried to buy reliable 'bangers', preferring to use our savings rather than get a loan or hire purchase for a newer car.

I knew other men who always took a set amount out of their wages each week for their 'spending money', but this is something I have never felt the need to do. Similarly, I never had the inclination to smoke, but rather the both of us diligently saved our money for necessities and family holidays. Being careful as we were, some of our holidays might have seemed cheap, but we enjoyed camping and caravanning with the kids and, being just ordinary folk, we always liked the sense of freedom that such holidays gave us. More importantly, the kids seemed to enjoy these types of holidays too and, like most parents, our holiday planning would always centre around what was available for them to do.

I was always on the lookout for a better job, and that was especially the case now with my growing frustration regarding Stan's haphazard payment of wages, and so it was that, in 1979, I left his employ and went to Grosvenor Engineering, a subsidiary group of Mowlem Builders. One of the things I have never done is to simply walk away from a job without having another one to go in to.

That same year had seen a general election, which led to the Conservatives gaining power and Margaret Thatcher becoming prime minister. I had no political education, so I had no firm party convictions and so, like so many others in 1979, I voted Tory believing that as a working man I was serving my interests as well as those of my family. I was no different to the other men that I worked with in that, at break and lunchtimes, we would pull out our red top newspapers and most days immediately turn to the back page to read the sport.

At key stages of the soccer season, I would have been able to offer a good analysis about the games in hand, along with both goal and points differences regarding certain teams, along with keeping abreast of the latest transfer news and changes in team managers. In the on-site *snap cabins,* sport, and especially soccer, was the main topic of conversation and, once having absorbed the back pages, I would turn to the telly page to review the channels and the programmes for the coming night's viewing.

In my world then, I was no different to everyone else, whereby the emphasis in life was on one's family and work. Occasionally, someone would mention a politician or some random political topic from his paper and this would likely be responded to in such language as "what a load of crap", or some other berating comment often sprinkled with four-letter expletives.

My new job was on a new building site at the bottom of Cemetery Hill and Malvern Road in Beeston, Leeds. The new houses being built were for the city council and, at the time of writing this, was perhaps the last local authority housing estate to be built in Leeds since that period. Other housing developments have been built via the Housing Corporation, the umbrella organisation for housing associations.

The plumbing foreman was a chap called Tommy, and I was fortunate to know both of the other plumbers working on the site. Peter was a lad I had gone to building college with and still carried with him the unfortunate nickname of *Tom Noddy,* which apparently he had been given at school, the other one was Phil, who I had worked with at Kelly's.

The individual bonus scheme was put together with the employer, allotting a certain number of hours to different plumbing and central heating tasks, such as so much for a bathroom, boiler, radiators, and so on.

As was the norm, it was a thirty-seven-hour working week and the bonus payments worked like this: if one earned eighty hours bonus in a particular week, then thirty-seven hours would be paid at the plumbing rate, with the remaining forty-three hours being paid at £1 per hour. This was a fairly standard scheme and by now I knew that I could earn bonus and still turn out work to a good standard.

Very early on in that first week, both Peter and Phil explained to me how things were running, which was that they started work each day a little before the official start time of 8.00am and grafted continuously throughout the day. They explained that by Thursday teatime they had accumulated a satisfactory number of hours. They would then simply advise Tommy accordingly and then had Friday off. At this juncture, the reader can be forgiven for thinking ""Well, that's just plain lazy! Why not go in on the Friday and earn more bonus?"

Whilst this might sound logical, we need to understand the reasoning of Peter and Phil; if an employer saw that a plumber or plumbers were making a lot of bonus, they would immediately believe that the bonus prices they had initially determined were far too generous and hence reduce the number of hours for each task. The psychology between employer and employee often works both ways.

As things stood, the three of us were arriving around 7.45am each of the four days and grafted continuously with our individual tasks, hence we were then able to have the Friday off. I personally never went down to the site *snap cabin* and had no morning or afternoon breaks, but I did stop at lunchtime, where I happened to be working for ten to fifteen minutes so that I could have a bite to eat and a drink from my flask.

I had tried working through, but my empty stomach told me that I needed food and without any I would feel lethargic. In contrast, Phil was able to work through the day without taking any breaks whatsoever. In the winter time on the run up to lunch I would turn my blowlamp on and place it in the smallest bedroom and close the door (if one had been fitted) so that when I stopped for ten minutes the room was warm.

Though the work was essentially physical, there were times when it became exceptionally hard – for example, when a wagon came with a delivery of cast-iron free-standing boilers (ones that stand on the floor as opposed to being wall mounted) for the houses that were ready, we would in turn stand with our backs to the wagon whilst the driver lowered a boiler onto our backs. Then, crouched over, we would trample over the rough, uneven ground to the house designated for a boiler and then, once in there, we would back up, wedging the boiler between us and a wall and then 'shimmy', gradually lowering it down to the ground. Some of the radiators were equally as heavy, but it was unheard of to ask another plumber for help to carry one. There was more than one occasion that, having sprained an ankle, I would simply strap it up at home and be in at work again the next day.

Overall, the money was good, and much better than what I had earned with Stan Storer. I began to pride myself that over the years, each time that I had moved to a new job, I always succeeded in securing better wages. As a family, we were going on holiday every year and I still had no inclination to drive anything other than an old, economic and reliable car. Things went along nicely with Grosvenor for the better part of a year, but as the final houses were being built, things began to change dramatically.

There would soon be insufficient work for me and the other two plumbers on site, but we were told that the firm had plenty more work on other sites that was waiting to be started. Then they started putting more plumbers onto our site, which was perplexing to say the least, but I had been happy with the firm so I was prepared to go along with their promises of new work.

However, one day Peter, who had worked for the firm a long time, said that he had seen this influx of plumbers onto a site before; Grosvenor were simply trying to sicken lads off so that they would leave because the promises of more sitework was false.

Not long afterwards, I experienced how this 'sickening off' process further operated. Throughout all of the time I had worked for the firm, Tommy the foreman had always ensured that there was an excellent supply of materials for all of us in order to make for good continuity of progress, and allowing the three of us to make bonus. Under any bonus scheme, the ideal is always to go into a house, have all of your materials to do the work and then be able to complete and move onto the next house. Bonus schemes were not overly generous to allow for plumbers to keep going back to houses to complete them when materials came in 'dribs and drabs'. Continuity was essential if one was to avoid losing both time and money. This was now changing.

I went down to the plumbing cabin one day to get some materials and was met by Tommy, along with Mick the plumbing supervisor, who occasionally visited the site. After the initial greetings, I looked for the fittings that I wanted and then turned around, simply saying, "Tommy, we haven't got any fibre washers. Have we got some on order? If so, when are they coming?"

He replied, "Oh okay, I'll order some then."

I responded frustratingly saying, "But if we don't have any, I can't fit them."

He snapped back, "Well, if you don't fit them and there is a leak then you'll have to come back and sort it out, won't yer?"

He had always been amicable and never used such an attitude over the past number of months, so this sudden change frustrated me. I said, "But the washers are a bog-standard item and we don't have any, so how can I fit them?"

Receiving no reply and feeling utterly frustrated, I began walking away when Mick shouted after me, "If yer don't like it, then yer know what yer can do!"

I swung around and shouted, "And if you don't like it then you know what you can do!" I have never liked being threatened or bullied in that manner with the implied expectation that I must 'kowtow' to them.

The following day, I went seeking Tommy again and found him having his morning break in the site *snap cabi*. Peter was there too and in the same way that I had been the day before, he was becoming frustrated by not only having to ask Tommy about the shortage of materials, but also the blasé response he was receiving.

Filled with dissatisfaction, Peter and I both came out, and my mind was beginning to think that, as it appeared, I would have to seek another job as it was better to jump before I was pushed. That evening, I bought a copy of the evening paper and looked in the jobs section. Within a couple of days, I had secured another job with the York based company J.H. Shoulksmith, who also owned the Leeds-based mechanical pipe-fitting firm – Morfitt's in Headingley.

At the end of the week I gave Grosvenor one-week's notice of my intention to leave, but I took both my annoyance and frustration with them to another level. For that week, I only booked thirty-seven hours to cover my weekly basic wage and carried forward the bonus I had to my final week, with the intent of doing as little work as possible.

During my final week, I was fitting what was known as an Elson water tank and the space designed for these in the houses was very confined within a cupboard. Due to this cramped space, the only way to commence what in completion would be a labyrinth of pipework was to begin with the very back connection, solder it and, in turn, work one's way to the front plumbing in the relevant pipework. This I did, but instead of soldering the 22mm fitting at the very back, I fitted it dry but, at the same time, I was saying to myself, 'sort that out when I've gone', because it was sure to leak.

My naivety then was such that I just didn't understand how or why I had been treated in such a derisory way because, over the twelve months or so that I had worked for them, I had worked diligently, not given them any trouble regarding the quality of my work or my attitude to the job. In the future, I was to lose such naivety and see that, when it suits them, a firm will string plumbers along with false promises of further work when things are looking bleak. Years later, I was to read that when some dissatisfied workers expressed their frustration by committing such acts as I had done above, it is regarded as industrial sabotage.

Away from the unsettling events at work, as a family we had settled really well into our home in Broad Lane Close. There were quite a number of young families in the street, just as we were, and both Colin and Teresa had no problem with making new friends. Wendy had made friends with Gale Schofield, a mother of three young children, and overall people got along well with everyone.

However, there is always one and, in this instance, it was someone that the kids in the street came to nickname '*Morngey Manders*'. The chap was possibly aged around thirty, married with a baby, and he lived towards the top of the cul de sac. He worked on the city council buses and, on one occasion, he repainted his house green and cream, the same colours as the buses, leaving many in the street to wonder where he had got the paint from. He was always complaining about the kids playing in the street and, as a consequence, they had grown to dislike him.

Colin was friendly with another lad called Stephen MacDonald and, along with a small number of other kids, I used to go onto the soccer pitch adjacent to Sandford School and we would all have a kick about. On one occasion, I had just arrived home from work and gone upstairs to change when I heard a knock on the front door, which in turn was answered by Wendy. When I went back downstairs, she chuckled and said that, upon opening the door, it was young Steve MacDonald who had said to her, "Is Colin playing out?"

She replied back, "He's already playing out in the street, Stephen."

Then he replied back, "No, I meant his dad."

Over the years, this instance has given us both some merriment. There were occasions when Colin, Teresa and I would play shops and to do this we would nigh on empty the food cupboard of tins of beans and such, employing trays used for baking buns as the cash till.

In February 1980, I began work for Shoulksmith's and was dispatched to a new sheltered housing complex at Keighly, West Yorkshire. The firm ran a 'collective bonus' scheme, which from the outset I didn't like because no two people work the same and, as I commented above, I knew that I could work at speed and still turn out good work, hence I didn't want to be 'carrying' anyone else that was unable to work to the same standard as myself.

An example of this problem occurred one lunch time when one of the six or so plumbers on site proudly announced to us all in the *snap cabin* that over the morning he had fitted something like thirty immersion heaters into the copper cylinders. The foreman prompted, "Did yer put jointing paste on and tighten e'm in wi' t' immersion key?"

The doleful reply came back, "Aw no, I din't." He was then told by the foreman to go back in the afternoon and fit each one correctly.

After a month or so, I was moved to a Laings building site at Bingley and this was also another older persons' sheltered housing complex. The site was just beginning to take shape and, besides myself, there was George the plumbing chargehand, along with two apprentices in their late teens. There were also two lads from Morfitts doing the heavy mechanical iron pipework that was associated with the central heating.

The job with Shoulksmith's was proving to be less profitable than my previous job, and that bugged me and hurt my pride. Although I was persistently looking in the newspaper for alternative work, to both my ongoing frustration and surprise there was nothing.

Chargehand George was a somewhat portly chap in his mid-to-late fifties and I got along with him really well. After a while he confided in me that he suffered with high blood pressure and really shouldn't be doing plumbing work anymore. He went on to explain that he hadn't informed the firm for fear they would get rid of him and, in turn, I assured him that his secret was safe with me. He was very much a level-headed man and the extra ten pence or so per hour for being the chargehand never caused him to become delusional about the realities of matters.

The builders' site agent, John, was somewhat unusual because, rather than having the customary site agent experience of being a bricklayer or joiner, his background experience was from working in the Laings' offices and therefore, at times perhaps because of this, he seemed to find it difficult to relate to the lads on-site, and he was disliked for his authoritarian ways. Because the *snap cabin* wasn't large enough to accommodate all of the Laings' workers and ourselves, we used to go in for our breaks when the buzzer sounded to signal the end of theirs.

As was customary, the site agent, along with certain foremen, would eat in their own site office. One Friday lunch time, we had just got into the snap cabin at 1pm and been joined by John the site agent for a 'natter', when a car pulled up outside carrying three or four joiners. Seeing this, John immediately ran out and we all heard him challenge the men and then shout loudly, "Each of you are all quartered." This meant that he was deducting fifteen minutes from their wages for being late back from lunch. It was about three minutes past 1.00pm.

Having demonstrated his authority, he came back in to rejoin us and continue the 'natter'. However, to his surprise, he was immediately followed by a tall joiner who, without saying a word, walked past John and took a seat in the far corner of the cabin. John's gaze followed the lad as he sat down and took out his flask from his snap bag.

"What do yer think you're doing?" snapped John.

"Have yer quartered me?" the man growled back.

"Yeah," John retorted.

"Well I'm havin' a cup o' coffee in my quarter of an 'our, okay?" the reply came back.

For just a few seconds it was tense, but John, not wishing to escalate things, simply said, "Aw okay."

Shoulksmith's itself was, for me, a somewhat unusual firm, due to the high number of plumbers that had been working for them for varying lengths of time. I was thirty years old then and there were a couple of lads employed at the firm that were my age and had been there from leaving school. There were also a number of middle-aged lads that had over twenty years' service with the firm.

As plumbing firms go, they were a big company employing quite a number of lads. I had been with them for about five to six months when Joe, their van driver, who visited periodically to drop materials off, began commenting that certain plumbers who he named had been given three months' notice of redundancy. This of course was a real source of concern, especially to those lads that had a lot of service with the firm, and for the rest of the year Joe became a constant source of similar bad news.

Joe himself was around fifty years old and had a very hoarse voice, and one day I asked George if he knew why this was so and the explanation given was that as well as driving he carried out a lot of welding back at the main offices in Headingley, fabricating parts for various jobs. Seemingly, this welding was undertaken in a shed with little or no ventilation, meaning these fumes over the years had taken their effect on this poor chap's voice box.

On the run up to that Christmas, we were grouped around the van driver, as he had not only come to deliver materials but also bad news about more redundancy notices for men that had been with the firm for a significant number of years. His news was followed by what had now become his common follow up refrain of, "What about loyalty? These lads have given the firm years of loyalty, and that should count for something!"

On this occasion, he turned to me and said, "How long have you been 'ere? You haven't been 'ere twelve months, have yer? How come they're keeping you?"

"I don't know," said I. Well, what could I say? I had no answer to offer and thankfully he didn't pursue the matter and, added to this, I was also grateful that I received no resentment from George or the other lads. Given this, and the fact that the firm was losing a lot of plumbers, I purposely avoided the firm's Christmas 'do', as I knew what some lads could be like once they had some beer down their necks and I didn't want any trouble.

Away from work momentarily, when we were all in the *snap cabin,* George illustrated to me at least that he was rather different to other lads that I had worked with. He was very much a thoughtful man who rarely 'lost it' and enjoyed hobbies such as opera, ballroom dancing and listening to music on good hi-fi equipment, and there were occasions at break times when he would regale us all with stories about one or more of these topics.

He seemed better informed than most of us surrounding current affairs, and I naively put this down to him reading *The Daily Mail*. It appeared to offer more in-depth news than any of the red tops, but at the time I had no idea about the political stance that it took on certain matters of the day, believing rather that all papers were unbiased.

I remember the Monday after Remembrance Sunday, during our lunch break, Mick (one of the pipe-fitters) asked George if he had watched the event on the telly. George replied that he never watched the event because it evoked too many bad memories of his own experience in the Second World War. Briefly, he uttered words about having to clear bodies following an armed conflict and the almost surreal experience of feeling the weight of single limbs such as someone's leg or arm.

He ended the conversation by explaining that, towards the end of the war, he had joined the Military Police (MP) and was told by some of the more experienced MP's that some British soldiers who were suffering from *shell shock* – now known as post-traumatic stress – had on occasion been taken into the bush by them and shot. This he was told was due to the logistics of returning such men back from the front for appropriate medical assistance and hence their families received letters in due course saying that their loved one had been killed in action. George said that thankfully, as an MP, he was never called upon to carry out such killings and, if he had been, then he simply had no idea what he would have done.

The job situation was not improving from my own personal standpoint, with nothing being advertised in the evening newspaper, and it seemed that the news was reporting daily about the steady increase in the numbers of unemployed. Very slowly, I began an attempt to take more notice of what was going on around me.

For some reason which I can't recall I decided to join the public library in Bramley and one of the first books I borrowed was about the Battle of Culloden in 1745. I had liked history at school, though I hadn't realised that the teaching of history for our consumption was really about kings, queens and so-called famous battles. The teaching had concluded in the mid-to-late nineteenth century, with a summary of factory conditions and how these had been ameliorated through the good works of philanthropists and wealthy benefactors.

The aforementioned book really gripped me, not for the description of the battle itself, but for the persecution of Scottish communities that followed. It evoked within me a sense of social injustice, causing a degree of indignation. As a consequence, I pursued further reading about people's social conditions across the eighteenth, nineteenth and twentieth century, taking in novelists such as Elizabeth Gaskell and Alexander Cordell, along with a number of non-fiction books. This reading caused me to stumble over the topic of economics and I was introduced to laissez faire thinking: Alfred Marshall, Thomas Malthus, Karl Marx and John Maynard Keynes. That Christmas came and went and, whilst thankfully I was still in work, my search for alternative work proved fruitless. Then, in March 1981, came a bolt from out of the blue.

Chapter 10

What About Loyalty?

The project was coming to an end and, having seen a number of long-serving plumbers being made redundant, my turn came around in March 1981, when I was given one-week's notice of redundancy. The word circulating was that Shoulksmith's, being the large employer that it was when I started a little over twelve months previously, had reduced in size to just six plumbers.

At the end of the week's notice, I went into the firm's offices in Headingley, Leeds to collect my wages and holiday pay and was greeted by one of the directors. I remember it well as he said to me, "You'll have seen a lotta plumbers go over these past twelve months."

I simply nodded in acknowledgement to this fact.

He went on to explain, "We worked it like this. We kept those plumbers that were making us money and their work was okay."

I said little in response to this and, along with my wages, I was also given almost three weeks in holiday stamps. As part of the Joint Industry Board for Plumbing and Electrical Work in England and Wales (JIB) framework, those employers signed up to the JIB scheme – and very many were not – would each week put a holiday stamp on a JIB Holiday Card and would then cash them in for the employee when they subsequently took their agreed holidays.

As we parted company, I could hear Joe the van driver's repeated refrain all last year about 'loyalty' and that it should – as if according to some high ground moral law – always count for something. Alongside this, at the same time, I remembered what was said to me as a young apprentice: *he who works and does his best goes down the road like all the rest.* Given this, I felt that loyalty was and is meaningless when confronted by employers and the cash nexus.

I had exchanged telephone numbers with George and rang him a few weeks later, and he told me that, when he came to turn the water on at the job, it had been a pleasure to test my work out because there had been only one or two very minor leaks. That was really nice feedback. I went on to ring him two to three months later, but his wife answered, sadly telling me that George had recently died and, being stunned at the news, I felt disinclined to ask how or why, but instead I wished her well and was left wondering if his high blood pressure had played a part. I remembered that he had confided in me that the firm was unaware of his condition as he feared they might dismiss him.

Initially, I had to 'sign-on' with the Department for Social Security (DSS) in order to claim benefit. This was my first ever period of unemployment and there is one memory that stays with me. Both Colin and Teresa were still attending Wyther Primary School and each day I began walking them there and then back at the end of the school day. This enabled me to chat with both about what they might be doing at the start of the day and then at the end of the day; as we walked home, they were able to share with me what they had done. This stands out for me as, usually with them both being young, I might see them for a couple of hours when I got home from work.

After a couple of weeks or so out of work, one mid-week day I went to get my haircut. Not having a regular barber, I ventured to one on Stanningley Road. It began with the usual conversation but then veered off into something else as the barber asked, "Arr yer on holiday this week then?"

"No," I replied. "I've just been made redundant."

"Aww right, wot is it that yer do?"

"I'm a plumber."

"Aww right," he said. "There's no demand, is tha?"

He was merely mouthing what political apologists were constantly saying on the telly as an explanation for the rise in unemployment. "No demand"? I said. "My sister-in-law lives just off Dewsbury Road and where she lives there are rows upon rows of back-to-back houses that all have an outside toilet. So ya can't say there's no demand for houses to be modernised."

He came back with more apologist drivel, stating, "Well, it's all that new technology, in't it?"

Again, I politely responded, saying, "Well no, you can't blame new technology either because I have never seen a machine lay bricks or put plaster on a wall, and I certainly have never seen a machine do any plumbing work."

It was all a frank but friendly exchange of views and, when I got home, Wendy looked and remarked, "What have you done to your hair?"

The barber had become so engrossed in the discussion that he had cut my hair much shorter that I would normally have had it! We both had a good laugh. I was out of work for seven weeks and then I managed to get a job with a small plumbing firm in Stanningley.

The owner was a chap named Cheatem and he had about four or five other lads working for him. At the interview, he told me that he didn't fully operate the JIB scheme, in that though he paid the proper rate he didn't run the same holiday scheme. When I mentioned that I had almost three weeks holiday pay in stamps on my JIB Holiday Card, he suggested that I submit them to him; he would look at them with a view to possibly adopting the scheme for everyone else at the firm. He added further that, as and when I wanted holidays, he would cash the stamps for me.

I thought nothing of this as it was routinely the employer's responsibility to retain hold of the card and ensure he put holiday stamps on your cards accordingly. When we then agreed holiday dates, they would cash in the cards and, in turn, pay you the due holiday money.

Cheatem had no office as such and ran his business from his home. Very early on, through observation of his interaction with others, I became aware of his surly presentation and volatile temper, though I had not, at this stage, been on the receiving end of the latter. There was no bonus scheme, so my wage comprised of a thirty-seven-hour working week at the JIB rate. His friend also worked at the firm and it transpired that this chap, John, was a joiner by trade, but had picked up some plumbing skills by working for Cheatem. I had been working there for a couple of months when Cheatem informed me that he had got the plumbing and heating contract for a round twenty to thirty flats in the Burley area of the city. I was designated as the plumber for the site.

I was content that I had got a job, as it had become increasingly clear to me that I was unable to secure any new building work due to a nationwide slow-down in the construction industry. It was generally a decent group of other lads on site and I had my breaks along with them in the *snap cabin*. There was one joiner called George, who was perhaps in his early to mid-thirties, and he presented as somewhat naïve and gullible, both potentially dangerous traits to have on a building site.

One day in the cabin, during a light-hearted discussion about the soap *Coronation Street*, George was demonstrating great awareness and insight of current events in the programme, along with an in-depth knowledge of characters from yesteryear. This was to the point that several people began taking the 'Micky' out of him and, after a period of time, he had had enough and simply clammed up, becoming totally unresponsive to any comments directed at him.

The lads seemed to go back to their newspapers, but I looked at the lad across the table from me and simply said, "Do yer remember Arthur Lowe being in *Dad's Army*? Well, wasn't he also in *Coronation Street?*"

"Yeah that's right he was," he replied, seeming to understand where I was going with this.

"Now didn't he work in some kind of clothing shop with Miss Nugent?"

"That's right. I remember that they both did work together in a shop," the reply came back.

I probed further. "Yeah, but neither of them owned that shop, did they? So who was the owner?"

There was a short pause for several seconds before George, who had clearly been following the conversation and unable to contain himself, shouted out the answer: "It was Mr. Papadopolous!"

The cabin was in uproar and George realised he had taken the bait and been had. Poor George was also one of a number people that simply should not wear trainers to work due to the fact that his feet absolutely stank. If you were working near him, or when he was in the *snap cabin,* more often than not the smell from his feet was simply appalling. No one had the heart to draw his attention to this, but over the summer, when he took his holidays, he left his work trainers in the cabin and one chap got hold of them, took them outside and nailed them to the wooden cabin wall with four-inch nails saying, "that ought to kill 'em."

On-site security storage for the plumbing materials comprised of what can only be described as a flimsy domestic six-foot by three-foot garden shed that Cheatem had provided. Almost immediately, I spoke to the site agent and asked if overnight I could store the plumbing fittings, along with the six metre lengths of copper pipe, in the builders' steel container. He agreed on the condition that each evening I put everything in the steel container and then first thing every morning, to avoid feet trampling and damaging the copper tube, I took everything out of the container and put it in the building.

As the summer progressed, I agreed with Cheatem dates for one-week's holiday that Wendy and I were to have with the kids. I reminded him that he was still holding my holiday stamp cards and he commented that he would have to find out how he could cash them for me.

As my holiday loomed nearer, I asked him on a couple of occasions if he had made himself aware of the process for cashing the stamps. On both occasions, he was clearly irritated and offered me blunt short-shrift responses.

Now, it is worth pointing out that, as part of the attempt to regulate the industry, plumbers were graded into three categories. 'Trained' meant that you had served an apprenticeship, but got no qualification. 'Advanced' confirmed that, along with your apprenticeship, you had gained an Advanced Craft City & Guilds Certificate. The third category was 'Technician', which I came across very rarely. I was in the 'Advanced' section and held a JIB card to prove it.

On the Friday, I was due to finish for my holiday and Cheatem's friend, John, was also working on the job. For many years, it had been a weekly custom for me (as well as other plumbers I knew) to have one's wages and, in this case, holiday pay too already worked out beforehand, because it wasn't uncommon for some employers to make 'mistakes'. When Cheatem arrived on site and met me the following conversation ensued.

"Ere Colin, there's yer holiday pay ere."

I looked and saw the deficit straight away. "This is one-week's holiday pay at the 'Trained rate'," I said.

He came back immediately and said, "I don't know how to cash yer holiday stamps and I'm fed up of yer going on about 'em. Anyway, I don't have a lot of work on, so when yer come back off holiday it's more than likely you'll be getting a week's notice!"

"That's great," I said. "Sounds like Victorian values!" And off he went.

I felt completely despondent. Later, as we set off from site in John's car, I related events to him and expressed my dismay at Cheatem's attitude and the 'downer' it would place on our family holiday due to being underpaid. I related to John how I had extended an element of loyalty by looking after Cheatem's on-site interests by storing the plumbing materials, not in the 'garden shed', but in the builder's steel container.

He suddenly stopped the car and said to me, "Where are all the fittings and pipe now?"

"Still in the building," I replied.

In an alarmed tone, he said, "We had better go back then."

I simply said, "Well, if yer going back, I'm getting out 'ere."

He drove on, but I had no doubt that he wouldn't waste any time in telling the tale on me once he met up with Cheatem. Well, we had our one-week family holiday and, when I went to Cheatem's house first thing on the Monday morning, he was true to his word and gave me one-week's notice of redundancy. However, he also promised to sort out the holiday pay that he owed me and hand it over when I was paid the following Friday. This never materialised and I received nothing.

For some reason that I fail to remember, I had joined the union in late October 1977, though I had never had any inclination to attend the meetings. In fact, it was later that year that I became aware that the Leeds Plumbing Lodge held no meetings whatsoever. Anyway, having explained matters to someone at the union office in Wakefield, I was promised that they would look into it but, in the meantime, I was unemployed yet again. About ten days later, I was sat at home when one afternoon the telephone rang and I had a most extraordinary telephone conversation.

I picked up the phone and a male voice at the other end said, "Is that Colin Potter?"

"Yes, that's me."

"Hi Colin. It's Mr. Scott here. I am ringing from my plumbing business in Selby. You've sent me a completed application form for a job."

"Yeah, that's right," I replied expectantly.

"Well, this is just a courtesy call, Colin, as I understand you've been working for Mr. Cheatem…"

"Yes, that's right," I concurred.

"Well, he's putting it about that you're not to be touched with a barge pole because you're too 'uniony'."

I was astounded and attempted to explain about my holiday stamp card and how Cheatem still owed me money. Mr. Scott responded by saying, "Well, there are now a number of employers who won't employ you."

I asked who he meant and he offered two or three names, to which I said, "I have never worked for any of them, so how can this be?"

Mr. Scott went on to explain that "The thing is, every so often employers have meetings and, at one such meeting, Mr. Cheatem has told those present about the problems that he is having with you and that you are too 'uniony'. As a consequence, you are quickly gaining a bad reputation."

I felt so indignant and dumbfounded at receiving such a telephone call out of the blue, with such scurrilous comments, and then Mr. Scott said that he was willing to consider me for a job, but he would want to interview me to assess my suitability. With this last comment, his voice had a cautionary tone as if to denote that there might be more than a hint of truth in the things that he had been told about me. I was still feeling aghast, but I thanked him for his call and declined his offer of an interview "to assess my suitability".

When I spoke to Wendy, she too couldn't believe it; I had, in effect, been placed on an employers' blacklist for trying to legitimately get monies owed to me by a rogue employer. Having gathered my thoughts, I called the union to explain what had transpired and they agreed that, along with the monies owed to me, they needed to deal with the 'blacklist' matter also.

Approximately two weeks later, there was an occurrence that Wendy and I found both strange and alarming. One particular day, the postman pushed a large brown envelope through our letter box and, upon opening this, Wendy found a number of smaller ones, each addressed to one or both of us. Each envelope had been individually opened in order – we presumed this was to establish the nature of their contents. Overtime, I have increasingly become aware that, especially in the construction industry, employers will collectively organise to keep blacklists of individual workers deemed for one reason or another to be 'troublesome'. Such lists would include names of individuals who were members of trade unions, and/or took part in trade union activity, or those that have raised health and safety concerns.

Given such clandestine goings on, had our mail been intercepted due to me also being judged as 'troublesome'? It remains a mystery, but as Wendy has often stated over the years, yes, "it's a democracy as long as you don't rock the boat".

With the situation I now found myself in, the fact that the construction industry wasn't completely co-ordinated and regulated by employers proved now to be a double-edged sword for me. Whilst on the one hand there were firms that were affiliated to the JIB and paid appropriate rates and holiday pay etc., others were more autonomous in paying what they needed to in order to recruit plumbers. In this latter group, many of these autonomous employers never bothered attending collective meetings with other bosses, probably because in many instances they had begun as a sole trader and grown their business by taking on more plumbers, and by working this way they often made up their own rules accordingly.

Luckily for me, this lack of overall regulation across the industry meant that, after three weeks of being out of work, in September 1981 I secured a job with a company on Easterly Road, Leeds. It was sometime later that a meeting was convened to hear my case about the matters relating to Cheatem. Present at the meeting, besides Cheatem and I, was his employers' representative and the trade union official there to represent me.

The meeting initially dealt with the holiday matter and, following some prevarication by Cheatem, there was full agreement that he did indeed owe me money. On the blacklisting matter, it appeared that the official had forgotten about this and I had to whisper a reminder in his ear. At this he simply said, "It has come to our attention that someone had been spreading scurrilous rumours about Colin and these must stop with immediate effect."

There was no reply from Cheatem or his representative and for myself, rightly or wrongly, I felt disappointed that he should get away so lightly with the matter, given the upset that he had caused both Wendy and I. With this episode now behind me, I now had my new job to look forward to.

When I attended the interview, Mr. Scammer the employer informed me that the work was likely to be temporary as my recruitment specifically concerned a project in Manchester and after that there might not be any additional work. He went on to inform me that it was a thirty-seven-hour working week, paid at the JIB rate, but this was the only bit of the JIB scheme that he operated. Not realising the full implication of his following comment at the time, for some reason, he made a specific point of telling me that he did not pay over the JIB hourly wage rate.

The firm had around ten plumbers in total, along with a chap who undertook the office work. In due course, I became aware that two of these plumbers (Peter and Harry) had been at the firm a number of years and that I was to partner Peter on the Manchester job.

The job in question was a smallish hotel that was now empty of guests and undergoing significant refurbishment. With an agreed meeting point, I met Peter each morning and, with him having the firm's van, we used the M62 motorway to travel to and from Manchester at the end of the day.

He was a chap in his fifties, who was seemingly pleasant enough. I remember one day he asked me what my hourly wage rate was, and not giving it a thought, I replied that it was the flat JIB rate, and then I commented further, saying, "Yer probably on a little more given your length of service with Jack?"

He offered no reply and I felt disinclined to pursue the matter further. After a couple of months, there were rumours that money problems of some sort revolved around the Manchester job and, subsequently, the work came to a standstill and I began fearing the worst. However, Scammer had me calling in to the office on Easterly Road each morning, where he gave me various small plumbing and heating jobs to do over the course of the coming working weeks.

The official start time in the plumbing/building trade has always been 8.00am, but here Scammer had everyone starting at 7.30am. One day, another plumber explained to me how this had come about. Peter and Harry, as the two longest serving plumbers, were in competition with each other so that one of them would be more noted and appreciated by Scammer than the other.

Historically, it *had* been an 8.00am start, but Harry and Peter would attempt to get to the office much earlier than the other. Therefore, if you were working with either of them, then inevitably you were getting to the office much earlier too. As a consequence, this 'crawling' led to them both turning up at 7.30am and in tow was the hapless plumber/s who happened to be working with one or both of them. Because of this, one day Scammer announced to everyone that, given some plumber's were turning up at 7.30am, that was to be the new start time. However, the 'crawlers' failed to stop there because the sad fools still attempted to outdo the other by now turning up at the office just after 7am.

The chap relating this pathetic and juvenile activity to me went on to explain that, on one occasion, he had been designated the previous day to work with Harry and, the following morning, Harry was to pick him. He explained that Harry arrived at his house at 7am and proceeded to sound the van horn and, having heard this, the chap went over to the window and lifted his cup of tea to indicate to Harry that he was concluding his breakfast.

A couple of days later Scammer took the plumber to one side and pointedly asked, "Are yer having problems getting up on a morning?"

"What do yer mean?" replied the plumber.

"Well, according to Harry, yer can't get out of bed on a morning and yer keepin' him waiting." The point was made clear to him.

One thing which used to irritate me was a sign on Scammer's office door which bluntly read, '*Will all operatives please have a bath daily as the only way we can get you to do any work around here is to kiss your arse'*. The overall sentiment I found particularly offensive and the non-person term 'operative' is something that I, both then and now, intensely dislike. It implies that individual workers are merely an appendage and, as such, their humanity is somewhat stripped away.

Scammer himself had never been 'on the tools' and, having taken over the firm from his late father many years ago, one might want to be kind and suggest that having never been 'on the tools' was the reason for his crass attitude towards skilled tradesmen. I have never found this to be a valid reason and many such employers – and indeed their foremen – adopted such trite attitudes.

Around this time the firm was carrying out a lot of contract work for Bass Charrington, as the brewery were proceeding to upgrade the living quarters across many of their pubs and that meant a lot of central heating work for us.

On one particular day, together with two other plumbers, we were working in such a pub in the York city centre when it was the day of a planned royal visit by Prince Charles and Princess Diana. The pub was adjacent to the route the couple would be taking and, when we arrived that morning, the crowd barriers had been erected and people were already beginning to gather, though they would be waiting at least three hours for the couple to pass by. We had to install a metal flue liner for the gas central heating boiler, so we proceeded to get the ladder up and begin our work and, from the rooftop, we were musing over the crowd that was steadily building at the road side and no doubt eagerly anticipating, when the time came, a glance of the royal couple.

Without being initially aware of it, our position on the roof was seemingly giving rise for concern and, at one point, we noticed a number of plain clothes men looking rather disconcertingly at us from an upstairs shop window across the street from us. Sensing that they might be security guards, we hastily grabbed hold of the metal flue liner and, as we gradually lowered it down the chimney, this seemed to allay the men's concerns and they disappeared from view, leaving us to get on with things.

All the time, the crowd was building up and they waited patiently, staring at the ever-vacant road, and then around 11am any tedium that was being felt was broken and there was a tumultuous roar from the crowd further on up the road, a little out of our view. As it happened, this wasn't, however, for the royal couple, but for some random cyclist, and he came down the road to more tumultuous roars and applause which went up like a 'mexican wave'. Having broken the lingering monotony of nothing happening, he brought some light relief to the patient crowd as he waved back in royal style.

Around thirty minutes later, the royal cavalcade had come into view and passed again within seconds, leaving the crowd with a mere glimpse of the couple. That was that and the crowd all slowly dispersed.

It was lunchtime one day and the other two plumbers and I were chatting when one became quite disgruntled as he spoke about not being paid anything extra, though he had the extra responsibility for being in charge of the job. It was common practice that someone with this kind of situation got a little extra.

I said to him inquisitively, "So don't you get anything for extra responsibility?"

"Nope, I just get extra on the JIB hourly wage rate, like everybody else at the firm," the reply came back.

This threw me as I had been specifically told by Scammer when he took me on that he did not pay anything other than the flat JIB hourly rate and, being unable to hide my instant surprise, they both went on to explain that every new starter was given extra on top of the rate after one to three weeks.

On reflection, Scammer had taken me on specifically for the job in Manchester, thinking I would not find this out and, whilst working down Manchester with Peter, he had gone out of his way to ask me what my hourly rate was, but he had then said nothing when I had told him.

I was feeling really hacked off for the rest of the day, so that evening when we went back to the office I broached the matter with Scammer. He was taken aback, almost like a naughty child that had just been caught out for telling lies, and then having gathered his response, he said, "Ah, well yes, but I was waiting to see how you turned out before giving you extra."

"Look," I said, "I have been here a couple of months whilst fellas I'm working with have got the extra on their rate after one or two weeks. I only want what everyone else is being paid."

"Okay, Colin," his reply came back and, from that point on, I was put on the same rate as everyone else.

A short while after this, I was placed on a job at Scarcroft and each morning I drove to the office for 7.30am and met with a plumber who had the firm's van and, on the way to his job at Wetherby, he would drop me off and pick me up at the end of the day. This work at Scarcroft involved a large detached house that had had a big extension built and there were various pieces of plumbing and heating to do there.

The couple owning the house had a daughter aged around two and two boys, one around eleven and the other perhaps thirteen years old, both of whom went to Leeds Grammar School. Apparently, the couple had their own frozen food business, which allowed the chap to run a Bentley and his wife a black Ford Capri. During the first day, the woman brought me a cup of tea and, though she tried her best to speak posh, it was obvious to me that they hadn't always lived in such surroundings.

In an attempt to make conversation, I asked, "Where did you live before here?"

"Oh, at Roundhay (generally a 'posh' area) in Leeds," came the reply.

"Aw right, we've friends up Roundhay, where abouts did yer live?" I queried further.

She made some excuse to end the conversation and went on her way. A day or so later, she had gone out, but her retired father had arrived, who she previously told me used to work as a painter and decorator. Around mid-morning, he shouted up the stairs, "Do yer want a pot o' tea, lad?"

"Please," I replied.

Minutes later, he shouted me to come downstairs saying the tea was ready. We both sat at the kitchen table and this pleasant chap pushed a plate of biscuits towards me saying, "Ere have a biscuit."

We chatted generally and then I asked, "You live up Roundhay, don't yer?"

"Yeah, that's right. We live in't Brackenwoods, do yer know it?"

I nodded and reflected on the fact that the day before his daughter had made some excuse to end our conversation as I was asking her where in Roundhay she had previously lived, presumably not wanting to admit to me that she had lived on a council estate. I presumed further that she was apparently ashamed of her parents and their family background. I remember thinking to myself "how sad". This couple owning the house employed someone to clean their home and another person to look after the garden and, on one particular day, I casually asked the gardener if he was treated okay by his employers.

"Gi' mi workin' class people any time," he sourly replied.

"But these *are* working-class people," I replied back, but they were trying their damnedest to run away from their roots.

Towards the back end of the job, I arrived as usual one morning and began straight away working in the kitchen. Then I overheard the following exchange of words as the mother, in a posh voice said to her son, "Timothy, get your plimsolls please."

However, there was no reply as the young lad ignored her request a couple of times more in the way that children sometimes do.

Again, she asked, "Timothy get your plimsolls and put them in your bag."

"Yer wot!" he enquired.

"Git yer pumps and put 'em in yer bag now," she bellowed back in a manner that led to the dropping of the 'posh' façade. I can only assume that the lad had no idea what plimsolls were and the 'show' had been put on to impress me of their social finesse. Instead, I was amused by this exchange, although I also felt sorry for the woman because she felt the need to deny who she actually was and where she had come from.

Oh, the shallow and utterly ludicrous subjectivity of the snob has to be understood and pitied. It is not how one speaks that matters, but rather what one says and added to this the commonplace crass belief that living in the 'right' area, having the 'right' job, the 'right' car and ownership of the 'right' house with nice things automatically makes one a good person is but an illiterate expression of both thought and attitude.

Whilst I was still working on this particular job, there was one morning that I slept in so, as quickly as possible, I telephoned the office and explained that I would be late and, by doing this, I alerted them that there was no reason for the other plumber with the van to wait for me. Because I needed some fittings for my job, rather than go straight there I called at the office first. I got there at around 8.50am before getting what I needed and travelling on.

Several days later, when I completed my time sheet, I thought nothing of it as I booked £1.50 for using my own car that day travelling to and from the job. Again, I thought nothing of it when I received the payment with my wage. However, several days later, when I was completing my weekly time sheet along with the rest of the plumbers, Scammer shouted out to me, "I paid you that £1.50 last week, Colin."

Unaware of the significance of his comment, I asked for clarity, "Yer know, the other week, when yer slept in and yer booked £1.50 expenses..."

"Oh yeah," said I, still unaware of any significance.

"Well, I won't pay it next time. If yer can't get to work on time, then that's your problem." Well, that was me told, though I thought his judgement and comments petty given that I had used my car to carry *his* materials to my job even though I did not have any business insurance to cover me.

Several weeks later, Scammer was absent from the office and the clerk said I was to travel in my car and go to a property in Cross Gates in order to put a new shower in at the house in question. He went on to say further that, once I had arrived at the job, could I measure up what materials I required and then go collect them from the plumbers merchants – about a mile away – at the end of Manston Lane, and then return to complete the job.

At this, I quietly shook my head and explained to him Scammer's recent comments over the small sum of £1.50 expenses. I went on to state that, because my car was *not* insured for business use, I would go to the house, ring through to the office the required materials, and Scammer would have to arrange for them to be delivered to me.

Later that morning, a plumber came with the materials I had ordered, stating that Scammer was fuming with me, but I wasn't too troubled by this. My personal experiences were leading me to look more objectively and critically at my employment situation. My schooling had apparently failed in some respects because I wasn't prepared to be subservient and deferential to hucksters and I was learning the hard way from bad experiences.

Any radicalism that I might have been labelled with had been in the main socially constructed, and this was leading to a slow development of my distaste for social injustice and the lack of fair play – not only throughout society, but especially in the work place. I believe the other factor now at play was the recognition by some employers of the deteriorating environment that the building trade as a whole was experiencing, and therefore this allowed some plumbing bosses to exploit this situation because they felt that their staff were likely to be fearful of losing their jobs.

After approximately five months of this employment, I was made redundant and, on this occasion, my period of being out of work lasted seven weeks before I got a job in Farsley, Leeds with a small firm comprising of the boss, Mr, Thinksmall, three other plumbers and an apprentice. I was told that I would not need to use my own car once I had arrived at the office/yard as it could then stay there until the working day had ended. The firm seemed to be part way through a small maintenance contract with the NHS. I say small because the work was across the smaller outlying hospitals such as Airedale and Wharfedale. Initially I was either being dropped off at some hospital by someone driving one of the 'rust bucket' vans, or I would be working alongside them.

As is customary with many small firms, we would meet at the yard each morning in order for work to be allocated and materials to be collected. Indeed, I remember one such morning when I asked Thinksmall for a large hacksaw blade. There was a brief moment's silence from everyone and Thinksmall gave me a cold stare before taking the blade out of a drawer and, as he handed it to me, he told me the cost of such a blade and stressed upon me that I needed to take care of it. This was a brief but bizarre moment and, once out in the yard, one of the other plumber's told me that Thinksmall. had 'a thing' about large hacksaw blades and was always chiding them for allegedly using too many.

One particular day, he drove into the yard in a big brand new, top of the range Rover. We were all invited to gather around as he opened the doors so that we could peer in and be mesmerised by the gadgets and supposed grandeur before he went on to demonstrate the – innovatory in 1982 – electric windows. As he stepped back to admire its splendour there was tacit understanding that we should all do the same and so we dutifully complied, but I couldn't help having a sideways glance at the two 'rust bucket' vans that were the workhorses for the firm.

I guess it was only a matter of time and before long I was asked to use my car in order to carry out his plumbing work and carry his materials, and these requests increasingly grew and grew because one or both of the vans were on their last legs. It was always the case, when one was asked to use their car for work purposes, the level of expenses the boss was prepared to pay was derisory, amounting to as little as they could get away with barely covering the cost of the additional petrol, with nothing towards the wear and tear of such privately owned vehicles. Wherever I have worked this arrangement was always a bone of contention for plumbers.

After a while of using my car for works travel, I did speak to Thinksmall, pointing out that when I began working for him he had said that I wouldn't need to use my car, but his excuse was the poor condition of both vans, as if that should be of concern to me. After three to four months of employment in January 1982 I was again made redundant on the premise that the NHS contract had come to an end and he had nothing in the pipeline. Luckily, this time I was only out of work for one week.

I thought my luck had changed when I got a job with Recruitem & Usem Homes, a well-known and relatively large building firm in Roundhay, Leeds. The first couple of days were spent going to different sites, working through lists of snagging work (repair work) and, around the middle of the week I went to one site where for the first time I actually met another plumber employed by Recruitem & Usem. Again, I had been sent there to carry out various snagging work, and the site plumber expressed his surprise that I had been so recently set on by the firm because, as far as he was concerned, they had very little work on or indeed any work to start.

After another two days of snagging, I was made redundant on the Friday. I had simply been set on for one week and crudely used to help the firm catch up with their snagging list and then tossed back on the dole! Around this time, Wendy and I once more resurrected the idea of emigrating to Canada where her older sister lived. Following telephone discussions between Wendy and Jenny, I was advised that Canada too was in an economic recession and, whilst they were still accepting immigrants, it was on the basis of them taking up work that indigenous Canadians either wouldn't or couldn't do. Wendy and I completed the application forms and followed these up by going to The Canadian Consulate in Manchester, but our application failed because at the time there were plenty of plumbers already in Canada also wanting work.

Disappointed, but still determined to seek a better quality of life for our family, we began researching the possibility of emigrating to Australia. Again, we completed the necessary forms and much to our delight Wendy and I were then asked to pay for and undergo private medicals and X-rays. We were both a little concerned that we might be refused due to Wendy having the polycystic kidney condition, which from the outset we had been upfront in divulging. It was with such a relief and joy when we were duly informed that we had both passed our medicals and X-rays and the final stage now was to pay for our own GP to write to the embassy with an overview of our medical history.

At the time he expressed a hint of pessimism about the polycystic kidney matter. He was very much aware that Wendy was not taking any form of medication. Wendy and I had discussed things ourselves and were of the view that, with her having a degenerative kidney disease, there would be every chance of us being able to settle in Australia before her kidneys presented as a problem requiring her to have medical treatment.

Disappointingly, it appears that our GP thought differently and, a couple of weeks after his letter had been sent, we received notification that our application to emigrate had failed. Though we were both disappointed, Wendy was especially more so, blaming herself for the rejection and for a short time it was difficult to dispel this from her thoughts.

Meanwhile, my job search bore fruit and, following two weeks of unemployment, I managed to get a job with the Leeds Public Works Department in October or, as they were also called at the time, a Direct Labour Organisation (DLO). Different trades' personnel were employed in order to carry out routine maintenance of the 80,000 or so rented council homes as well as undertaking what was commonly termed 'whole house improvements'. Prior to this new job, I had become a member of the Bramley Branch Labour Party and leading up to and informing this decision was my understanding and awareness of what I had at that point read of post-war Britain.

The period from 1945 until1979 is regarded as one of 'consensus politics', due to the implementation and influence of Keynesian economics, both in the United Kingdom and across the industrial, developed world. Broadly, this meant the adoption of a mixed economy, with key utilities, such as gas, electricity, telephones, the railways and coal, being taken into public ownership along with the creation and introduction of the British Welfare State, which included the bringing about of a National Health Service. It would be free at the point of use, offering free prescriptions and dental treatment, local authority personal health and social services, the building of quality and affordable council homes and a network of subsidised local public transport. The term 'consensus politics' came about as both successive Labour and Conservative governments continued to broadly adopt the above approach to managing the economy.

It was perhaps a naïve view then, that any new Labour government would reverse the draconian policies that had and still were being introduced by the Tory government. Around this period, a number of leading Tory Ministers appeared on the television declaring that Keynesian economics was now over and, as Michael Heseltine said, "It had been a useful experiment."

The right wing of the Tory party had gained ascendancy over a number of years and now, in government, they were ideologically altering the economy in order to bring about the return of pre-war 'laissez fairre' economics now re-branded as 'free market' economics. Pre-war laissez economics is widely viewed by many as proving itself as being completely bankrupt of ideas as it dismally failed to offer anything towards resolving the 1920s slump and the Great Depression of the 1930s. In 1936, John Maynard Keynes published his book entitled *The Grand Theory of Employment*, but from 1979 onwards the Tory government purposefully set about gradually cutting public spending wherever possible, thus reducing the role of the public sector in favour of a free market-orientated private one.

After several weeks of being a Labour Party member, a lad called Neil had apparently been informed that I was an unemployed plumber and one evening struck up a conversation with me. He suggested at one point that I might want to read a novel entitled the *Ragged Trousered Philanthropists (RTP)*, written by Robert Tressel. I subsequently bought a copy and over the years I have re-read it on four or five occasions. Many of the characters within the book I have worked with and having read it herself at the time Wendy dismally concluded that nothing has changed. Whilst material surroundings change the essence of some social relations remain the same.

On a personal level, job insecurity coupled with short periods of unemployment meant that Wendy and I would find it difficult to plan things, such as any additional housing expenditure and family holidays, due to my unstable employment situation. It was seen then, as it is now, that being out of work was often viewed as a failure of the individual. Wendy and I didn't see it that way as we were both beginning to see that unemployment was a structural phenomenon. Nevertheless, I had a number of people say to me "What? Yer a plumber and yer out of work?"

It was in this context that I was pleased to get the job with the DLO and, though the pay wasn't very good, there was an ongoing bonus scheme and, knowing my ability to earn bonus, I felt I could make my wages up that way. Moreover, I was looking at the possibility of more enhanced job security. As with other employees my contract of employment stated that I must participate in the bonus scheme and if I failed to make bonus then I would be disciplined or perhaps even be dismissed. The DLO was then situated in a post-war building on Sweet Street and on my first day I remember sitting in the reception and finding, in one of the other chairs, there was another chap who turned out to be a new plumber by the name of John Light. Later, I discovered that John also lived in Bramley on the Raynville estate, which was about a two-minute walk from where we lived.

Following our induction with a large general group of other new starters, John and I were allocated to a project in Bramley with several other plumbers, where we were to fit new baths and sink units on the Broadlea Estate. A steel container was sited near the Sandford Middle School with all of our equipment inside and we were advised by the 'off-site' foreman that, to earn any bonus at all, each day you had to fit two items (for example, two baths or a bath plus a sink).

I had ten years' experience of working on bonus so I had a good idea as to whether a scheme was good or bad and, though I was able to fit the obligatory two items per day, one or two lads persistently struggled. After a week or so, following a group discussion, we were all of the same opinion that, for a number of reasons, it was very hard work for the level of bonus on offer. When the foreman came to the site, we put our concerns to him, but his immediate response was to say, "Well, Peter's mekin' money."

Peter was aged around thirty and he was always on the fringe of the group, being something of a loner, always working through his breaks, including lunches. It soon became apparent that the foreman was using him as the 'yardstick' in order to deflect our collective concerns and therefore he would simply shrug his shoulder's saying, "Well, he's mekin' money."

Individuals who, whether consciously or not, allow themselves to be used by management as a 'yardstick' will often inadvertently do their colleagues a dis-service because employers will use them to undermine any legitimate concerns from other workers. The bonus formula was complex and convoluted and I couldn't possibly go into detail, other than to say, for example, that all bonus prices were based on a hundred minutes to the hour! For the first time ever I, along with the other new starters, all brought calculators to work our bonus out.

The Broadlea Estate itself had a bad name, but working in many different houses, I found that most people were trying to eke out a living just like anyone else. Hence, there is relevance in the two aphorisms: "give a dog a bad name" and "don't tar everyone with the same brush".

John Light and I soon struck up a good rapport as we both shared many similar political views and, in fact, for me this was the first time that I had ever worked with anyone that had a good understanding of current affairs and politics. Indeed John was very much on the left with his political views. We were both members of different unions and, having spent much of his working life undertaking mechanical services work, his union was the Heating, Ventilation and Air Conditioning Trade Union (HVACTU), whilst I was a member of The Electrical, Electronic, Telecommunications and Plumbing Trade Union (EEPTU). Over time, we became good friends, and that remains so to this day. At that time, he had more party political and trade union involvement and experience than I and, whilst I was keen to listen, I have always liked to explore and assess things in my own way.

On site, apart from Peter, there was still ongoing collective discontent and, following a group discussion early in 1983, I agreed to the other plumbers electing me as their shop steward. One of the first things I took up with the foreman was a health and safety issue relating to the need for appropriate face masks, because many of the old baths being removed were enclosed with asbestos panels and, invariably when attempting to remove them, they broke, releasing asbestos dust into the immediate working environment. Initially, he brought to site simple cloth-type masks, but I informed him that they should be specific for asbestos and thus have the right filtration element.

Later on in the year, I began a regional Trades Union Congress (TUC) one day per week Shop Stewards' Training Course at the Leeds Polytechnic College. Over this ten-week period, I found the course very educational and I gained much benefit, which hopefully helped me to be more equipped at representing members. This course was run by Eric Preston, an excellent tutor, who much later I became aware was also a member of the Independent Labour Party.

The thing with being a plumbing steward is that, on a day-to-day basis, you are taking instructions from management and then, as and when with your union hat on, you can be challenging them over certain issues. This being the case, initially I was told stories from some plumbers that indicated some stewards found this dual role difficult, often resulting in the poor representation of a plumbing member.

One salutary lesson that I learned, also on the course, was to never argue from the top of one's head, and instead always refer to the relevant policy or procedure, and this is of wider benefit in life in general when trying to address problems with all types of organisations. This however wasn't common practice within the DLO and many managers failed to take any cognisance of this. Before the Bramley Project came to a conclusion, I was informed one day by the foreman that I was being moved to the Sheepscar Maintenance. John suggested that, because I was increasingly becoming recognised as an 'active' steward, this move may have been a ploy to strip me of my steward credentials.

Sure enough, this proved to be the case after a couple of weeks of working at the depot. I received a telephone call from the full-time trade union convenor based in the Sweet Street Offices, informing me that a particular plumber was facing a disciplinary in a couple of days' time and, though I didn't know the lad, he had asked for me to represent him on the day. I went to the depot manager's office to explain that I would need time off to represent the lad on the due date, but was immediately told that "We already have Des here and he is our plumbing shop steward, so we don't need another one."

Expecting this response, I replied, saying "That's fine, but I am not a steward for a site, rather I am an EEPTU plumbing shop steward for the whole of the public works dept." Following John's comments, I had checked out my position beforehand pending the move to Sheepscar, but within a week of me speaking to the manager, I was moved to the Morley Maintenance Depot.

After a number of weeks working there, I happened to notice one day two plumbers unloading a load of broken asbestos guttering and fall pipes and simply throwing it into the general skip at the depot. I went in to see the manager, who appeared ignorant of the potential hazard and was trivialising the event until I advised him about the dangers of working with asbestos if it was potentially going to break, thus emitting dust on the worker who, in this instance, had to be working from a ladder under the gutter, so any dust would fall on to his face. I further told him that there was a legal duty on the council to ensure that any type of asbestos must be safely disposed of at a designated 'safe site'.

After a short period there, I was moved to a project at Halton Moor, probably due to me challenging the depot manager about the hazards of plumbers working on the removal of asbestos guttering and fall pipes. The work at Halton Moor was a 'whole house improvement' project that was very close to being completed. One of the lads in the bonus office at Sweet Street had told me that the council was increasingly finding it difficult to win new projects such as these and he went on to explain that in 1980 the government had introduced the Local Government Planning and Land Act, which amongst other things, saw the introduction of competition in relation to council services.

To help the process along, since the Act's introduction, the government had compelled all DLO trades within a council public works dept. to make a year-on-year increase in their profit margin. The current annual increase meant that the figure was now 5% for each trade working within the DLO. He went on to point out that currently Wimpy Builders were carrying out 'whole house improvements' in Morley at an annual profit margin of possibly around 1.5%. Not exactly a level playing field and therefore the council was unable to win new contracts and it didn't require a mind reader to see that the future of the DLO was precarious to say the least.

I have since learned that the Conservative Party does not as such have any overall ideology, but one of the historical cornerstones is that *social change* should be gradual in order to avoid social disruption and unrest. The ramifications of the Tory rejection of Keynesianism meant that, throughout the 1980s and onwards, there was the constant drive to rid the economy of publicly run services in favour of private sector involvement and, as a consequence, people began using the term *privatisation by stealth*.

The government imposed other financial constraints on local authorities, including that of rate capping, which had the effect of restricting the amount they could spend and this no doubt impacted on the ability of councils to build any new homes for rent. Across the DLO there were five EETPU plumbing shop stewards, including myself, and the senior steward, who was an older chap called George.

I was very surprised to find out that the stewards never held any periodic meetings in order to consult with their members, other plumbers. This would allow them to air any issues that they might have and, at the same time, the stewards could share information concerning plumbers that might come from the joint shop stewards committee meetings held periodically at Sweet Street. I felt that this state of affairs was undemocratic.

At this time, the city-wide Leeds Plumbing Lodge also held no meetings either, leaving many plumbers adrift of relevant events concerning them, but whilst I was unable to do anything about this, I felt that I could make progress with the former. After discussing things with John, followed by a diplomatic word with George – as I wanted him to be onboard rather than feel alienated – he agreed with the idea that an evening meeting should be arranged at the Trades Council Club at the bottom of Chapeltown Road.

All plumbers were notified of the event and John quite rightly suggested that, as matter of courtesy, I should also invite the EETPU full-time official, adding that he probably wouldn't turn up anyway. John was right; on the night of the meeting the official never showed, but about twenty plumbers did, which was very pleasing.

With the meeting being a success, further ones were subsequently held over the year and, at one of these, I put it to the meeting that there should be no change in the employment conditions of DLO plumbers without a meeting being convened for *all* to attend, with a full discussion followed by a vote to accept or reject any offer. It was good that everyone was in agreement because I had learned that historically within the DLO too many things affecting plumbers had simply been introduced without any consultation and a democratic vote. Some time later, this new policy was to be tested.

It was becoming common knowledge that a new bonus scheme for the 'whole house improvement' projects was being considered in order to help the authorities' competitiveness in winning any new contracts in the face of private opposition. At this time, I was working on the only 'whole house improvement' site across the city though I was unable to earn any bonus due to the persistent 'snagging work' that I was being given to do. Then at some stage I became aware that a meeting of all trades was to be convened in order to outline the new bonus proposals that were to be implemented. I went to see the site manager beforehand and informed him that, whilst plumbers (including myself) would attend the meeting, this would be for information purposes only because the proposals would have to be put to a full meeting of all public works plumbers and then voted on.

Present at the meeting were bonus/works study staff from Sweet Street, several full-time officials from other unions (but no one from the EETPU) and a number of lads working on the site. After a broad explanation of how things were going to work, I responded by making the following points. "We all know the current difficulty that we have in winning 'whole house' contracts and, alongside this, the authority has a policy of no redundancies. The current bonus scheme is known to be a bone of contention within all trades, yet we are being told that the new bonus scheme will offer more financial gain to tradesmen. How can this be? There will be no redundancies, an increase in bonus payments and we will win more new projects. How does that square when we are unable to compete at the moment?"

The Union of Construction, Allied Trades and Technicians (UCATT) official reared up at me saying, "Ah, so you want to see redundancies, do yer?"

"No, I don't. I am simply asking the question; if we are unable to compete at the moment and a new bonus scheme will pay men more money, how does that make us more competitive?" There were further exchanges, but lads present were now picking up on my argument and the meeting closed without any real agreement about the new scheme.

Sometime later, I was chatting to the convenor at Sweet Street, along with the chair of the Joint Shop Stewards Committee. During this discussion they suggested to me that I should become senior shop steward for the plumbers because, although the current incumbent was a nice guy, for him it was anything for an easy life. I knew that they were right as he hardly contributed at any meetings and, on one occasion, upon his return from a week-long training course, I had asked about the training to which he replied, "It was okay. It's a week away from the wife."

To oust him, it was suggested that I call one of the evening meetings and, at some stage in the course of events, someone from the floor should put forward a vote of no confidence in George. I later spoke to John and we agreed that the removal of George in favour of myself would be a good idea and serve to enhance plumbers' interests.

An ordinary meeting was scheduled and, as usual, I invited the EEPTU full-time official, although he had, as yet, never turned up to any meetings. On the evening of the meeting, as people were gathering, John explained that he had only confided what was to take place with the plumber who was to put forward the vote of no confidence.

Minutes prior the start of the meeting, to my surprise, the full-time official walked through the door and almost immediately asked if he could speak to me outside of the room. Once we were in the corridor, he bluntly said to me, "If you stand against George tonight, I will make sure that you lose your shop steward's card."

I don't recall saying anything, and what could I say? However, before re-taking my seat, I had a quick word with John to call things off. Later, John and I discussed matters and he felt that the convenor and chair of the Stewards Committee had set me up because he believed that my active role as a steward, allied with being a Labour Party member, was seen as a threat by them. I believe he was right and, though I had been politically naïve, I never confronted them. Both were also Labour Party members and, within their respective roles, both spent all of their time on DLO union duties, so I was mindful that the previous convenor had also been a Labour Party member and had got a nice job within the Leeds Civic Hall.

People often have their own agendas, lack integrity and their own self-interest is frequently at variance with the people they are supposedly and democratically representing. Sometime later, at a Joint Shop Stewards Committee Meeting, we were told by the convenor that senior management had recently met with full-time trade union officials and agreed that a thirty-two-year-old Travelling Time and Expenses Agreement was to be amended. This would mean that in the future all newly employed staff would receive new (and reduced) payments. I could see the pitfalls of this and I, like some other stewards, were annoyed that the full-time officials had agreed this. Pressure was put on the convenor and I suggested that he should call a full meeting of all DLO tradesmen to properly discuss the new deal and its implications.

An evening meeting was duly held at the Trades Council Club and there was an impressive attendance of individuals from all trades giving up their free time to hear about what was an important issue. The convenor outlined the proposals and then invited other contributions from the floor.

At some point, I got to my feet and said, "Now, on the face of it, these changes to travelling time and expenses will only affect those new recruits to the DLO so initially these people receiving the reduced travelling and expenses will be in a minority. However, we all know that there is a big staff retention problem and therefore a situation is likely to occur in the not too distant future whereby those enjoying the existing arrangement will become the minority. At this point, what will stop management from arbitrarily placing everyone on the new arrangement? A division between staff is being created and those on the new travelling time and expenses won't in the future offer their support to you all here when you are about to lose out."

I got quite a bit of support from the floor and a proposal was put forward and agreed that, to show our protestations with the arrangements, a half-day stoppage should be planned. That half-day stoppage was planned and on the day a protest was staged outside the Sweet Street Offices. I always remember one lad brusquely saying to me, "What's the union doing about this?"

I simply replied, "You are the union."

Any union is only as strong as the membership. History tells us that progress has only come about when people have taken collective action and that no one can have an understanding of British history without having read about the introduction of combinations and their development into unions and the many struggles of working people. Many people assume that much of the things that they enjoy today, broadly wrapped up in the term 'social democracy', have historically been freely given by successive governments and that at times politicians have been tripping over themselves to expand the very nature of social democracy. History tells us otherwise.

In 1984, the EETPU Office at Wakefield arranged for the appointment of a new plumbing lodge secretary. I had heard about this on the grapevine and, after meeting with the lad in question, I agreed to become the lodge treasurer in the hope that together we could bring about regular and active meetings. It was well regarded in the trade union and political world that the EEPTU was right wing and, some years later, they withdrew their affiliation to the Labour Party. With this in mind, I was guarded about my comments with this new lodge secretary, who I saw was merely using the post as a stepping stone towards some full-time union job. At home, money was still very tight and no doubt due to my union activities I had been unable to participate – as required by my contract of employment - in any bonus schemes to enhance my weekly wages. Indeed at one point Wendy and I considered making a claim for the Family Income Supplement (FIS) benefit, but we were a mere several pounds adrift of the qualifying amount. Therefore one night close to Christmas Wendy and I had a chat about our financial situation and I decided that although I enjoyed my role at the DLO it was time to start the job search once again in order to earn more money.

Chapter 11

Hoping for a Change of Luck

Success finally came in January 1984 when I secured work with a biggish Leeds plumbing firm called John N. Dunn. They primarily carried out new house build work and operated a reasonable bonus scheme.

It was with some regret that I left the public works. In the fourteen months spent there, I had become respected by many plumbers and I believe they saw that I was genuine and sincere in the work I undertook as a shop steward. It was a number of years later that the Leeds DLO was drastically reduced in size, with work being outsourced to the private sector, and the Tories' policy of privatisation by stealth finally worked.

My new job was proving okay and very soon the extra cash enabled Wendy and I to buy a new family car. Now that I was again working out of Leeds, I needed a car, and one that was reliable, so we took the plunge and, for the first and only occasion in our lives, we bought a new car on hire purchase. Due to the insecurity of employment that I had experienced over the past several years, we decided to take out the added protection of insurance so that, in the eventuality of being made redundant, then the car payments would be taken care of. The car was a Lada Riva and at the time they were relatively cheap to buy and therefore quite popular. We were all quite excited at the prospect of having a new car to travel in.

Lada cars were manufactured in Russia and over time, following our own purchase, they rapidly became the brunt of many jokes, for example: *"What do yer call a skip on wheels? A Lada."* The car had rear seatbelts and that was something of an innovation at the time, offering a definite attraction for us, having two kids. Initially, the kids really enjoyed the smell of the new car and driving around in it seemed cool.

Several months after we had purchased it, their attitudes changed. Wendy and I still remember driving down Bramley Town Street with Teresa sitting in the back seat and, as we passed a bus stop with a young girl standing at it, our daughter suddenly flopped down. Seeing this in the rear-view mirror, I asked what the problem was. She replied that it was a school friend standing at the bus stop and Teresa didn't want to be seen in a Lada!

Just like my dad had done with me, I had introduced Colin to fresh water fishing and it became a firm hobby for him for a good number of years. This meant that, as and when we could, we took ourselves off fishing. At times, Teresa would help us dig some worms in the garden, but over a period of time, she became a little squeamish of them.

I had also introduced Colin to Leeds United and again we would go and watch home matches. On one job, I found a small wooden crate and, thinking "this will be ideal for him to stand on and getter a better view of matches", I brought it home and subsequently painted it white. It went on to serve him for some time until he gradually became taller.

Teresa became interested in ice skating and, on occasion, I would take both her and a friend to the Bradford Ice Skating Arena. Around this time, and after some discussion, we decided to buy a Jack Russell puppy who we named Patch. We hadn't realised it when we bought him, but the poor thing had mange. Following several visits to the vet, and a number of times bathing with a medicated shampoo, we managed to rid him of his problem and Patch became a welcome addition to the family.

Later that year, Wendy and I decided that it was time to move house and, following a search, in July 1984 we bought 16 Calverley Gardens in Bramley. Though the house wanted quite a bit of work doing to it, Wendy and I could see the potential, and this was reflected in the price. When young Colin and Teresa saw it for the first time, I remember one of them saying, "Oh, we're not moving here are we?"

The house itself was a pre-Second World War semi-detached with three bedrooms, bathroom, kitchen dining room and living room. The good-sized garden encompassed front, side and back. There was no central heating, but we had a gas fire in the living room, along with two gas wall heaters, one in the hall and the other in the dining room. Prior to the move, I project-managed the carrying out of essential works that included all new softwood window frames and two new hardwood doors that were fitted by a joiner with myself cerrying out the glazing. The house was completely re-wired and a good deal of new plastering was carried out.

We eventually had a new fuse box fitted and Yorkshire Electricity informed me that they needed access to the adjacent property in order to alter the supply, but Mr. Parkin the neighbour in question was, according to YE, proving awkward. Within a day or so of hearing this, I went to the house and popped around to see Mr. Parkin and, after apologising for any inconvenience that was being caused, I gave him a bottle of cheap wine, to which his reply was, "Oh no, Colin. You shouldn't have, you've got to have the work done. In fact, I had a visit the other day from Yorkshire Electricity and I told them they can come in anytime to carry out the work that needs doing. Cheers, Colin, and oh, by the way, my name's Phil."

With the neighbour problem solved, I duly informed YE that they could go ahead with no apparent problems. I myself also fitted a new pompadour-coloured bathroom suite, which were all in fashion then, and upgraded the rest of the plumbing. Due to the physical appearance of the house, we had a structural survey carried out which revealed that some roof spars to the front of the house were rotten, so I recruited a roofer who one day stripped the roof slates back accordingly so that I could cut out and renew the defective roof spars.

Pamela, Wendy's sister, looked after the kids for one week to enable Wendy and I to decorate certain rooms, beginning with Colin and Teresa's bedrooms. After this, though there was other work that needed doing, we had almost run out of money so we simply moved into our new family home.

Quite early on, I set about painting the outside in order to protect the new window frames and doors, which being new only had a coat of primer paint. On one particular evening, having got home from work, I got the ladders out and I was applying the pink undercoat to the front bedroom window when Linda, one of our neighbours, who had been walking up the street, stopped and said to me, "Peter said, with the pink undercoat, you must be painting it red, but I said to him no. No one paints their house red. What colour are you painting it?"

"Red," I replied with a broad grin and she walked on.

Linda and Peter Kitson were about a year older than I and we had all gone to Armley Park Secondary School. Along with the other kids, Colin and Teresa would come to dislike them both due to them moaning constantly about kids playing out in the street. As it happens, all of the house, windows, doors, gutters, fall pipes and waste pipes were all painted bright red, possibly causing some irritation to our neighbours in the process.

Following the move, Colin transferred to Broad Lane Middle School and Teresa went to Stanningley Primary. Her new teacher was Kevin Richardson (also a member of the Branch Labour Party) and he soon became aware that she was somewhat withdrawn at school, so each morning he gave her the task of going to the different classrooms in order to collect the school registers. Colin too became withdrawn and we eventually discovered that he was being bullied at school. I made representations to the school's headteacher and, having spoken with him, things settled down with seemingly no more problems.

Rather ironically, the bully's father was also a member of the Branch Labour Party. Stanningley Park was only a short walk away for us, so we would all frequently go there for some enjoyment and, on some occasions, Colin and I would go by ourselves with a football and have a kick about there.

Janet and Laurence, Wendy's sister and brother-in-law, had a number of fruit and vegetable stalls in Leeds indoor market and she was now working part time for them five days a week. The ongoing monitoring of her polycystic kidneys meant that periodically she was attending St. James's Hospital and, at some point in the mid-to-late 1980s, due to an increase in her blood pressure, she began taking medication to combat this; after all, high blood pressure has a damaging effect on the kidneys.

I myself had become quite active in the Labour Party and was on a couple of committees, along with being a union branch delegate to the Constituency Party. The good money that I was earning was a refreshing change, allowing us to enjoy some stability as a family and it was around this time that we bought a new three-bedroom canvass frame tent. Wendy's mam and dad had also taken up camping several years previous and, on Sunday afternoons, all of us would often drive out to Casey's Camping Shop, Wakefield, and then on to Mitchell's Camping Shop at Horbury. We would simply enjoy looking at different tents and equipment and, at times, this would evoke thoughts of our next camping holiday.

It was common knowledge, even with the kids, that Wendy's dad just had no sense of direction and, on one Sunday afternoon, he was driving with me sat alongside in the front and, at one point, he had missed his turning and went around a roundabout a couple of times with the kids giggling away in the back. I bit my lip so as not to giggle too whilst he just sat stony-faced, staring straight in front of him.

It was around this time that we spent two weeks camping at Stepaside, near Saundersfoot in South Wales. Wendy's mam and dad joined us, along with her eldest sister, Irene, and her husband, Alan, and we all stayed on the same site. However, whilst we all camped, Irene and Alan were in a static caravan. Her mum and dad's tent was a little like home from home for in the living area there was a large table with a bowl of fruit and a telly on it.

Just like now, tents then would have *storm pegs* firmly securing it down, yet early each morning we would hear Iris saying to Frank, "You'd better go outside and bang them pegs in cos' it seemed a bit breezy last night." There would usually be a little resistance from him before he dutifully came out and banged the pegs down some more.

Wendy's mum and dad would often amuse us with their antics, and the year before they had come with us to Newby Bridge in the Lake District. Several days prior to us arriving, it had steadily rained to the extent that there were ducks swimming around in the huge on-site puddles that had formed.

Her mum and dad had recently bought a new trailer tent and, after the first night, Iris informed us that two of the legs supporting the bed had sunk into the ground overnight, causing some discomfort. However, Frank was going to go underneath and put something in place to support them. Iris was a plump lady whilst Frank was quite slim and the plan was that, once he had placed the two supports in position, then he would shout so that she could lie on the bed to ensure that it was sturdy. However, after a couple of minutes, Iris mistook Frank's grunting and groaning for the awaited 'sign' and flopped onto the bed, much to the dismay of Frank as the poor man became almost pinned to the wet ground.

Now in Wales, Iris and Frank were pleased to be with Irene and Alan as they themselves lived in a village called Barton Stacey in Wiltshire, so visits were few and far between. It was probably on this holiday that Teresa was bought a little Welsh bag that, over the course of the holiday, became filled with shells and suchlike, and this she still has today.

The following year saw us all go on holiday again and, though we enjoyed Wales, it was agreed that we would go to South Devon, where we each rented a caravan. It was agreed that Teresa would bring her friend Samantha along and, for some reason, Wendy and I didn't travel down to Wales on the same day as her mam and dad.

Colin had decided that he wanted to travel down with his nan and grandad and, when we arrived the following day, Iris told us that their journey had been somewhat calamitous. It seems that, having reached the M6 and travelled along it for a good number of miles, her dad decided to pull in at a service area and ask for directions to Wales. To their horror, he was informed that he was on the wrong side of the motorway heading north to Blackpool, so he had to drive further on and find somewhere for him to turn around and head back down south!

We enjoyed the holiday and Irene and Alan were always very good company to be around though, by the middle of the second week, as was often the case, Iris always seemed to be *'chomping at the bit'* for home and began talking about what she would be doing when she finally did get back. There would be times when she would ask Wendy if she had started packing things away yet.

We always enjoy our holidays and are never in a rush to get home. This particular site had been selected because it had a fishing pond and, along with Colin and I, his grandad had also become interested in fishing. Indeed, he had accompanied us on a number of fishing outings to the Leeds and Liverpool canal and a pond at Cawood near Selby.

One day we were all sat fishing around the holiday pond, catching lots of small fish, when Frank was reeling in yet another his catch was seized upon by one of the number of ducks also sharing the pond. For a good number of minutes, he tugged away frantically, trying to release the duck's grasp on the little fish until the latter finally let go of its intended meal.

On another day's fishing at the pond, Colin caught a carp, which put up a fight for him. However, having 'played' it for some time, he finally landed it, much to his satisfaction. Before being released it was weighed at a little over five pounds and the lad was really pleased.

One day during the first week, Teresa spotted a 'tie die' T-shirt in a shop window. She ended up spending most of her holiday money on the item.

At the start of this holiday, upon seeing Irene, Wendy had commented to me that she looked really unwell and there were times throughout the two weeks that she seemed to be struggling when out walking with the rest of the group, though not once did she complain. Several months following the holiday, Irene, who had been in her early forties, died from a secondary cancer, having some time earlier undergone a double mastectomy. On the day of the funeral, all of the West Yorkshire family members made the long solemn journey down to Barton Stacey and then back home later that same day.

Meanwhile, work for me began to look gloomy towards the end of 1984 as rumours were going around suggesting that Dunn's were running out of work. After several months, I was moved to a site at York where a new Sainsbury's supermarket was in the stages of being built. I learned sometime later that, to secure the work, rather than price the job accordingly, Dunn's had simply undercut the lowest bidder.

Every so often, a Dunn's quantity surveyor would arrive on site in order to keep a track of what materials were being used, no doubt with the aim of someone gauging at some point if the firm would be making a profit, and if so how much it would be. It soon became evident from a resource standpoint they were ill-equipped for such work, with some of the plumbers bringing to work their own electric drills – no cordless drills then – and one lad was left complaining because his drill became burnt out and the firm was reluctant to repair it.

One day I asked an electrician that was working close to me if I might borrow his drill and he reluctantly consented, but borrowing other tradesmen's equipment didn't bode well and I felt embarrassed asking the lad. At one time there were perhaps six plumbers on site, including Dave the chargehand, and there had been several times that I had been ten minutes or so late, though each time when this had occurred the lads hadn't started work, but instead were stood outside the plumbers' cabin having a smoke.

On each of my late arrivals, Dave had made some sarcastic remarks, always at the same time turning to the other lads as if demonstrating his authority, and this was starting to irritate me. So on the next occasion of me being slightly late, as I entered the site with the other plumbers stood smoking outside the cabin as usual, upon seeing me Dave came out with more sarcastic remarks in an attempt to belittle me.

I quipped back saying, "Do you take nasty pills?"

To which he replied, "What do yer mean?"

"Well," I said, "nobody can be as nasty as you without tekin' summat for it!"

Hearing this retort, he went on the defensive saying, "Oh do't be like that." Still, that was the last time he was ever sarcastic towards me.

One day, Mick, one of the 'shirt and tie' managers, came on site and informed us all as a group that the company was finding it difficult to win contracts against smaller firms because presumably our competitors had smaller overheads. A gloom seemed to permeate through the workforce and, sometime later, we had another routine visit from Mick the manager, and this time he proudly sat in his new company car showing it off to us all as we were tacitly expected to gather around and croon over it.

"I thought things wer' tight," said one lad.

"Ah yeah, but life goes on, doesn't it"? Mick responded with a broad grin on his face.

I was in earshot as one lad muttered under his breath, "It does for some."

In January 1985, a number of us, including myself, were made redundant at the end of the week. The following week, John, a plumber who had worked at Dunn's for a number of years and who I had become friendly with, rang me to say that he and a number of others had also been laid off that week. He went on to say that over the past two weeks the firm had made fourteen plumbers redundant, which was useful to know, but of little consolation.

I was still continuing to avidly read books – with a dictionary still by my side to learn the meaning of certain words and hence the overall meaning of a particular sentence – as well as keeping up with day-to-day political and economic events. I had also come to question the system of bonus working.

As I explained earlier, most firms operated such schemes whereby plumbers were given so many hours for doing the various aspects of plumbing work concerned. For example, if I earned eighty hours bonus in a week then – with it being a thirty-seven hour working week – the first thirty-seven hours were paid at the JIB approved rate with the remaining hours being paid at £1 per hour. In effect, the employer was getting a second week's plumbing work carried out at a miserly rate of £1 per hour. Not only that, but given the precarious employment situation those on such schemes were rapidly working themselves towards unemployment.

Historically, this speeding up of the work process has massively benefited the employer. The 'carrot' for workers is that, with existing hourly work rates being kept artificially low, many would inevitably seek out bonus schemes to supplement their earnings. Arguably, in addition to this financial imposition, there was then an increase in accidents and incidences of ill health for workers. There have been a number of occasions whereby, having suffered a sprained ankle at work, upon getting home, I merely strapped the injury up and returned to work the following day. Over summer periods, there have been several times when, at the cessation of work, I have gone home feeling thoroughly exhausted, had my evening meal and then gone straight to bed, only to wake the following morning for another day's work.

One of the issues facing the incoming Tory government in 1979 was the high level of inflation, which at its peak was around 17%. The use of unemployment was an insidious strategy to reduce the amount of available money in the market, stifle the demand for goods and thus help to bring down inflation. On a more down-to-earth level, I once more had to sign-on as unemployed.

We were lucky in some respects because our monthly mortgage payments were primarily the interest on the initial loan, so the benefit I received did enable these payments to be made. Yes, I had insurance to cover the car payments, but these only kicked in following the first thirty days of being unemployed so, in the interim, we had to bite the bullet and find the money to cover this because I needed a car for work. Indeed, when enquiring about any plumbing job one of the first things asked of you is 'have you got a car'?

Over the ensuing weeks and months, there was little work around, with the few jobs on offer being poor pay. In a nutshell, the wages on offer weren't sufficient to pay the mortgage along with other household expenditure whilst also resuming the car payments. Bills such as renewing the house insurance were simply put to one side as unaffordable and therefore momentarily deemed not important. We looked at our income and expenditure and cut back on the latter where possible – for example, cheap biscuits became the norm when shopping.

Over a short period of time I had occasion to repair the washing machine more than once, but some months later it packed in altogether and, for some time, we had to do the family wash in the bath and wring the clothes out with our hands before pegging them on the washing line. Back then, the DSS deemed that a washing machine wasn't an essential household item, therefore we were unable to claim a *Discretionary Payment* from them and get a new one. We had to seek help to clothe Colin and Teresa in new school uniforms and endure the humiliation of going along to the shop with our vouchers. Both were also now receiving free school dinners.

As for making progress with the decorating and furnishing of the rest of the house, well that too had to be put on hold. I carried out a few bits and pieces of 'work on the side' when asked, but I was very careful when doing so. I was prepared to do anything to bring money in and, on one occasion, John, a lad that I knew – who was a self-employed plumber and had recently moved into Bramley – asked me to dismantle his garden shed and then dig the earth out in readiness for a garage base. We didn't have a garden shed at the time so he agreed that I could take the frame from his old one and I subsequently used this to build our own one. When the need arose, John would ring me and I would help him out with plumbing work.

On one occasion, Philip Hardaker, our older neighbour's son, being aware that I was unemployed, asked me if I could give him a quote for central heating in his own home in Rodley. For some reason I felt uneasy so I replied that I didn't do work 'on the side' because I told him that I read that the DSS had fraud teams who, having the names of tradesmen, would carry out surveillance on their homes in an attempt to catch them going out to work.

To my surprise, he instinctively responded saying, "Oh yes they do. My wife works for the DSS and has told me about it." I don't know to this day whether he was trying to catch me out or not.

It was difficult to get away from the fact that there was still much work to do in the house, yet it was impossible to do any due to the overall shortage of money. To make the dining room bigger, we planned on knocking out the existing chimney breast and I set about this one day and plastered the wall accordingly to finish it off.

When we moved, almost immediately, Mr. Hardaker, the neighbour opposite, used to knock on our door complaining about our car being parked on the road outside our house. Apparently, because the old lady who had lived here previously hadn't owned a car, Mr. Hardaker was used to driving up the street and straight into his driveway, but with our car being parked outside our house, it seemed to be a great source of distress to him, for he apparently had never had to reverse his car onto his drive.

Even his son tried to remonstrate with him one day, saying that I was merely parking the car outside *our* house, but this was to no avail. In the end, to put an end to the hassle, I knocked an opening out in the garden wall, where the eventual drive would be, and began parking our car off street. To form a temporary driveway, I used the bricks from the chimney breast fireplace along with those from the garden wall. Neighbour problem solved.

Though the national problem of unemployment was a structural phenomenon, for so many being out of work is internalised as individual failure and throughout the 1980s one would read or hear on the telly about the numbers of unemployed people that had attempted or committed suicide. Moreover, unemployment can place an immense strain on immediate relationships, causing some marital breakups due to the financial pressure.

There were continuous Tory attempts to scapegoat those without jobs, with Norman Tebbitt, a senior minister, saying in his Tory Conference speech that the unemployed should get on their bikes and go look for work, implying that they sat at home on their backsides. The Tories like to use statements designed to 'divide and rule' and ministers would frequently make public comments about the amount of benefit money that was being fraudulently claimed. To counter this, opponents would point to the amount of money that goes unclaimed by those on benefit. Added to this, one would read or hear about the vast sums of money that, far exceeding that supposedly claimed fraudulently by claimants, never went into the government's coffers due to tax evasion and avoidance.

Fortunately, Wendy and I never attempted to play the blame game regarding our situation because, just like me, she too was becoming more politically aware about the 'social forces, factors and influences' that were affecting not only us, but millions of other people. Often, we would hear some mealy-mouthed politician offering a mere 'jabberwocky' response (the term comes from a conversation between Humpty Dumpty and Alice from *Alice in Wonderland*, Lewis Carrol) to an important question of the day.

We both noticed – and it is so today – that when the government wanted to spend money, it was referred to as 'government money', but in order to justify cuts in public spending and resist spending money that it didn't want to, then they referred to it as 'tax payers' money' a subtle nuance of words designed to enter people's consciousness and make them feel resentful towards the wrong people.

Indirectly, one thing that did help us overcome our financial position, though at first we hadn't realised it, was the fact that we lived a short walk from the Leeds and Liverpool Canal and enjoyed regular walks there with our Jack Russell dog, Patch. We used to enter the canal at the part that is situated in the Aire Valley and it was a relatively peaceful and scenic setting with the occasional glimpse of a deer or a kingfisher. After a time, such walks – with no cost involved – helped us both to momentarily escape from our situation and what at times represented an oppressive house. We both still remember that, on one occasion, the ice cream van made his regular visit to our street and, as expected, both Colin and Teresa came running in for money, but we were unable to give them both the required 10p each for an ice cream.

Around May 1985, I went to 'sign-on' as usual and was given a slip advising me that, from June of that year, my benefit would be taxed, but this wasn't to be direct, but indirect taxation. Let me explain further. Prior to this, when a person was unemployed they drew a benefit – against their weekly contributions of National Insurance – and upon returning to work they would receive a tax rebate for the period that they had been out of work and not earned any wages. But now, as of June, their benefit would unbelievably be classed as 'earned income', which upon restarting work, would lead to either no or a significantly reduced tax rebate. Today, it is very much the case that the majority of welfare benefits are now indirectly taxed in this way and in Chapter 20 I shall return to this.

Several years later, I was reading some research highlighting the fact that those who graduate from the top five public schools in the country feed into the higher echelons of society; banking, industry, commerce, the judiciary, politics and so on. Fair enough and no surprise there, but in addition the research went on to reveal – well, it was news to me – that all public schools are registered charities and, as such, receive massive tax concessions from the Inland Revenue. What an inverse system of educational welfare, with the clear argument that, as tax payers, those on benefits are subsidising the education of the children of the most wealthy in society so that they may gain top jobs and thus contribute towards the perpetuation of a privileged and elite class.

In 2003, the then Labour government set out to look at this massive historic anomaly, but soon let it drop on the grounds that public schools offer a handful of scholarships to those from poorer backgrounds. Much was written about life on the dole in the 1980s, and it was frequently said that anyone returning to work after around twelve months on the dole would spend another twenty-four months catching up to where they and their family had been before being out of work.

Around this time, one summer's evening in 1985, I attended a meeting of the West Leeds Continuing Education (youth, community work and further education) Committee and, with a Labour city council, I attended as a local Labour Party representative. This wasn't my first meeting, but I ended up sitting alongside a chap from the Labour Party branch in Pudsey by the name of Mike Stein, who I had never met before.

At some point, Mike and I were chatting and he asked me what my area of employment was and, upon hearing that I was unemployed, he explained that he was a tutor with the Leeds University School of Adult Continuing Education. He went on to say that in September they would be starting a one day a week Social Studies Access Course in Pudsey that was aiming at help adults into higher education or vocational training.

I was already periodically undertaking work on a TUC Correspondence Course regarding Basic Trade Unionism, but following a subsequent chat with Wendy, it was decided that if I was still unemployed nearer the time, I could enrol. Time passed and I enrolled on the course that was set to run one day a week over thirty weeks.

The teaching was set into two halves, with Mike Stein teaching the class for one half day and Moira Ashley the other half. The subject area was really interesting and, with essays being set periodically, I looked forward to the weekly sessions.

It was around this time that I also began two evenings work as a volunteer at the Intake Civic Youth Club. The club was held inside the nearby intake high school and, after a short while, I had managed to build up a rapport with not only the staff, but many users too. Through the Labour Party, I also knew one of the officers from the Gamble Hill Community Association and I obtained volunteer youth work there for several months. I began to explore the possibility of training to be a youth and community worker and as a result I was able to source the relevant course information from Bradford and Ilkley College. I completed the application form and posted it off.

September came around and it was the start of the political parties' conference season. Since I had left the DLO, John Light and I had remained good friends and we would see each other on a fairly regular basis. There was a huge demonstration being organised for the Tory Conference being held at the Winter Gardens in Blackpool. This was the first Tory Conference since the end of the year-long miners' strike in March 1985.

During the strike itself, I had been on a couple of the early-morning picket lines – one at Kellingley and then at Ledston Luck – with another Labour Party member. As I recall, it was during the strike that Wendy and I started getting a daily copy of the *Morning Star* newspaper, simply to get a different point of view to the daily misinformation that was being fed to people in the country.

Accompanying John and I was one of his friends, a chap called George who was perhaps in his mid-seventies and lived in the Seacroft area of the city. Arriving in good time at Blackpool, it was interesting to see the steady gathering of so many people from all over the country. As we were all about to set off on the designated route, John suggested to George that, at any time on the march, he should drop out if he was feeling exhausted. He said that he would be okay and was keen to march all the way, but partway round he did indeed drop out and we met up with him later.

Police helicopters were flying overhead as we marched and, as we approached the Winter Garden, I had never seen as many police as were gathered outside to 'protect' the Tories. The huge demonstration passed without any incident and, in due course, people began to disperse and make their way back to their disparate homes around the country.

As we made our way out of Blackpool, the traffic was heavy and moving slowly and at one point we were travelling behind a police minibus when a small coach creeped up on us in the outside lane and, as it passed the police minibus, there were multiple bare backsides pressed up against the coach windows in a symbolic gesture.

In order to build on my interest in youth and community work, in November 1985 I attended a one-week residential course at Northern College, Barnsley, titled 'Organising Your Community Group'. On the first day during the induction we were asked over the course of the week to write a 300–500 word essay about poverty. There was no obligation to do this, but for those who did then at the end of the week before leaving the college they would be offered an individual tutorial with a member of staff regarding their essay.

When the end of the week arrived, I was one of only a few people from the group who had bothered to write an essay and my tutorial was with a college tutor by the name of Ed Ellis. After reading my essay and asking me a number of questions regarding it, he asked me what my future plans were and I commented that I was fed up with being periodically unemployed and the hassle that it caused and, as a consequence of that, I was aiming to enrol on a Youth and Community Work Course. He shook his head and said that I should aim higher and he went on to encourage me to enrol for higher education at university.

I was delighted with his encouraging comments and to this day he is someone that I shall never forget, as this tutorial proved to be something of a turning point. When I next attended the course at Pudsey, I couldn't wait to tell both Mike and Moira what Ed had said. As the course progressed into 1986, I recall that in one class, during a group discussion, one of the students openly remarked that, "Colin is very much a self-educated person." I was a little shocked as the comment simply came out of the blue, but I proudly accepted this praise from one of my peers. It was years later that I learned her statement meant that I was considered as being an autodidact.

Early in 1986, I began part-time paid work in the evening as an Assistant Youth Leader at the Tyersal Youth Club in Bradford and, once again, I was able to build up a rapport with both the leader and the users. It was also around this time that Moira Ashley introduced the class to a full-time lecturer from the University of Leeds by the name of Kirk Mann. He was a friend of Moira's and they had both taken the mature student route through university. Kirk had been an engineer and was now working in the Social Policy Dept. and, having spoken with Moira after the session, she arranged for me to meet with him informally at the university in a few days' time.

I was still buoyed up by the comments of Ed Ellis when I met with Kirk. We had a good chat about university and the necessary requirements. I remember him asking me if I liked economics and I replied that I did enjoy reading about different theories to which he shook his head, making the point that if I applied for the Social Policy and Administration Course then the economics content was heavily influenced by mathematics. I said that I wasn't keen on maths, as I had always found the subject rather 'dry'. Kirk acknowledged that he held a similar sentiment hence, when he had been an undergraduate, he had opted for a Social Policy and Sociology Course.

I subsequently applied for the three years full-time BA Joint Honours Degree in Social Policy and Sociology and, by doing this, it meant that I now had two options. Much to my surprise, in due course, I received an interview at the university. The day itself arrived and, as is often the case with interviews, I came away feeling very unsure as to how it had gone – although before I left I asked if I might leave some of my essays with them, which they agreed to.

I remember going home feeling somewhat despondent, but as I went into the house Wendy was beaming and said, "You've got it then?" Feeling a little perplexed, I began to dolefully explain what had transpired. "No, you've got a place. They have rung up to say so." It was a while before I could take it in.

"They must have read the essays that I had left and then decided to offer me a place," I muttered.

The place at university hinged on me passing a Mature Matriculation Exam, due to the fact that I had no GCE's or A-Levels. Within days of this good news, I was somewhat brought down a little when I received a letter from Bradford and Ilkley College saying that I had been unsuccessful with my application. When I saw Mike and Moira the following week, they were genuinely pleased for me over the university offer, but regarding the rebuttal from Bradford and Ilkley, Moira said that I should take up their offer of an interview just to find out the reasons why my application had been unsuccessful.

When I attended the arranged meeting, I was quite perturbed that sat alongside me was another unsuccessful candidate. The tutor went through this chap's application in front of me also and then advised him to gain certain specific additional academic qualifications before reapplying. He then turned to my application and, turning the pages over quite quickly and with a smirk on his face, he looked at me, saying bluntly "Well, basically you don't have any qualifications."

I promptly responded by saying, "I have an Advanced Craft City & Guilds Qualification." At the same time, I was thinking to myself 'why do people fail to acknowledge that a skilled trade qualification such as this involves both theoretical and technical reading?' To achieve a good standard of practical work an understanding of the theory is essential. Anyway, I digress and suffice to say a City and Guild's qualification failed to impress him and he reiterated his earlier comment.

"Well," I said, "it's funny you should say that because I have been accepted for a degree course at the University of Leeds."

Upon hearing this, he shuffled about feverishly in his seat and quickly flicked through the pages of my application again before asking, "Well, how can that be?"

I looked at him and simply said, "Well, clearly they are more willing to accept mature students than you are."

That was the end of the interview and in hindsight embarking down the youth and community vocational route would not have offered the sustained employment that I now wanted. The co-ordinator for continuing education across West Leeds was a chap named Angus Ross and he was also a member of our Branch Labour Party. During one conversation that I had with him, he tried to steer me away from thoughts of a youth and community career. He went on to explain that when the authority was compelled to make spending cuts, youth and community services were amongst the first to be affected.

I have since learned now myself that indeed whenever there is an economic recession such 'soft' targets are often the first to financially suffer. For example, this was what happened following the 2008 'banking crisis'. I did however still retain an interest in both youth and community work and around the spring of 1986 I was approached by some local residents who knew of my Labour Party membership and they informed me that they wanted to set up a local community group. Following some discussion, I expressed an interest in working alongside them. Being hopeful of starting university later in the year, I didn't want to become too involved so I spoke to one of the group members and gave him some educational papers that I had from my TUC Correspondence Course regarding the practice of committee skills (e.g. chairing meetings, the role of the secretary, taking notes/minutes, resolutions, amendments and addendums).

As an informal group, we began to make good progress, so I introduced them to Angus Ross, who was a great help in explaining the process of setting up the group and, as a consequence, in late 1986 the Intake Community Association was formally created. As the Social Studies Course came to a close, Moira, who also lived in Bramley, suggested that I should obtain recent Mature Matriculation Exam papers in order to gauge which questions might crop up and then write a number of mock essays. In turn, she would look at them and pass comment.

She was true to her word and, having advised me accordingly, I subsequently passed the Matriculation exam. It seemed a little surreal that in September I would become a three-year full-time student undertaking a BA Joint Honours Degree in Social Policy and Sociology. Wendy was fully supportive and we both acknowledged that, in employment and financial terms, up to now the 1980s had been downright crap for us.

On the run up to enrolment day, Moira loaned me two sociology books, one by Peter Berger and the other C. Wright Mills, *The Sociological Imagination*. The Mills book really resonated with me, so much so that in my final year a quote from Mills is in the forefront of my dissertation. Again, looking back, Moira Ashley and Mike Stein are two people I have to thank for their support and encouragement. At home we still had things yet to do in the house.

Mam, sister Gill and Me. Filey 1954

Mam and Dad

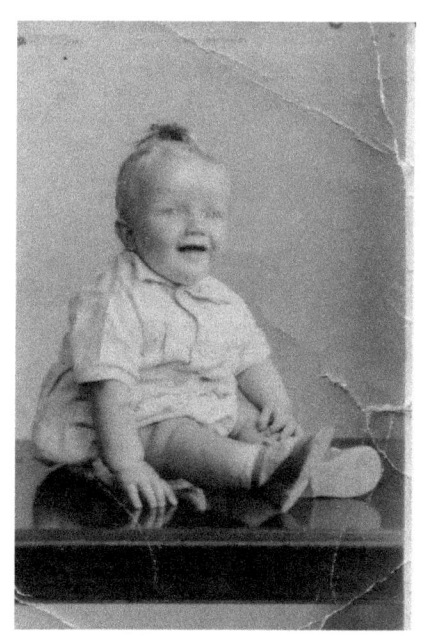

Me when a baby

Castleton Junior football Team. I am just to the right of Mr Jowett

Me and Fred Tasker. Dixons Mill circa 1958

'The Boys are back in town'. I'm in the middle bottom row. Circa 1968

Colin on camp site near Filey 1968

Colin, Gerald, Ian, George and John. Shaftesbury Pub 1969

York Teds visit Leeds. Outside the 'Slip Inn' 1969

Briarbank, our home 2005

View of Loch Ness from front of Briarbank 2005

University Graduation Day 1989. Colin and Wendy

Colin and Colin Jnr. First holiday at Primrose Valley 1973

Wedding Day 1972

My Mam and baby Colin 1973

My Mam with Teresa and Colin Jnr at her flat 1987

Teresa at Peasholm Park, Scarborough 1983

Colin at Blair Athol BMW Rally 1996

Wendy at Scarborough 1970

Colin and Wendy 1970

Colin, Cassie and Tetley camped in the sunshine on the shores of Lock Broom
Ullapool 1995

Wendy, Isle of Arran, part of the Glenluce long weekend 1994

Colin's 3rd Scottish solo tour. On A944 near Strathdon, Cairngorms

Colin's 2nd solo tour Scotland. Camped at Braemar with Koat and Werner, two German bikers Sept. 1997

Chapter 12

Being a Full-time Student

We had bought the house on the understanding that, from the estate agent's paperwork, our home was "partially central heated" and this comprised of a gas fire in the living room and two wall-mounted gas heaters, one in the dining room and one in the hallway. It was around mid-1986 when a leak was detected on the dining room gas wall-heater and the matter of the cost of the repair was raised with the DSS. They paid out accordingly and without any quibble so, as far as I was concerned, that was that, or so I thought.

Because an element within our benefit covered household costs (e.g. water rates), when in April 1986 we got a new increased water rates bill through the post, I contacted the benefits office, expecting that because our household costs had increased slightly then there would be a corresponding increase in benefit. To my surprise, when I rang and discussed the matter with them the outcome resulted in a reduction of our weekly benefit. I decided to get a second opinion, so I visited the local Citizens Advice Bureau (CAB) on their relevant day at the Waterloo Lane Community Centre.

Having perused the paperwork given to them, the worker agreed with me that our benefit should have been increased and suggested that I visit the Pudsey Benefits Office in order to sort matters out. I was a trifle concerned about doing this and, knowing that such visits can potentially be problematic, I asked the CAB worker if, once I was there and potentially reached an impasse, did I have any rights? The worker said that if the person on the desk was being unhelpful then I had the right to ask to see an executive officer in order to pursue my case.

Armed with this knowledge and my relevant papers, the next day I caught the bus and went to the Pudsey Benefits Office and sat down in the waiting queue. Through my observation, I quickly became aware that the worker behind the desk was a little abrupt with some people and, at times, offered what was no more than 'short shrift' to their representations. When it was my turn, I had drafted a concise summary of the points concerned and, following a brief introduction, I offered her the paper.

She merely pushed it back, saying, "What is it that I can help you with?"

After verbally explaining the problem, she carried out a written calculation, arriving at a figure showing that in effect I should be getting fifty-odd pence per week extra benefit. And then to my complete and utter surprise, she said, "What you will have to do now is go back home and ring the benefits office up, tell them that you have called here today and ask them to increase your weekly benefit by this amount."

I couldn't believe what she was saying and queried, "Can't you just update my file now and then it's done?"

"No," she replied, and she repeated again what I must do.

"But," I insisted, "I rang your office from home and they have actually reduced my benefit and that is why I have come in person to sort things out."

She repeated once more what I must do, so I said, "I want to see an executive officer."

She bluntly said to me, "Wait in the green seats at the back."

As I made my way past other seated claimants, one woman said to me, "Yer'll be waiting now, luv. You've rattled her cage."

I duly sat in one of the green seats, somewhat deflated with feelings of being powerless and frustration. After about twenty minutes, a door opened along a wall and I was called through. A chap took his seat behind what I could only view as a sort of bank cashier's desk, with strengthened glass going almost down to the countertop separating us.

He asked, "How can I help you?"

I instinctively pushed the flat palm of my hand towards him on the surface of the countertop, but it stopped abruptly when it reached my knuckles. He looked a little surprised as I said to him, "Just feel that, will yer?"

He looked even more perplexed and I repeated, "Just feel that, and when yer do yer will see that, just like you, I am flesh and blood. The way that your colleague out there is treating people is disgraceful. Being a plumber, I am used to earning good money, but I now find myself in a position that I don't choose to be in."

I went on to explain the reason for my visit and what the outcome had been with his colleague on the desk. He too then carried out a paper calculation and announced, just like his colleague, that I was entitled to fifty-odd pence extra per week. He then altered my file accordingly. Before leaving, I said to him "that fifty-odd pence extra per week is merely my bus fare home."

The reader may be thinking, 'I couldn't be bothered for fifty-odd pence'. Ordinarily they would be right, and under normal circumstances I wouldn't have been either, but in our current dire financial position it was not insignificant.

There was one period that I had to leave the car on the 'brick drive' for a while because the brake discs were so worn that they were metal to metal on the brake discs, and we had no money to get them seen to. Months earlier, on the run up to Christmas, the chairman from the branch had called around selling fifty-pence tickets for the Labour Party Christmas party. Chris, the lad in question, ran his own small clothing business and was in our hallway asking me to buy two tickets and, although several times I politely declined, his irritating persistence led me to pointedly explain, "Look Chris, even if I bought the tickets, we can't afford to go."

His trite reply was, "Well, just buy the tickets then." I didn't and, after he had embarrassed me with his crass persistence, he left.

That is just how tight our financial situation was, and living under these circumstances, one could be forgiven for thinking that some organisations and people justly feel that you don't have enough stress and hassle in your life already, so their purpose is to make amends for this by piling more on to you. Not too long after my visit to the benefits office, I received a letter from them referring to the repair I had claimed for several months previously, regarding the gas wall-heater, and that my claim was false because on my initial application for benefit I had said that we have 'partial central heating'.

Wendy and I both felt that this was a case of victimisation arising from my recent visit to the benefits office and the fifty-odd pence increase in benefit. At that time, housed within the Leeds Market Buildings was the Trade Union Community Resource and Information Centre (TUCRIC). I decided to go see them for advice, so I walked the five miles or so into the city centre in the hope of being able to sort matters out and gain some advice. There had been several previous occasions that I had done this walk, either to save money or because we didn't have any. Having discussed the matter with the TUCRIC worker, she too felt that it was a clear case of victimisation and that I should appeal After walking the five miles or so back home I subsequently wrote a letter of appeal.

A couple of months prior to our appeal being heard, I had commenced university. Upon my receipt of the date of the appeal, Karen (one of the mature Social Policy students) offered to accompany me because she had previously spent some time working for the CAB. Though I was more than confident in my own ability to deal with matters myself, I agreed that we go together. On the day of the appeal, as Karen had suggested, we both carried briefcases and I had a shirt and tie on, so as to present ourselves in a business-like manner, or what might be referred to today as 'power dressing'.

As we entered the floor of the building, a chap introduced himself as the usher and seated us in the waiting area. Within minutes, a somewhat dishevelled couple came out of a room and, just as they were about to sit down with us, the usher said, "Oh, there's no point in waiting, you will get the decision in due course and in writing."

Karen and I entered the room and there sat before us was a panel of adjudicators, who seemed surprised to see us both looking smart and business-like. Commencing proceedings, the worker from the DSS presented their case against me. When it was my turn, I confidently referred to the estate agent's original specification of the house – which I had with me – showing that we had in good faith bought it as being 'partially central heated'.

I pressed on further, but increasingly the DSS Worker was interjecting until I stopped and very politely said to her, "Please, please, I have allowed you the decency and courtesy of being able to present your case without me interrupting, will you please allow me the same courtesy?" Immediately, I noted the panel's annoyance as they looked at her disapprovingly.

Case presented, we were ushered out and, to my surprise, unlike what the dishevelled couple before us had been told by the usher, he said to us, "Do you want to take a seat? They will have a decision for you shortly."

After about five minutes, we were told that my appeal had been upheld, therefore the DSS case against me had been dropped. It was around a month or so before starting at uni that I learned that, with regards to my student grant, the government, as of that year, had cut the Mature Student Allowance element some £600 – just great. However, in the second year this was reinstated due to national lobbying from university vice chancellors.

Wendy and I changed from Yorkshire to the Midland Bank in Bramley for my grant to be paid into them, solely because they offered student overdrafts whereas Yorkshire didn't. Being prudent with our money, we didn't intend to readily use the overdraft facilities, but if needed then it would be there.

My first day at uni was spent going around and visiting the relevant lecturers in order to pick up lecture and tutorial timetables, along with recommended reading lists. All first-year students had to undertake a one-year subsidiary course and I had previously opted for politics, which was a course split into two sections: British Government and Political Theory. By the end of the day, my head was in a whirl. I remember going home and lying on the settee with Wendy saying to me, "Do you think that you've taken too much on?"

In that instance, I thought that perhaps I had, though I answered, "No."

Students had all been notified the day before who their allocated personal tutor was and, in addition, that they should regularly check their 'pigeonholes' for any communication. Upon my morning arrival for my second day at uni, I dutifully went to check my 'pigeonhole' for messages and I found a note from Kirk Mann, who was my personal tutor, which read, 'come and see me when you can'. I popped along to see him straight away and, after sitting down, he said that "In this next week or so, you might start to feel a little overwhelmed."

To which I replied, "I do already."

He went on to say that, in contrast to students coming straight from A-level, universities thought differently about mature students, because they tend to work consistently at their studies. He explained further that the younger students are often adept at cramming for exams and therefore may miss lectures tutorials and sometimes drop essays. His advice was to consistently work at my studies. Good advice, which some time later I would draw on.

Besides myself, there were only about another five students doing the same degree as I was, and the one other mature male student was a lad called Mike – over the following couple of months we got on well. We all used the Social Policy common room for relaxation between lectures and tutorials.

For some unexplained reason, following the Christmas break, Mike didn't show at the university and finally word came that he had still been stupidly 'signing on' even though he had started uni. Over the three years, there were times when I missed having him around, as I was the only mature chap on the course. Throughout my first year, I diligently completed every essay that was set and, when the end of year exams came for first-year students, it was a case of either pass and go on to the second year or fail and you had to leave the course.

Thankfully, I passed, but a number of the Social Policy students had to subsequently re-sit the Economics exam, some of whom had studied the subject at A-level. I was thankful for the earlier advice offered to me by Kirk about the difficult maths content in the subject. Whenever the chance came along, I continued to do plumbing work 'on the side' and, when the first term at uni came to an end, I spent the summer break working full-time for a plumber in Horsforth named Des.

He was a decent chap and I had made him aware of my situation from the outset. Des had one other lad employed with him and I enjoyed working for him over the holiday period, with the extra money being very handy.

Wendy was still working in Leeds Market and Colin had moved from Broad Lane Middle School and was now at West Leeds Boys High, with Teresa still at Stanningley Primary School. At the start of our second term, when we were in the common room, the students that were a year above us began reminding us that at the end of this year there were no exams, so they repeatedly suggested that there was no real need to do much work; we should all just chill out, cruise through the year, enjoy ourselves and not worry about work.

In the first few weeks of the second term, this was repeatedly said whenever one went into the common room. Quite early on in the term, I dropped a couple of essays and I fell into a malaise, until one day I remembered the advice given to me by Kirk on the second day at uni. I decided to buckle down and catch up with the two outstanding essays and, having completed both of these, I felt much better about things. I realised that, for me personally, being on top of things was the answer.

Kirk lived near Gotts Park, close to Bramley, and I had previously carried out some bits and pieces of plumbing work for him when I bumped into him one day at uni, along with another lecturer called Malcom Harrison, who like Kirk was a nice chap, but very much the academic.

"Ah Colin, I'm glad I've seen you. I am wanting a plumbing fitting, but I don't know what to ask for," Kirk said.

Having then described to me the threaded fitting in question, I then said, "The fitting you want has an external thread and that is called a male fitting. A fitting with an internal thread is called a female one. Now, unlike the world of academics, in plumbing there is no sexual division of labour, because both male and female fittings have equal parts."

Kirk laughed as I advanced my argument, but Malcom was nodding philosophically. He was taking serious note of every word I was saying, presumably believing that I was making a genuine academic point.

Each weekend at home, for the most part, I was writing essays. I realise that this must have been difficult for Wendy and the kids, but I had undertaken this three-year course determined to achieve a good degree and stable employment at the end of it.

Around this time, we decided to go vegetarian, due to our growing awareness of the E number additives in foodstuffs. As I was usually home before Wendy, I took to preparing the evening vegetarian meals, but the kids overall were not impressed and often responded with the classic comment, "It's like rabbit food." However, some years later, Teresa did comment to me that she used to enjoy my vegetarian lasagne.

On one occasion, I called into the Leeds Fish Market and bought some fresh mackerel. When I got it home, I had to gut it and clean it out. When Wendy came home the kitchen stank to high heaven of fish, she admonished me and instructed me not to buy any again.

There were times when money was really tight and, on a couple of occasions, Wendy's family organised a box of food that was delivered to us, but she never took me to task for being a student and we never argued about finances. In fact, she gave me total support even at the point when Pamela and Stuart (her sister and brother-in-law) bought us a new bed due to our own dropping to bits. As the end of the second year came nearer, as students, we had to choose our ten-thousand-word long dissertation subject and title, along with the name of a lecturer who would offer guidance and support. The dissertation itself was to count as one of our nine final examinations.

Given that I had become interested in issues surrounding old age, I therefore decided that would be my subject matter. After initial discussion with two lecturers, who wanted to take me in a different direction than I intended, I passed them over and agreed matters with a lecturer who would offer the additional support. On the run up to the end of term, I made certain preparations in advance of my dissertation.

During the summer break, we managed to take time out for a one-week family holiday at Rhyl in North Wales, where Wendy's mam had told us about a flat that they had used and had a very enjoyable time. The flat itself was above a downstairs one that was the home lived in by the owner of the two. The flat wasn't really our cup of tea and, though we found bed bugs and then silverfish in the bathroom, we made the best of it as it did offer us all a break away.

As part of my overall interest in social justice, I had never come across the term ageism and, indeed, my support lecturer said that at that time there were very few definitions of the concept. Through my extensive reading, I became aware that in the 1960s the Grey Panthers had emerged as a group primarily to further the interest of older people, though they openly and correctly stated that anyone could be discriminated against on the grounds of their age.

Many people today erroneously associate the concept of ageism only with issues affecting older and elderly people. Because of my continued interest in how ordinary people can effect change, I had titled my dissertation, 'Ageism and the Role of Pensioner Groups'. The particular methodology that I used involved a literature review of published texts along with the implementation of research to gather empirical data.

Three questionnaires were constructed and used as the basis for interviews regarding the organisation of four pensioners' groups, three in Leeds and one in Sheffield. As far as possible, the questionnaires were constructed to enhance the gathering of qualitative information. I also attended five separate meetings of pensioner groups and these provided me with additional insight regarding the mechanics of how they operated. The second questionnaire was used for an interview with Leeds social services adviser to the elderly, and the third questionnaire was used to interview the secretary of the Leeds Western Community Health Council. I worked hard during the summer break to the extent that, upon my return for the start of our final year, I had completed my dissertation.

During the first few days, we were all catching up with each other about the holidays and who had done what, and a number of fellow mature students were startled when I revealed that I had completed my dissertation, as some hadn't even started theirs. Consequently, I was met with comments from some such as, "Oh we've been enjoying ourselves over the summer whilst you've been stuck working." Some said that I was "a swot". Some of the comments such as this I found to be juvenile and it was like being back at school with 'classmates' deriding someone because they had done a piece of homework or something that a teacher had asked for.

I wasn't too bothered by such derision because by now I knew what worked for me and that was producing what was asked of me in a timely manner. It was about this time that I was beginning to realise that I was drawing on some transferable skills from my plumbing days (i.e. self-discipline, ability to organise myself and to use autonomy to good advantage).

As we moved closer to the exams, panic started to set in for some of those who had derided me. For example, one woman heavily plagiarised on a written assessment exam paper, was caught out and told that she would not be allowed to sit her exams that year. She could return the following year and sit them, but even if her work was of first-class standard the best she would be awarded was a Pass. She subsequently left the course, with someone saying that she had moved down south somewhere.

Another person who throughout the course had left everything to the last minute had some kind of a meltdown and missed the exams, but she returned the following year. The former of these two individuals had previously asked if I could loan to her all of my essays to help her with her revision, but it was my view that, knowing I had completed every essay assignment over the three years, she and her small – what I had progressively viewed as a 'trendy' – group merely wanted to photocopy my work to help them with their own revision. I declined the request, but I did share my essays with a Social Policy mature student, who had taken a year out due to her husband suffering a heart attack.

At home there was personal upset because, towards the end of my final exams, Wendy suffered a breakdown and ended up being off work with depression. She had been still working in Leeds Market, but she was now managing a frozen food shop for Fultons. Being in a relatively isolated manner at home perhaps just proved too much for her, though at no point then or now has she pointed the finger of blame at me. Suffering with depression caused her to be off work for a period of six months.

At the time of her falling ill, I mentioned the situation to Kirk Mann, who at the time cryptically said, "Well, as long as you don't want a First degree."

It wasn't until much later that I understood what he had meant and how he was attempting to make me feel better because the outcome of the exams was that I achieved a Class II Division I (2:1) Degree. With the conclusion of the exams, talk in the Economic and Social Studies building was now turning to the ceremony for graduation day.

Over the previous three years, I had always stopped to have a joke and a natter with the two porters for the Social and Economic Studies building and now, with the graduation ceremony looming, they asked me if I would be attending the event. Answering no to this, they expressed surprise and then asked why and I simply said that I wasn't able to afford the hire of the gown and hat etc., which was around £100. They attempted to convince me otherwise and that, having worked hard for three years, the ceremony would be the culmination of this, not only for me, but Wendy too.

I had similar conversations with them over a number of days and then one day they called me over saying, "Colin, we have been informed that the company hiring out the gowns and hats are to use one of the lecture theatres downstairs to store everything inside. On the morning of the graduation day, if you come down here between 7.30am and 8.00am, we will take you down and get you kitted out for free."

I couldn't believe their kindness so, as requested, on the morning of the ceremony I went into uni early with my plastic bag and met the porters, who promptly took me down to the relevant lecture theatre where, just like being in some up market tailor's, they fussed about until they had a hat and gown that fitted me. I duly offered them my thanks and folded the items before placing them in the plastic bag that I had brought with me.

Later that day, Wendy and I attended the ceremony along with her sister Pamela who videoed the event. Afterwards, there was wine and nibbles in the Social Policy area of the building and at one point I was approached by the head of department, Alan Deacon, who said to me, "Well done, Colin. Though I must say I have never seen you looking so smart."

I was wearing grey trousers and a navy-blue blazer that was reasonably well covered by the sleeveless gown and, upon hearing his comment, I stood up and pulled the gown open to reveal the badge on my jacket, which read 'West Leeds Boys High School'. Not having a jacket at all, I was wearing our Colin's school blazer, which raised some laughter from Alan and those around us.

Having concluded my time at uni, I once more had to sign-on as unemployed whilst looking for work. Having graduated with the idea of becoming an adult tutor, I applied for a Postgraduate Certificate of Education (PGCE) course at what was then (in 1989) Huddersfield Polytechnic. I was informed beforehand that the course had received approximately one thousand applicants for what was, in reality, only a small number of available course vacancies and, with this in mind, I considered myself very lucky when I was subsequently offered an interview.

Sometime later, a letter came through the post to say that I had been successful in gaining a place on the course. However, having recently met Moira Ashley, she offered a cautionary note advising me that upon successfully completing the course there was no guarantee of gaining permanent full-time employment because, just like her, many other tutors had the insecurity of trying to pick up courses, often at different colleges, in order to accumulate one-week's work, and this was difficult. Some courses may not recruit sufficient students and thus not run, whilst others might close after a few weeks if students dropped out and left the class sizes too low.

I remember visiting the FE College at Horsforth and speaking to at least one tutor there who confirmed what Moira had said and more. One of the things he had encountered was that when the college holidays began he received no holiday pay and then, when trying to 'sign-on' as unemployed, he was informed that, "Well, if you're resuming work at the college when the holidays end, then you are not unemployed."

My aim was to get away from job insecurity and so reluctantly I gave backward to the place on the course. I was beginning now to realise that nationally graduate unemployment was something of a problem. My being unemployed passed into months and, at one time, someone said to me, "You know what BA stands for, don't you?"

I shook my head.

"Bugger All," came the reply.

I had been out of work some three to four months when I responded to an advert for a Probation Services Assistant (PSA) at Waterloo House, Wellington Street. During the interview, I was told that the team covered Gipton and I responded by saying that, in my teenage years, I had had friends there. I remember some raised eyebrows, not so much as when I mentioned being at uni, but I commented specifically concerning the transferable skills I realised that I had from undertaking plumbing work, such as self-discipline, ability to work on my own initiative and good organisational skills. Later, I put this down to their lack of knowledge and understanding of what I had been, meaning in relation to plumbing.

Anyhow, later on in the day I received a phone call from Peter, the senior probation officer (SPO), saying that the job was mine if I wanted it. My response threw him somewhat when I asked if I could ring him the following day with my decision because I had concerns about the low salary. The problem was that the money wasn't too good, so Wendy and I had a discussion that evening. On the face of it, the job offered some employment stability and, if I wished, then I was aware that I could do one of the existing one-year postgraduate courses to become a qualified probation officer.

I rang Peter the SPO back the following day confirming that I would take the job. And so it was that, following four months of unemployment since my graduation, on 16 October 1989 I began work with the West Yorkshire Probation Service (WYPS).

Chapter 13

From Blue to White-Collar Work

Waterloo House had five floors in the building with the probation team. I was to work situated on the third. The team comprised of Peter, the SPO; nine probation officers (POs); four clerical officers; and myself. When I started, they were regarded as a community-orientated team working across Gipton and Harehills and, to facilitate this work, there were also several small local offices, some of which were in local community centres.

The team members were a friendly bunch and the idea of my role was that as and when they might ask me to help them with particular offenders, concerning issues such as housing or welfare rights, I would. We still had our trusty Lada car, which was useful because I would often have to carry out home visits across the area and, on one occasion, I remember pulling into the car park at a block of flats in Lincoln Green that had a group of teenage lads standing outside, who looked at me suspiciously as I parked up.

As I exited my car and approached the entrance to the flats, they all quietly eyed me up so, to break the ice, I asked them, "Will my car be okay here, lads?"

"Yeah, why?" came the reply.

"Well, it's just that I've heard some performance cars have been stolen around here."

There was some laughter and someone shouted, "Who'd want to steal a f*****g Lada?"

I smiled and went into the building. I hadn't been in the post long before one of the PO's suggested that I might want to try and specialise in an area. For example, I might choose welfare rights, due to the fact that most ex-offenders had such problems.

Much later, I remember being asked to assist an offender who was living in a ground floor 'cottage' flat on the Gipton estate because he had received an eviction notice. I arranged a home visit to see the lad and was staggered at the amount of stuff that he had in his downstairs flat besides the old car outside. There was a canoe in his kitchen along with a multitude of engine parts and other numerous bits and pieces throughout. The place was solid with junk.

As I spoke to him it became clear that there was no way I was going to prevent eviction because I had been brought in too late and he had not responded to any of the letters that he had received from housing. His had been the typical 'ostrich approach' in dealing with matters. He now had a County Court Eviction Hearing to attend.

On the due date, I went with the lad and, inevitably, after hearing the case the judge said that the lad was to be evicted that day. At that point, being mindful of all the stuff in the house, I couldn't help but think that it would take much more than today for that task to happen!

Not long after I had started work, I was with John Light one Friday evening in the Bramley Band Club, along with a small group of lads, when one of them asked what work I was doing now. When I replied, "Working as a PSA", he responded by saying, "Oh, so you're just a dogsbody then?"

I was slightly hurt by this remark as I hadn't seen myself that way, but as time went on, I saw that, quite often on a daily basis, I was treated differently to others in the team. Speaking to other PSA's in the building and beyond, they all had various anecdotes to tell that had resulted in them feeling put down. It was simply the case that the organisational culture was such that there were perceived status differences, as there would be in most organisations.

The problem is not so much the actual status differences, but how people internalise them and use their perceived superior status to deride or put another person down, and this can be done both consciously and subconsciously. The sociologist Max Weber saw status bringing about 'social closure', with others being differentiated against and excluded from the status group.

For myself, I simply viewed this as employment snobbery and, after several months of being in the job, there were a number of occasions when I felt uneasy with my treatment as a PSA. However, at the time I naively felt that newly qualified PO's would be different, somehow more progressive. I was to be proved wrong.

At one stage, the team gained a newly qualified PO and, after a period of settling in, he too made a number of subtle and nuanced remarks that caused me some irritation. Then one day in the clerical office he came in and said something to me that I considered naff, so I politely asked him, "How long does it take to train to be a PO?"

He looked back, clearly thinking 'well, you already know', but then answered, "Two years".

"Well," I responded back, "it took me five years to train in plumbing practical and theory work." As I walked out, I added, "Speaks volumes, doesn't it?"

By and large, we all got on well, but it was just this negative use of status differences that got to me. Perhaps part of my resentment lay in the fact that, for many years, I had worked as a plumber journeyman, something I was proud of because it inherently meant that, over such times, I had been entrusted with a significant amount of autonomy.

From wider discussions that I had with other PSA's, I had no doubt that at times it not only upset people, but was tantamount to discrimination. This ran counter to the existing WYPS Equal Opportunities Policy, which stated that discrimination should not occur on the grounds of perceived negative status differences. The problem was that it was firmly embedded in the culture of the organisation, and it was a problem that I and others constantly wrestled with. Apart from this, I enjoyed being part of this community-orientated team.

Over time, I had indeed immersed myself in the wider field of welfare rights, which I found both stimulating and at times challenging, so I liked it very much. In part, Gipton was considered to be a deprived area so, in partnership with other agencies, such as the Police and Educational Welfare, we would co-ordinate and hold play schemes in the school holidays.

On one of these play schemes, we took the kids to Temple Newsam park and, when going around the small animal area, one child asked what one particular animal was. I believe it was a duck and I was a little shaken that they had never seen a duck before and secondly, with Gipton only approximately one mile away, many of the kids had never visited Temple Newsam before.

On another occasion, I recall one police officer being utterly disparaging about Gipton as a whole and, along with two or three others, we listened to him for a while before picking up on his remarks and I then tried to unravel with him what he was saying. I suggested that the implication of his comments was that at some stage God had simply reached down to earth with Gipton in the palm of his hand saying, "Here, have this estate with all of the numerous and rotten problems that go with it."

I suggested that to understand matters more fully, one would have to consider the history leading up to the social construction of Gipton itself. In other words, what over time had contributed to the deterioration of the estate. For example, it is widely acknowledged that housing allocation plays a big part through a decision that had been made at some stage that 'difficult' individuals/families should be housed there.

I told him that, in the late 1960s, the estate had a good reputation and many people came into Gipton to use the facilities at the leisure centre in the Ambertons. I put it to him that, although Alwoodley (a well-to-do part of Leeds) was not part of his remit, if he was to respond to an address there due to a burglary incident, along with another burglary committed at an address in Gipton, he would deal with both burglaries differently.

He immediately responded back by saying, "Of course I would. For a start, I would call the homeowner in Alwoodley 'sir', but I would never call anyone in Gipton that."

I commented that, "You have just gone some way in justifying my point."

Still, I don't believe he grasped it. Indeed the problem we had in housing homeless offenders and ex-offenders was that the only accommodation was in 'hard-to-let' areas and, a number of years later, the Home Office declared that one of the criminogenic factors leading to both offending and re-offending was that of 'neighbourhood'.

Peter, my SPO, continued to encourage me to apply for the postgraduate course and, later that year, I enrolled at Park Lane College for a one-year's Psychology undergraduate course that was held in the evening. The three core academic disciplines counting for the postgraduate course were Social Policy, Sociology and Psychology, so I saw my enrolment for the latter as part of my building towards this.

Later that year, I learned that nationally these postgraduate courses were ending and, though I was reluctant, Peter urged me to travel to Liverpool (the nearest one at the time) to speak to someone at the uni there. I arranged a meeting and made the trip to Liverpool, but left the informal interview feeling somewhat dejected because the tutor, having broadly explained the syllabus to me, had then made the point that, for me to make a go of it, I would have to have accommodation in Liverpool itself. For me and Wendy this was not practical; as a family we had endured enough disruption.

With the postgraduate course ending, a new two-year qualification was being introduced nationally in order to train and recruit PO's, and this was the Diploma in Probation and Social Work (DPSW). I rejected this option also for the same reasons: another two years as a student was just untenable. I settled back into my work and, as and when I could, I participated in a range of internal training courses.

My welfare rights knowledge developed and, besides working with a range of offenders on such issues, in 1990 I became a member of the Yorkshire Electricity Monitoring Group. The group included a range of welfare rights workers, from both statutory and voluntary organisations across Leeds, and with senior YE managers we would meet periodically, specifically relating to issues affecting those on benefits and low-income users, which of course included probation clients.

To prevent electricity disconnections, YE had recently introduced token meters, but ironically, though these tend – both then and now – to be targeted at those on a low income, those using such meters actually pay more for their electricity. One argument that was frequently put to the YE managers at the meetings by colleagues was that we all knew of users who at times have had to 'self-disconnect' due to not having enough money to purchase tokens. The response from YE was always the same, in that the additional charges for those having to use a token meter were to offset the costs of developing and installing the metres.

Sometime later, I joined the city-wide Leeds Welfare Rights Support Group, which included a similar range of workers. From a probation perspective this partnership, or 'networking' as it became commonly known, was deemed to be beneficial and I was increasingly being given greater autonomy, which I like to believe was due to the fact that I was being both trusted and respected. At home, Colin had now left school at the age of sixteen, though both Wendy and I, along with the school, had urged him to stay on and do his A-Levels.

On the run up to leaving, I remember him coming home saying that Mr. Carrington, the careers teacher, was going to take him and a group of other lads along to visit Farnell's, a light engineering firm in Armley. At best, the firm offered semi-skilled work and both Wendy and I felt that schools were more bothered about their statistics as to how many kids left school with jobs, as opposed to what kind of jobs these actually were. In other words, a measure of quantitative over qualitative.

One of the changes in the 1988 Education Act was the introduction of league tables and schools, then and now, have become overly preoccupied with statistics, targets and their league-table position. When he did leave, however, it was for a job with an accountancy firm in Armley. After a number of weeks, he would comment that the most technological thing that they had in their offices was an adding-up machine. Periodically, he was given the task of duplicating a number of papers and the work was carried out in an unventilated room with the fumes from the machine causing him to become nauseous.

After a number of months, he left and went to work full-time in Leeds Market at one of the stalls owned by his aunt and uncle. Teresa was now at West Leeds Girls High School, preferring not to go to the nearby intake high school. Wendy herself was now working full-time in Leeds Market, but around this time, she became very ill.

She had previously seen her GP, who had dismissed things as no more than a chill, but a short time later she was laid up in bed, so I requested a home visit by the doctor and his diagnosis resulted in some medicine being prescribed, along with a referral to the Leeds Chest Clinic. In due course, she was diagnosed with pneumonia and treated accordingly.

Sometime later, she confided to me that, prior to the appointment at the chest clinic and the following diagnosis, she thought that she had cancer. Being a smoker, she had made the erroneous link and then of her own volition decided to stop, and this she did and has never smoked again. Whilst I wasn't enamoured with the level of wages that I was receiving, the regular money was now enabling us to make progress with things in and around the house and pick up the threads of family life again.

One of the PO's that I got on really well with was a chap called Malcom and, having introduced me to the idea of playing golf, we subsequently enjoyed a number of games together and, in turn, this is something that I then introduced Colin to and a good number of our games were held on Gott's Park course. This became another hobby for him, along with fishing and Leeds United, though today his main interest is actually golf.

Malcom and I went on a number of prison visits to see clients of his and, on more than one occasion, he said I should use my car in place of his and thus enjoy receipt of the expenses. Around this time, the Birstall Urban Motorcycle Project for Young People (BUMPY) had been set up for young persons who were deemed to be in danger of or had actually committed motorcycle offences. One of the leaders of the project was a chap called Bill Swallow who at the time still raced classic motorbikes at the Isle of Man TT races

Malcom and I paid the project a visit and seeing the machines brought back memories of when I owned one myself. I commented to him about how I had once been a motorcyclist, and he told me that he had a Honda 70cc motorcycle at home that he hadn't used for some time. If I wanted it then I could have it.

I later collected the bike and took it home, got it taxed and tested and began riding it and, though it was only a moped, being back on two wheels resurrected my interest in motorcycling and this began to grow once more. Following a number of discussions, and looking in bike shops, in June 1992 Wendy and I agreed to purchase a 1000cc BMW K100 touring bike. We still remember the precise month because, having bought the bike, throughout June it rained every weekend, so we were unable to go out for a ride.

With Wendy now working every Saturday, that was the day I would carry out the cleaning up and then, Sunday's weather permitting, we would be out on the bike to places like the east coast, Yorkshire Dales, North Yorkshire Moors, the Lake District and so on. Over the years, I have commented to a number of nonplussed people about the difference between cars and motorcycling, which is that, when travelling A-to-B in a car, your enjoyment begins when arriving at B, but travelling A-to-B on a motorcycle *is* the enjoyment.

Colin and Teresa were now old enough to look after themselves and we also now had two Jack Russell dogs added to the family. At the age of only eight years old, our first dog Patch had been euthanised. He had undergone surgery for a snapped tendon in one of his rear legs and, during the long recovery, his other leg also suffered the same injury.

With the house being so quiet, through not having a dog around, we bought Tetley as a puppy privately and, approximately one year later, we rescued Cassie, a four-month-old Jack Russell/Corgi cross, from the RSPCA on Kirkstall Road. Wendy and I had never been to Scotland and, having heard so much about it from other motorcyclists, in 1993 we booked a long weekend in a bed and breakfast in Fort William and made our first trip.

As we travelled over Rannoch Moor and approached Glencoe, I noticed that on the reverse of a sign on the other side of the road, someone had written in spray paint, 'Settlers out'. Then underneath it another person had written 'Rennies in!' The humour tickled me and, several years later whilst talking to a Scotsman, I reiterated what I had seen. He was from Fife and said there is a place there called the Crook of Devon and underneath one road sign someone had written in spray paint, 'Twinned with the Thief of Baghdad!'

Moving on from Rannoch Moor and seeing the beauty of Glencoe for the first occasion was really stunning. Over our weekend in Fort William, we both recall coming out of a pub on the main street on the Saturday evening, at around 11.00pm, and it was still daylight. At this point, we hadn't realised that the more north one travels, the lighter it remains on an evening.

The following day we headed off west to enjoy a day on the Isle of Skye. We journeyed the forty miles or so to Mallaig, where we intended to catch the ferry for the twenty-minute crossing over to Armadale on Skye and, whilst waiting, we got chatting to a couple of bikers. Once aboard and having secured the bikes, the conversation was rejoined, but after several minutes I noticed that Wendy had disappeared. Whilst the ferry began slowing down as it entered the port, she suddenly re-emerged and confessed that, because of her aversion to boats, she had taken solace in the ladies' toilets.

Having been to Scotland many times over the years, Skye appears to be the one place that many tourists want to visit. Perhaps, as someone once remarked, this is due to the widespread popularity of the Skye Boat Song. We found Skye okay, and indeed have been a couple of times since, but for us it is too 'touristy' and busy.

We eventually had to tear ourselves away from what had been a great Scottish weekend being hugely inspired by the beauty of the scenery and its vastness. We didn't realise then that this was to be the start of our love affair and passion for Scotland.

In between trips out on the bike, I was always giving it a clean or a polish and, quite early on in owning it, I was out in the garden with my duster and polish when Wendy came to the door. She said, "I knew you'd be just the same as before once you got another bike."

"What do yer mean?" I replied back.

"Always bloody cleaning it!"

We eventually joined the BMW national bike club and, though we never took advantage of the regional fortnightly rides out – preferring instead to do our own thing – over the years we attended many national rallies, such as the annual May camping one at Blair Atholl in Perthshire.

At that time of year, there were a number of occasions when we woke up to find a light covering of frost on the tent. These were always really enjoyable events giving us the chance to meet other like-minded bikers.

Though I had been an active member of the Labour Party for around ten years, I took the decision to leave in the early 1990s. Something that had developed throughout the 1980s was the level of both my awareness and understanding of politics. There is a misleading understanding that politics exist in Parliament and is carried out between parties, such as Labour and Conservative. In reality, politics exists wherever there are relations of power and subordination; therefore politics are ubiquitous.

I recall attending a Labour Party constituency meeting around the mid-1980s and listening to a talk given by a local councillor, which she concluded by saying "at the next general election, let's get a Labour government so that we can return to socialism." At the time, I found this to be a naïve comment because the Labour Party has historically set out to merely reform capitalism in order to ameliorate the lives of working people through the introduction of more social democracy and, though such measures are to be welcomed, they are after all highly tenuous and subject to the dictates of economic recession and right-wing governments.

Overall, though the Labour Party includes many members that are socialists, I had come to the conclusion that, as an economic system, capitalism could not be reformed, like many party members believed. For me and others like me, capitalism is an inherently flawed economic system, driven solely by an output fanaticism to constantly accumulate profit and hence is prone to periodic 'overproduction', with economic booms, and slumps, often euphemistically known as the 'trade cycle' or an 'economic downturn'. The post-1945 adoption of Keynesian economics following the economic disaster of the twenties and thirties across the developed world was a wholesale acknowledgement of this.

The developed countries of the world adopted Keynesian economies, with individual nation states managing their economies through a range of fiscal measures. This reformism of capitalism did not have the desired effect, believed by many, of being the absolute economic panacea, as there were still problems of poverty, poor housing and other issues. A literature survey of poverty in the United Kingdom throughout the fifties, sixties and seventies serves to illustrate that social conditions were very different to the comment of Prime Minister Macmillan in the later 1950s that Britain 'had never had it so good'.

A key factor of Keynesian-led economics was that governments, or the nation state, was seen as the main driver of the mixed economic affairs, operating a number of fiscal levers as and when the economy needed to be slowed down (to avoid overproduction and recession) or pushed forward for more investment and growth. However, the growth of transnational companies, with a head office in one country but operating in many others, served to contribute to the development of globalisation. This, in turn, reduces the ability of nation states to effect and influence their very own economies. Another factor was the huge increase by the Organisation of the Petroleum Exporting Countries (OPEC) of crude oil 1972.

Crude oil had remained at very low prices since the late 1950s, but OPEC was realising its economic power and influence and, at the same time, there was the aim (especially by Saudi Arabia) to reduce oil supplies to Israel because of the existing Yom Kippur War, involving Egypt and Syria in opposition to Israel. In any event, the oil increase had a drastic impact on Western economies and went some way towards causing the downturn of many economies, including Britain's. There are only two ways to run a capitalist economy: Keynesian economics or laissez fairre (which means leave alone) economics, now known as free market economics. Keynesian economics was overtaken by global capitalism and the re-branding of laissez fairre (now free markets) only offers greater social inequalities and social injustice.

Historically, and indeed now, 'free markets' have no regard for inequality and social justice and their sole purpose is the maximisation of profit. The more I asked "Why?" in relation to the issues and problems I was encountering then (and indeed now) the more analytical in my thinking I became.

Some may say that one cannot understand capitalism in any great detail without reading the voluminous works carried out by Karl Marx and, to a certain extent, I have done this. He was back then, and still is today, the only person acknowledged as studying and understanding capitalism in such a comprehensive and profound way. Indeed, at the start of the 2008 global banking crisis, at one stage it was reported that in Germany there was an upsurge in demand for Marx's book *Das Kapital*. Therefore, for me in this context to continue being a member of the Labour Party simply didn't sit with the way my political development was taking shape.

Three years following my graduation, my interest in further education teaching still remained and it was around 1992 that I wrote a speculative letter attaching my Curriculum Vitae (CV) to the University of Leeds Adult Continuing Education Unit, enquiring if they had any vacancies for a part-time lecturer/tutor. To my elated surprise, I received a reply back inviting me for an interview and on the due date, to my surprise, I was interviewed by Mike Stein.

Following this, I gained a part-time post as a sociology lecturer on a Combined Social Studies part-time degree course. The course involved teaching adults one evening per week and the central theme was social inequality across the three topic areas of: education, the family and social stratification. It was my responsibility for the putting together and planning of lessons, along with the setting and marking of essays, but none of this perturbed me because I was doing something that I really enjoyed and I thoroughly looked forward to each of the evening classes. Myself I had gained so much from further education and I simply wanted to give something back to other adult students.

Some years later, I overheard someone – not a student I hasten to add – comment that the discipline of sociology was merely individual writers simply offering different opinions on certain topics. Clearly, they had no idea and I felt disinclined to point out the error. In a crude deterministic way, they had – whilst not realising it – been conflating the work of metaphysicians with that of sociologists. Whilst the former offers no more than a general and abstract view of life, the latter, as is the case with other social scientists, are also empiricists. In the nineteenth century Marx heavily criticised metaphysicians due to their baseless reasoning.

Meanwhile, back with my day job, whilst I found much of the work challenging and rewarding, I simply couldn't accept some of the status-driven attitudes and behaviour of some PO's. PSA training courses would at some point result in someone complaining about something that had been done or said to them and, on such occasions, I would both dryly and sarcastically remark that, "Most people don't know this, but in this country there is a huge conspiracy whereby everyone at birth undergoes a lobotomy and the only time that's reversed is when you pass a DIPSW."

Ridiculous maybe, but to be on the receiving end of crass status-driven comments makes you wonder if some PO's actually thought this to be the case. For example, working in an open-plan office there are inevitably occasions when you can't help but overhear what other people are saying and one morning two POs sitting opposite each other and within earshot were recalling a documentary that they had both watched the previous evening on the television. They exchanged several joint perceptions about the programme and then, at one stage, in response to another jointly acknowledged point, one of them commented, "Oh, so you picked up on that too, so did I!"

And the other rejoined, "I think it's because we've both been trained."

The other person concurred.

I had seen the same documentary and arrived at the same points as them and sighed inwardly at their conclusions and crass delusions about where one derives intellect from. Both had recently qualified and were really okay people to work with, but oh dear me this goes some way in validating my 'lobotomy' theory. Because of my ongoing frustrations, I was beginning to look out for other jobs and was successful in applying for the position of community service officer (CSO) in August 1993.

Chapter 14

The 'White-Collar' Blues – from the Frying Pan into the Fire

A CSO carried the status equivalent to that of a PSA, though the role of the former appealed to me largely due to the enhanced autonomy, which included an offender caseload and the management of a number of CS supervisors. The latter supervised groups of around four to six offenders who would work on a range of projects for around six hours per day.

A community service order was a court order for a number of hours, depending on the severity of the offence, it ranged from a minimum of 40 hours with the maximum being for 240 hours. I remember, just before leaving for my new post, one of my PO colleagues wished me luck, but said that they didn't believe that I would find the work challenging enough.

Then the CS office was located in the old police station on Dewsbury Road, which was also shared with a probation field team. There were about ten CSO's divided into three teams, each having different duties for managing offenders and their orders. We also had four clerical officers. The existing CS manager was actually a PO, but holding this position automatically promoted them to senior PO, and some believed that that is why she took the post up – fast promotion.

She was relatively new to the post and Ian, the deputy manager, although being a CSO/PSA, had stood in temporarily as manager, but was overlooked for the job when the final appointment was made, much to his lingering chagrin. The work was interesting and involved court training, because if an order was revoked then we would have to prosecute the offender back in court for the original offence that led up to the making of the order in the first instance.

The team had two temporary CSO's and one of them, Mike, had undergone his court training with Ian. One day when they returned to the office, much to Mike's embarrassment, Ian revealed to everyone that, when in court and reading out the nature of this offender's original driving offence to the magistrates bench, Mike, who hadn't been wearing his glasses, had said something like this, "Yes, your worships, on such and such a day at such and such a time, the defendant was seen driving *erotically…*"

At this point, there had apparently been titters of laughter from those present, including the magistrates, before Mike had corrected himself "...erm, the defendant was seen driving *erratically.*"

No doubt the psychological impact of my previous periods of unemployment throughout the 1980s was at play as I was beginning to settle into the belief that the probation service was probably where I would stay indefinitely. Long-term unemployment can be a crushing experience. Also, when my friend John Light and I would meet he would offer anecdotes about the plumbing trade.

Around this time in the mid-1990s, he himself had taken an employer to a Small Claims Court due to leaving their employment and not being paid the wages and holiday pay that he was owed. Though the court found in his favour, they then informed John that the said employer had ceased trading under that particular name. John recalled on another occasion that, after being with a firm for several months, they moved him to Sheffield for what was supposed to be a 'big' job. However, after being there a week or so, he received a telephone call telling him that, because there was a lull in the job, would he mind simply taking the week off. This he did then, at the end of the week, because of the ongoing delay, he was asked if he would take take his two weeks paid holiday and then the job should be ready to go back to. Again, he agreed and then, following his two weeks 'holidays', they made him redundant.

When he then went to register as unemployed, according to John, when he was asked about the last day that he had worked, he had a difficult task in getting the benefits worker to accept that, at the firm's request, he had first taken a week off work with no pay, followed by the two weeks' 'holidays'. The common experience of many plumbers was similar to that of both John and I, in that jobs were often shrouded in lies and deceit. In the late 1990's John got off the *merry-go-round of chance* - that led to the periodic experience of working for a rogue employer – and went to work for the City Council undertaking maintenance duties in a older persons' home.

Many plumbers would talk of being 'scammed' by an employer, but rather than deal with the hassle, they had simply left the firm in question and walked away. Looking back, I had perhaps lost a little bit of self-belief and confidence, due to being in the probation service, which structurally had a very limited hierarchy for progression. If you were not a PO with the pre-requisite DIPSW, then your job opportunities were extremely limited.

After a number of months, we gained a new manager who was of CSO/PSA grade, and he had been managing the CS office in Wakefield. Mark came with a reputation of once working throughout the night in his previous office, and this was validated a short time later when we gained a second deputy manager, Marion, also from Wakefield.

In the first few weeks of Mark's appointment, there was a flurry of memos in everyone's pigeonhole each morning. The two deputies and the manager had their issues with each other and that was plain to see, with Ian just as resentful of Mark as he had been of the previous manager. The probation service had been under budget constraints and set targets for a year or two. There were periodic rumours that community service might possibly be the first sector to be privatised. We were all being frequently pressed to meet targets and one day Marion came into the office that I shared with my sub-team members, Brian and Diane, and attempted to brow beat us about targets.

At the point where she thought that she was wielding the 'sword of Damocles' over our heads, by threatening that if we don't meet targets then we could be privatised, I flippantly reacted by saying, "Oh good, well at least privatisation will alleviate all this uncertainty."

Somewhat surprised by this, she rejoined. "If we are privatised then there will be redundancies!"

Becoming more reactionary, I said, "Even better, a bit of extra cash."

"Well, how long have *you* been here?" she flew back at me. "You haven't been here too long, so you'll only get several thousand pounds."

Still being impish, I replied back saying, "Several thousand pounds redundancy! When is it all happening?" I had called her bluff and, without saying any more, she opened the office door and went.

The constant subtle and indirect comments aimed at intimidating us regarding targets proved, at times, to be a little more than irksome. At times organisations will attempt to achieve targets through the distortion of their processes and procedures. For example, one hears quite often that the number of pupil exclusions from schools is more to do with their own internal targets, especially regarding educational attainment. Thus, all three of our managers were on a mission and nothing, but nothing, could be allowed to cause failure.

One morning, as I arrived at work and entered the main office, Sheila (one of the clerical officers) was very upset and close to tears. Her fellow colleagues were trying to console her and when I enquired what was the problem I was told that Hilary, one of the temporary CSO's, had left and that Shelia had been given all of the additional admin work to do relating to Hilary's casework.

When I went upstairs to our office, Brian was already in and I remarked about what I had seen and the extra work arbitrarily given to the Sheila. Then he remarked, "Yes and you have been given half of Hilary's caseload to manage too!" That is how things were carried out, no consultation. I had for some time been thinking about the differences between blue and white-collar work.

Perhaps I was naïve in the first place to think there were differences, because I saw that there were very few. In the building trade, there was often a more direct and verbally forceful approach used by management and, indeed, between work colleagues too, with their frequent exchanges of four-letter expletives. I was finding that, in white-collar work, things were framed in more of a subtle and middle-class 'let's discuss this' manner, but quite often both differing approaches could end up leaving one feeling the same: upset and dejected. Still, I had more or less resolved that probation offered me both stable employment and remuneration and, though I was unhappy at times, I continued to bite the bullet.

Due to budget constraints, the probation service in Leeds had closed a number of outlying probation offices and a new centralised building was constructed at the bottom of Lupton Avenue in Harehills. We ourselves moved there too. Most of the CSO's had not worked in a probation field team as I had done – two had worked in the police force, one in the magistrates' court, with the others from different occupations. Given this, I was pleased that, following some restructuring, a number of field team PSA's joined the CS Team. Two of these, Alan Brown and Richard Nelson, had a background in the building trade and, because of this, we had some commonalities in our approach and thinking.

The disenchanted mood seemed to permeate across all the staff, and at any given time, it seemed that someone was aggrieved for some reason. The new office was fully open plan, though the managers had their own offices and one day our heads were lifted from our work to hear Richard in a really weird voice loudly announcing via a child's loudspeaker, "Will all you children please get on with your work!"

Each morning, individual CSO's would staff the meeting point (several miles from the office), take the names of individual offenders attending, and place them into teams with CS supervisors. The meeting point could potentially be a flashpoint, with the odd offender complaining of being ill or not wanting to do certain types of work. Their complaints could be exacerbated as some would be 'playing' to the crowd of offenders also waiting. In such instances, I would take a recalcitrant offender well away from the crowd and simply stress to them the rules that they had agreed to.

This would lead to them backing down, so the trick was gauging who to isolate and who could be dealt with in the midst of a crowd. For example, one lad standing in the crowd one morning said to me that because it was winter it was too cold for him to work outside and, after a bit if persuasion and banter, I simply said, "What's matter wi' ya? When I worked in't building trade at this time o' year, I always dressed in shorts and tee shirts!"

He strolled off for the outside work with the supervisor and the other lads muttering, "Yer mad, you." CSO's were also on a rota for working weekends, which was okay because of the time and a half paid for Saturday and the double time on Sunday. Following some resistance by CSO's and the Unison Union head office, management succeeded in introducing a new system of working whereby we had to work any five from seven days, for single time only!

It was only finally agreed on the back of management threatening to tear up our old contracts and re-start us on new ones that included the new provisions. Over the years, many workers nationally have moved on to similar arrangements, leaving many young workers today looking at you bewildered if you mention the time and half/double time payments.

Within the CS office, there was a clear divide between the majority of all staff and the management, and on one occasion I was in the manager's office with a female colleague and his blunt and aggressive behaviour brought her to tears. On another occasion, on the day that one of the clerical officers was going on maternity leave, she came out of the manager's office in tears, although I was left unaware of what had transpired.

I remember another colleague saying to me that each morning, upon his arrival, he would sit in his car looking up at the office windows, not wanting to come in. Without realising their true extent, matters were steadily building up, especially for me.

Chapter 15

Time to Dig Deep

It was around 1996 and I hadn't been feeling myself for some time, so I went to see my GP, Mr. Gilmore. He opened the conversation, as doctors usually do, by asking what he could do for me and, in response, I garbled something about work and then simply broke down in tears. I can still see the look of surprise on his face, but I don't recall what I said to him after that.

In retrospect, I had been experiencing a cumulative build-up of negative events, experiences and emotions that I was now demonstrably unable to cope with anymore. He put me on sick leave and diagnosed the problem as 'work-related stress'. I was in a very, very dark place and Wendy, who had suffered depression several years previous, kept telling me that, although it may not seem so now, there was indeed light at the end of the tunnel.

Initially, I had suicidal thoughts, but thankfully they stopped there with no real inclination to act on them. Because over the years I had become a person who likes to understand matters and what is happening, after a short time on sick leave I went to the local library and loaned a book entitled *How to Deal with Difficult People*. When I began reading it, I got no further than the first few pages because it was evoking thoughts about work and some of the negative experiences, so I put the book down and never picked it up again. However, I did retain a mental note of a number of points from the book that, over time, I never forgot and drew strength from.

The first was that we can choose not to accept negative comments and opinions that others might hold about us; secondly, there are occasions when we should remind ourselves and gain strength from our positive achievements. Perhaps most importantly, though, was a method or strategy for dealing with those who we find difficult for whatever reason.

Firstly, try to block out and ignore the person that you perceive as being difficult. Secondly, openly speak with the person who is being difficult and causing you distress by telling them how they are making you feel with the hope of getting a positive response from them. And finally, if neither of these two options worked, then seek employment elsewhere.

As I made some recovery, I got a call from Alan Brown and he told me that he too had just returned to work having had some time off due to stress. I had been off work for around four to five months when I decided that I didn't want to return to community service as the thought of going back simply filled me with dread, so I built up the courage and sought a meeting with the assistant chief probation officer (ACPO) in Leeds, as it was he who had the managerial remit over the CS unit. I had asked in advance if I could be found a different post.

On the day of the meeting, as I drove the five miles or so from home to Waterloo House on Wellington Street, I was filled with trepidation and my stomach was churning. I arrived about ten minutes early, so I stood on the street outside the offices, feeling daunted about the meeting and the fact that there might be no alternative post for me, meaning I would have to go back to CS.

I took the lift to the fifth floor and went into a meeting room with the ACPO, Mr. Indifferent. Almost immediately, I sensed that his attitude towards me was cold and aloof. There were some preliminary comments in which he queried whether my time off work with stress was actually work related. I replied that it was, and the sick notes signed by my doctor confirmed this.

The ACPO then talked about a post away from CS for me, but this would mean a drop in salary. I detected from his cold attitude that I wasn't going to achieve any empathy and, in response to his derisory offer, I said, "If I was sat before you as a victim of racism, you wouldn't be offering me a post with less salary because that is tantamount to re-victimising the victim. And that is what you are doing to me."

His cold response was such that when I was ready to return to work, he said that I could return to CS, but this was followed up with a negative comment by him about my attitude. This was proving useless and his whole demeanour suggested to me that, as far as he was concerned, he held all the cards.

I hit back by saying, "Under Section 2 of the Health and Safety at Work Act, as my employer, you have a legal duty not only to make provisions for my physical wellbeing at work, but also my mental wellbeing too. I know this to be a fact because a Leeds solicitor that I know recently won a case against a North East Local Authority for failing to take account of an employee's mental wellbeing. It was the first case to be won under the Health and Safety at Work Act. And yes, when my doctor says that I am fit to return to work, I will go back to CS, but I can tell you now that, if there is no improvement in conditions there, then I shall take a grievance out against you as my employer for breaching my rights under the Health and Safety at Work Act".

I left the meeting feeling utterly dejected, in despair and mentally worn out. Clearly someone had been speaking to the ACPO indicating that I was a problem. At least now I had some idea about what I would be returning to. The Leeds solicitor I had referred to was called John and he worked for Thompson's Solicitors, who in turn had been providing legal assistance to the trade union and labour movement since the 1920s.

A friend of John Light's, a chap called Frank Gray, was a legal executive for them and, along with John Light, we often met in the Bramley Band Working Men's Club. At times, John had also been present because, in the 1990s, John Light was found to be suffering from 'plural plaque' in his lungs, due to at some time having ingested asbestos fibres, and this was causing him to have a shortage of breath. Frank, who came from Middlesboro, had lived an interesting life, travelling all over the world with the Merchant Navy before becoming an engineer, active trade unionist, gaining a BA part-time degree then subsequently taking a course to become a legal executive. He was also very much in the forefront of setting up the West Yorkshire Asbestos Claimants Group and, when Wendy's eldest brother, Michael, was diagnosed with the terminal cancer mesothelioma in 1998, Frank was able, for what it was worth, to take on Michael's case and gained a compensation sum of approximately £45,000 for him and his wife, Julie.

Both John Light and Frank were also autodidacts. Several weeks before I did go back to work, I received a scheduled home visit from a senior probation officer who, apparently, was standing in for the CS manager who was on sick leave.

We invited him in and gave him tea and he asked a number of mediocre questions, putting my replies down on the pro-forma questionnaire he had brought with him. The one thing that stands out in my mind was that, akin to some pseudo-doctor, he proceeded to ask me what symptoms I had experienced whilst off work and so on. Afterwards, I wondered at his audacity, asking such specific and personal questions as, given that he had no qualification in mental health, just what realistic assessment could he make of my answers?

Eventually, I returned to work and, upon my arrival, the same stand-in manager gave me a pile of team meeting minutes and suggested, as a way of easing my way back in, I read through them to see what has been happening. Previously, one of the female colleagues of my sub-team had been nicknamed "Me-Me" by Richard, because she was so well known for putting herself forward for most things required by management. She was not only a 'crawler', but I saw her as someone who wouldn't hesitate in standing on any colleagues' heads to get herself noticed.

That day and throughout the rest of the week, "Me-Me" persisted in directing sarcastic comments towards me about how my being on sick leave had caused her and the other members of the sub-team real difficulty in managing their collective workload. I never rose to her baited comments and I noted that none of the other members of the sub-team had said anything. Come Friday, the end of my first week back, she again began baiting me about the undue amount of work that I had caused her.

Mindful of comments in recent team meeting minutes, in a quiet voice I replied, "You tell me how busy you've been, but I notice that you have recently volunteered for additional work."

I had finally been lulled in and had taken the bait. She jumped out of her chair yelling at me with the whole office gazing on before then charging into the manager's office and, following a short time, she came out. I too then went in to see the manager in an attempt to explain and present my side of the story, but he was dismissive and made it clear that, as far as he was concerned, it was 'six of one and half a dozen of the other'. I felt utterly gutted and demoralised.

When I finally got home that evening, I explained to Wendy what had happened and, the next morning being Saturday, when she had left for work, I eventually went to the telephone situated in the hallway. I rang the deputy manager, Marion. No sooner had she answered than I had broken down in tears.

I remember Colin beginning his descent down the stairs and I tried to pull myself together. Still sobbing, I explained to Marion what had happened the day before and that I couldn't face going into work on the Monday. When Monday morning finally came around, I went to see Dr. Gilmore, who subsequently assessed me as being depressed and gave me a three weeks sick note. The three weeks passed and I realised that the only person who would support me at work was me. I had not deserved to be treated in the way that I had, and I dug as deep as I could into whatever mental strength I felt that I had.

Remembering the book I had attempted to read about *Dealing with Difficult People*, I took to work with me a picture of Wendy and myself taken during my uni graduation day, as well as photos of Colin and Teresa. These I placed on my desk in order to remind myself of what really mattered in my life.

I knocked on the temporary manager's office door and duly entered. As I sat down and he asked me how I was feeling, I began in an assertive manner to take him back over the Friday that "Me-Me" had baited me on and then kicked off. I took him through what I explained was his woeful response to me and how his mishandling of it had compounded my feelings of negativity.

I remember saying, "I am working for an organisation that purports to be welfare orientated, yet for me, I have been treated in a lesser way than an offender might expect. If I had a broken limb with a cast on, then everyone in that office would see my situation, yet I have been off work for six months with work-related stress and I don't expect to go round each individual in that office saying so, whilst adding that it might be twelve months before my mental strength has recovered. You have dealt with matters badly, as far as I am concerned, and I now know that the only person that I can rely is me."

On several occasions, he attempted to make reference back to the Friday in question, so that he might revisit events in order to justify himself and gain some control over matters. However, I remained assertive throughout, telling him he had had his chance and his response had been utterly pathetic.

Over the next few weeks, there were no further upsets and I settled back into the work. The temporary manager gave way to the return of the post-holder, as he returned from sick leave. One day, Richard approached me saying that a letter was to be drafted and signed by all members, saying that the unit as a whole had no confidence in the manager and his two managerial deputies.

This letter would be sent to the Leeds ACPO asking for a meeting to be held to discuss the team's grievances, without the presence of the managers. I was asked if I too would sign it. I said I would, but only under the written qualification that I had recently been off work for almost seven months and, as such, over the time I had not been privy to some of the issues that were alluded to in the letter.

Over the next couple of weeks Mr. Indifferent, the ACPO, dragged his heels, despite several representations from individual members of the unit. Then the meeting finally was convened and I went into the room with everyone else, but I was determined not to be the spokesperson for the airing of the unit's grievances.

After listening to a somewhat muted response from several colleagues, the ACPO appeared to offer what he thought was an appropriate defence regarding the concerns of CS staff. He tacitly offered his support for the three managers by talking about the differing 'managerial styles' that individuals present and therefore the issue, as far as he was concerned, was more to do with the inability of staff to come to terms with these differing managerial styles.

I found his comments crass and, with no one offering any real response, I commented to him that, "In any workplace one can imagine it is extremely rare, if not unheard of, for there to be such unanimity of negative feelings towards management as there is here. Everyone is of the same view and, as such, it is incomprehensible that it is merely 'management style' that is the problem." I said no more and the meeting ended with the ACPO leaving to ponder on what had been said.

Not surprisingly, we never heard any more from him and I resolved that it was time to find another job elsewhere. It was only a matter of weeks following the meeting that I became aware of a position back at Waterloo House in the city centre. My interview was successful, and I was both relieved and excited to have a new job, which I started in June 1996.

The job was working within a probation field team as a probation services officer (PSO). A change in job title had taken place from PSA to PSO. Though I was to be working with PO's and certain offenders on their caseload, I also had a divisional 'first line management' role, concerning the contract monitoring regarding the three offender accommodation supported-living projects with the charities running them, e.g. Leeds Housing Concern, Stonham Housing and Foundation Housing.

Chapter 16

'Give a dog a bad name'

Over the coming weeks I settled into my new role and got on well with all of the other team members and then, after two or three months, a colleague said to me one day, just out of the blue "You're alright you, aren't you?" I looked back with an element of surprise and then there was a follow up remark, "Before you started we were told you were a right bastard, but you're okay."

I was a little surprised and chose to simply smile and say nothing in reply. However, inwardly I thought that clearly I had been negatively labelled by significant others. The lack of willingness to admit personal wrongdoing and then go on to abuse one's power is frightening.

Approximately twelve months went by when yet more structural change was announced, along with a number of meetings for the staff concerned. One of my current colleagues, Pim, was a middle-aged person and, following her attendance at one such meeting, she returned looking very upset. She explained that during the meeting she had asked a number of what she believed to be critical, but pertinent questions from the group of attendees. According to Pim, as the meeting ended and people began to disperse, Peter (one of the SPO's) passed her and made a really cutting remark to her without stopping for a reply. This left her feeling debilitated.

We attempted to console her, and I said, "Look, in my experience there are three types of people that attend meetings. Firstly, those who quite often simply coast through without saying anything. Secondly, there are those who listen and pick up on one point or more, but never ask questions. And the third type of person will listen intently and openly speak out, querying certain points. I personally fit into the third type and it appears that so do you. Managers like to be in control and quite often object to that third type of person being present."

None of these structural changes were going to affect me and I found myself working within a new partnerships team, alongside individual officers responsible for partnership work regarding mentally disordered offenders, drug and alcohol misuse and employment training. Steve still remained as the SPO, which pleased me because I got on well with him.

In 1997, the Crime and Disorder Act gained royal ascent. The act made it incumbent upon local authorities and the police to work together as *lead agencies* in order to carry out a thorough crime and disorder audit of their localities, collate the information and bring about approximately five priority areas. A strategy was to be published identifying the priority areas and underpinning this were relevant action plans for each area. Every three years a new crime audit would take place with corresponding priorities and action plans.

Essentially, the act recognised both the need and importance to establish key and relevant partnerships in tackling crime and disorder. Relevant partnerships, including both statutory and voluntary agencies, were eventually involved, such as the youth offending team and the Leeds Interagency Advice Project relating to domestic violence.

From the probation perspective, I was tasked with working part time alongside both Andy from the Authority and Sue a police chief inspector. In essence, we were the embryonic community safety unit, which in the future was destined to develop and expand, but in the interim it was the three of us that embarked on the initial task of undertaking the crime audit.

I came to thoroughly enjoy the work and, not too long afterwards, whilst attending a community safety residential training course, I picked up a flyer from the West of England University, Bristol. They were recruiting part-time community safety distance learning tutors, so I subsequently applied and succeeded in gaining a post with them.

Essentially, the work involved written student assignments being sent to my home, which I would then mark and offer constructive feedback. I found that, with community safety, I could draw on both my academic knowledge and practical work experience. As with my role as a sociology lecturer, I always gave full and comprehensive written feedback on student assignments and it was good that both institutions acknowledged this to me at different stages.

As a definition, community safety is an umbrella term covering crime prevention, crime reduction and anti-social behaviour. In Leeds, a community safety unit was eventually formed along with the development of key and relevant partnerships from across the city.

One day, my SPO spoke to me about the need to create an active volunteer group so that volunteers, via discussion and ongoing assessment, could be placed to carry out clearly defined work with low-risk offenders. I was thus given another role, that of volunteers co-ordinator, and after a couple of years we had a solid group of twenty-plus volunteers.

I had part responsibility for interviews, but complete responsibility for putting together a training pack for induction and ongoing group training and meetings, which were carried out in the evenings. When PO's expressed an interest in using a volunteer, I would convene a three-way meeting between the relevant PO and volunteer, so that I could assess the suitability of the work being proposed. If there was mutual agreement, then once the volunteer became actively involved with the offender concerned, I would have frequent contact with them to ensure that matters were running satisfactorily.

I now had three very different roles to carry out and, around the late 1990s, the partnerships team had a relatively new SPO, who at one point spoke to me saying that, in his opinion, the level of responsibility that I had was way above my actual paygrade. He resolved to speak with the ACPO and I was subsequently given the pay grade equivalent to that of a middle manager and, along with this, I was asked to attend the monthly district managers' meetings where, on occasions, I appraised managers on relevant matters. I recall attending one particular meeting, with the main topic being a presentation by the head office equal opportunities manager (EOM) regarding the new draft Anti-Discriminatory Policy (ADP).

All of the managers had been sent a copy beforehand and, for me, whereas the old policy included the issue of status, the new one chose to omit it as a potential area of discrimination. It also failed to mention anything about discrimination because of trade union activities and this was raised by one of the managers who was active in the National Association of Probation Officers (NAPO). When I raised the matter of status and my reason for doing so, the EOM scoffed at my comments and suggested that I wanted to turn the service into some kind of co-operative.

In order to push my point further I said: "One particular day, I had reason to visit the York Road office and, upon entering the building, I happened to bump into a black female PSO that I knew. She was upset and set about telling me about a PO who had derided her for being what he saw as a mere PSO. Being a PSO myself, I could relate to her story and offered her some words of comfort. Now, as a black female, if the cause of her upset and discomfort was due to sexism or racism then you would all agree that she would have just cause to instigate a formal complaint, don't you? However, *her* complaint was to do with the misuse of status differences and, because of a perceived inferior status, she was derided for simply being a PSO. When you go to any probation office around West Yorkshire, there are posters everywhere stating that the service does not tolerate sexism or racism, with other forms of discrimination not getting a single mention. In reality, what we have is an Unequal Equal Opportunities Policy. The fact that status causes inequality was recognised way back by the sociologist Max Weber."

There was a muted response and I didn't expect much more because they all knew that I was right and, given the organisational culture, perhaps some of them had been or were guilty of such discrimination themselves. One of the realities of life, I came to realise, is that the problem of common sense is that it is not always common.

Several years previous, during my first few years in the service, we had a black PO named G who had politely challenged me one day as I reflected upon my childhood for mentioning the Lone Ranger, an old 1950s children's Western, because he said it was racist, and yes I could understand his reasoning. He was of course referring to the subordinate role of Tonto the native Indian companion of the Lone Ranger. As a young infant in the 1950's I didn't feel responsible for the culure within which I grew up. However, one day as I entered the team's clerical office, the four officers appeared glum, so I queried what the problem was. One of them replied that G had just been in to the office and, upon his entry, he had asked what they were all talking about and, when the reply came that they had been discussing a disability awareness course to be held at the head office, his reply had been to derisorily comment, "Oh, I thought it was something important."

Little had he or even I known that one of the clerical officers, Christine, had a prosthetic limb below one of her knees and his comments had caused her considerable upset. Moreover, such a crass comment was totally inappropriate and not in keeping with the Anti-Discriminatory Policy of the service which quite rightly expected a holistic approach rather than a selective one when considering forms of discrimination.

In the early 1990s, at the time of the breakup of the despised apartheid regime in South Africa, I recall having a brief conversation with G about the situation where at one point he said that "what we want is more black businesses", implying that was all that was needed.

I replied that the left wing of the African National Congress (ANC) wanted far more for black people than that, and I remember asking him, "Do you want black people to exploit black people?"

As I recall, he didn't reply, and I don't believe he had ever thought things through other than the limited view that it is only white people who exploit black people. My own view is that there is only one race and that is the human race. Nelson Mandella joined the ANC in the 1940's and besides being an African Natonalist he was also a socialist. The same goes for Martin Luther King and both men being socialists recognised that capitalism had nothing to offer, but greed and grasping materialism coupled with the oppression and inequality for both black and white people. When the singer and actor Paul Robeson (the son of an American slave) appeared before the House Committee for un-American activities in the 1950's he was alleged to be a communist for visiting the Soviet Union. In reply Robeson said that because there was no racism in the Soviet Union actually being there was the first time in his life that he felt like a human being. The limited response from G just reinforced my view that advocates of single-issue politics are often guilty of adopting a mono-cultural or one-dimensional view of both history and contemporary life and this blinkered outlook is something that is quite common when listening to people. For example historically, in the realms of feminism, whilst the suffragette Emily Pankhurst is widely acclaimed for getting all women the vote, this was only after a change of heart because initially she only wanted the suffrage for middle-class women. In contrast, her daughter Sylvia – who was a socialist – not only wanted working-class women to be included in the fight for suffrage, but also she saw a need also for a campaign to be waged against the many social injustices that these women faced on a daily basis too. As a result of these convictions, her family distanced themselves from her and she was expelled from the Women's Suffrage and Political Union. Early feminists such as her recognised clearly the true sphere of women's politics.

At the turn of the millennium, my workload had become really excessive and I was having difficulty keeping on top of things, so I approached the person that was yet another new line manager on several occasions, in an attempt to address things, but in the end she simply said that I should let the volunteers remit slide in order to reduce pressure on myself. I felt very disheartened at this for, having built a group up of approximately twenty volunteers from nothing, I was now being asked to let it decline.

Around this period, the new National Probation Directorate had been created and, over the next two to three years, staff were gradually withdrawn from all partnership work due to the new and narrow emphasis on core targets. This was a clear contradiction in thinking by the Home Office who, on the one hand, given the Crime and Disorder Act and the clear and unambiguous emphasis on the benefits of partnership working, the introduction of a National Probation Directorate was now diametrically opposed to it in favour of simply core targets. Around 2002, my probation manager advised me that my part-time secondment to the community safety unit was to be brought to an end. Moreover, I would revert back to being a PSO and my salary would be gradually downgraded over two to three years back to that level. I was gutted and I expressed my dissatisfaction about this to my line manager during one supervision meeting, saying, "So much for striving for personal development!" I complained, but to no avail.

Several days later, I informed Andy the community safety unit manager. He was disappointed to hear my news, but a day or so later he had clearly given the matter some thought and he asked me, if he could get funding for twelve months, would I be prepared to stay in the unit on a twelve-month permanent secondment. I jumped at the chance, saying "definitely".

I had two reasons for accepting this offer. Firstly, as stated above, I really enjoyed the work, and secondly, my thoughts were that the hierarchy within the local authority offered far more scope for advancement than that of the probation service. The probation head office agreed to my secondment and I joined the unit as a training and development officer, with my existing salary still intact. I had previously undertaken a lot of training on behalf of the unit, often with colleagues from other partner agencies. A number of us had earlier attended a training for trainers course held at the police headquarters in Wakefield. I settled into my new role and thoroughly enjoyed the work, but as the year progressed, I was beginning to find some of the office politics extremely petty and began to question what my future was likely to be at the end of my secondment.

Around the turn of the millennium, my part-time lecturer's role with the University of Leeds had come to an end. Over the mid-to-late 1990s, the government had increasingly cut funding for further education and, particularly in the last two years, the uni was finding it difficult to sustain courses. Seeing this, and not wanting my lecturing role to end, I held discussions and offered them an overall synopsis about a potential new course with the central topic being 'Old Age in a Modern Society'.

I got the go ahead to develop the course more comprehensively and, though this was approved and subsequently advertised in the uni's course prospectus, when it came to the evening for student enrolment, my course failed to gain the required numbers. Given this, my role with the uni as a sociology lecturer would shortly come to a sad end.

However, I was still working as a part-time distance learning tutor and I received regular essays to mark, pass appropriate comment on and return by post. At home, Colin was now married and living in Pudsey with his wife Sara and the first of their two daughters', Lauren. Before they moved into their new home, I had fitted full central heating for them, and Wendy had undertaken lots of decorating. Prior to his wedding, he had left Leeds Market and taken a temporary position with Halifax Bank, a very brave move to make, but he worked at it and was eventually kept on, steadily progressing through a number of posts with them.

Like her brother, Teresa had left school early at sixteen and had done some part-time work, also in Leeds Market, on her aunt and uncle's fruit and veg stall. Then she had begun full-time working in the office of a chemist in Pudsey, before the place was taken over by Lloyds Chemists. She moved on to full-time work for a number of years in the offices of Edwin Woodhouse in the village of Farsley. The mill itself dated back to 1829, but in 1882 Edwin Woodhouse, who had been the majority shareholder, became the outright owner.

Wendy too had undergone some employment changes over the past few years. Having moved out of Leeds Market, she took up a part-time employment with T. Ball Footwear, who were then located in one of the city centre arcades. She had been there for several years when, along with the rest of the staff, they were informed that the store was to be relocated to York. Given that Wendy only worked fifteen hours a week, and at that time did not drive a car, she felt that moving to York was simply untenable. This was raised with the manageress who supposedly in turn spoke to more senior management, but the message that came back was quite simple in that the firm was not making anyone redundant, due to there being work for each and every one of them in York. Anyone that did not take up the offer of relocating to York would therefore be making themselves unemployed. Wendy indicated to them she for one would not be moving to York as it was not in her interests to do so.

One Friday evening, when I was in the Bramley Band Working Men's Club, I raised the matter with John Light and Frank Gray. After listening to things, Frank remarked that, under employment law, what the firm were attempting to do came under the 'reasonable test' and the three of us agreed that the firm's position was not consistent with employment law, given Wendy only worked fifteen hours per week.

That weekend, I discussed with Wendy the outcome of our discussion in the club and the following week, whilst working in the city centre, I went into the library by the town hall to carry out some research on the 'reasonable test' vis-à-vis Wendy's predicament. Then, armed with relevant information, I carefully put a case together on paper and Wendy appealed to an employment tribunal over what had now turned out to be her dismissal because of the issue.

On the day of the hearing, there was no representative from the employer and, having presented our case, within a short space of time the appeal panel found in Wendy's favour and she was allowed a sum for compensation, which I believe at that time, for some bizarre reason, was paid by the tax payer and not the employer! Not long after this, Wendy heard that the manageress had also lost her employment. According to Wendy, the woman in question – similarly to some of the charge hands/foremen I had worked with – had stupidly believed herself to be removed from her colleagues and closer to the actual managers. This is a common contradictory class position that baffles many people in such positions.

Being the type of person that she is, Wendy was not out of work for long and became employed with Chiltern Mills, who then were also in the city centre. It was perhaps around this time that Wendy needed a planned admission into hospital because the left shoulder that had been pinned in the early 1970s was now causing her some discomfort. Following surgery and a suitable period of recovery, she resumed work and she would tell me at the end of certain days how some of the other staff had unloaded deliveries in order to save her the shoulder discomfort. It wasn't just her shoulder giving her discomfort for, in the late 1990s, she began having problems with both her back and left hip, which would often flare up, giving her both pain and discomfort.

This job of hers too came to an end, as the store was relocated out of the city centre along with a number of staff. When she went to register as unemployed, she was asked a number of questions and the astute benefits worker decided that, whilst she had plenty of employment experience in retail work, the onset and development of problems with her back, shoulder and hip should realistically preclude her from this type of work in the future. As a consequence, she was placed upon a retraining scheme that would offer the skills for her to carry out a range of clerical and administrative duties.

After a number of months of being on the course itself with the accompanying work placements, Wendy then gained a qualification and also found a full-time position with Leeds Mental Health Services, based at St. Mary's Hospital. Not too long after this, she decided to take up driving lessons and, in due course, she passed her test on the second attempt.

Throughout the 1990s onwards, each year we had held our holidays somewhere in Scotland and I remember at work that, whenever the topic of holidays cropped up, someone would always say, "I suppose you're going to Scotland again, Colin?"

My usual reply was, "Yes, but not to the same place; Scotland is a big country."

So, in 2003, Wendy and I were once again in Scotland for our holidays, along with our two Jack Russell dogs, Tetley and Cassie. Though we had carried out a lot of camping holidays over the years, on this occasion we stayed in a cottage at an idyllic setting in Plockton, literally on the banks of Loch Carron. Having parked the car, we had a very short walk that took us over some train lines, and the front of the cottage was about fifteen paces to the shoreline. There had been occasions in the past when we both spoke about the fanciful idea of living in Scotland and the feasibility of how we would make a go of things. Perhaps we might buy a bed and breakfast (B&B) establishment. Wendy would have the main responsibility for running it whilst I had my trade as a plumber, which I could resurrect.

One day, when we were at nearby Kyle of Lochalsh and gazing into the window of an estate agent's, our attention was drawn to a B&B located north in Cannich, close to Glen Affric. We contacted the estate agent, who arranged for us to go view the property and, after doing so, we made further contact with the agent.

This conversation placed us on a steep learning curve regarding the Scottish property market. For example, estate agents and solicitors are more often than not one and the same. We were informed that, though the sale of our home in England would realise the capital required, that wasn't good enough because the money needed to be readily available due to the fact that, once your bid is accepted by the buyer, it can be a mere matter of weeks before one is moving into the new property. We would thus have to sell our house and move to Scotland with the money and rent a property until we were able to buy.

We were left with plenty to think about and at the end of the holiday, upon arriving back home, we discussed further the potential for moving to the Highlands of Scotland. In doing so, it made sense that I would return to my trade as a plumber and heating engineer, helping Wendy with the running of the intended purchase of a B&B in the evenings and weekends.

I would initially work for a firm and then, at the right time, start working for myself. Our son was now married and Teresa had set up home with her partner Simon in Armley. Added to this was the fact that we had grown tired of living in a big city.

There was also the matter of Wendy's kidney situation to take into account. Relatively recently, I had accompanied Wendy to what had been a pre-dialysis workshop, due to the fact that Wendy's kidney function was now down to around 18%. Neither of us felt concerned about this, as she was still working full time and living a full and reasonably active life.

Later that year, in 2003, we placed our home on the market. With Inverness being the proclaimed capital of the Highlands and Islands, whilst waiting for our house to sell, I began using the internet to view the *Inverness Courier* newspaper to look at potential jobs for myself along with suitable rented property.

Chapter 17

A New Chapter Begins

After some six months or so, we finally sold our house and, in February 2004, we were ready to move to Scotland. Our use of the internet had proved more than useful because we had secured a rented small bungalow at 7 Logan Way, in the village of Muir of Ord, about twelve miles west of Inverness and, besides this, I had the promise of a plumbing job with a small firm in Inverness.

We had formally said our goodbyes to family and friends and, early one Friday evening, Colin came down to help us load our belongings onto a seven-tonne wagon that we had hired for our self-move to Scotland. With the wagon loaded up, it was later that evening that Wendy and I, along with the two Jacks, set off on our new journey adventure. With the journey being one of around four hundred miles, along the way we stopped a couple of times for us to have a nap and we reached our destination mid-Saturday morning, just in time to visit the letting agent in the town of Dingwall, in order to complete relevant paperwork and collect the keys to the property. Logan Way proved to be a quiet cul de sac, with a mixture of both bungalows and houses.

Our bungalow had a detached garage so what we didn't immediately need was stored in there, with the essentials being taken into what was an extremely cold bungalow that hadn't had any heat throughout the winter months. The next day being Sunday, we drove back down to Leeds to drop off the hired wagon and collect our car from Teresa's home in Armley and then, after a short stay, we set off for our home in Scotland.

Early in 2003, we had bought a new Yamaha FJR 1300cc Sports Tourer, which had been garaged with a kind friend, Stewart McDonald. He was not only a biker but also the elder son of a former neighbour in Broad Lane Close. Indeed, it was his younger brother, Steven, who a number of years previous had knocked on the door asking Wendy if I "was playing out".

After several weeks, we had a weekend visit from John Light and Ken, his older brother, and they stayed in one of the local B&B hotels in the village. Taking my bike gear with me, I travelled back down to Leeds with them, collected the bike from Stewart and rode it back the same day to Scotland. Muir of Ord is a sizeable village and, from our bungalow, we were able to see the Wyvis mountains and, in particular, Ben Wyvis, which is one of the highest mountains in Scotland and towers over the surrounding area.

Within the first few weeks, Wendy had secured a part-time job working in the village Spar and, one week after our move, I began work with the job I had pre-arranged prior to our move.

The owner was a chap named Sean and he employed three men besides me: a joiner, an electrician and another plumber. The work was essentially refurbishing bathrooms and kitchens. On the first morning, I met my new boss, along with the others, I was given a blue T-shirt to wear that had the name of the business printed on it.

As the week progressed, each of the men gradually aired their irritations and concerns about Sean and how he ran his business. For example, contrary to what he had told me, there was no monthly bonus and one said that, at the end of one particular week, none of them received any wages. Another lad expressed his suspicion that Sean was failing to pay any income tax or National Insurance on behalf of his employees, and all of them shared a complaint that Sean daily took advantage of the fact that they all had personal ('pay as you go') mobile phones and they were expected to keep him updated on how jobs were progressing. He offered nothing towards the lads using their phones for his business purposes and one lad said that on occasion, not wanting to use his phone, he would tell Sean that he had no credit left.

One day, I had gone to the plumber's merchants and, upon hearing who I was working for, the lad behind the counter informed me that Sean had formerly been a butcher, but had run the business into the ground before declaring himself bankrupt. The lad went further, declaring that Sean was no more than a 'chancer'. By the middle of the week, alarm bells were clearly ringing, though I kept my thoughts to myself.

Having looked in the *Inverness Courier*, I rang about a plumbing vacancy and was invited to an interview on the Friday evening. Prior to moving up to Scotland. I had taken a number of photocopies of my Advanced City and Guilds Certificate, Apprenticeship Indenture and employment references, and at the interview I gave a copy of each to the manager.

I was offered a job and my new firm was called Corries and, though they appeared to be a big firm at the time, I had no idea how big. Although I had no obligation to work any notice and could have started the Monday after the weekend, I wanted to be fair with Sean, so we agreed that I work one-week's notice and then start the week after.

On the following Monday morning, with the other lads present, I advised Sean I had a new job and would therefore be working the coming week as formal notice. He immediately became angry and, at one point, he had stepped forward and his face was almost touching my face. I said nothing in return; what was the point? I was leaving and that was that. Over the course of the week, when he came on site, he made several sarcastic remarks and one of them was to the effect that "I might not bother paying you at all for this week." I didn't respond as I knew that he was holding 'all of the cards'. The end of the week came and, remaining true to his word, I received no wages.

Wendy and I had been here before with the antics of rogue employers, so I decided to ring the Citizens Advice Bureau (CAB) in Inverness and then proceeded to type out a letter, with much of the text being exaggerated for effect. I informed Sean that I had spoken to a CAB employment rights adviser who suggested to me that, in the first instance, I give him the opportunity to make amends and pay the wages owed to me. If he failed to do so, I wrote further that I had been advised that I should contact the Inland Revenue querying as to whether he had paid both tax and National Insurance on my behalf in relation to the two weeks that I had worked for him. In addition, I wrote, should I receive no satisfaction from him, then I would refer matters back to the employment rights adviser.

The letter made it clear that he had seven days to respond before I escalated matters further. Sean knew that in England I had been working for the probation service and perhaps this figured in his deliberations, along with his knowledge that perhaps he *wasn't* paying the due amounts of tax and National Insurance regarding the other lads.

Whatever it was, it worked because several days later, Sean's joiner, who also lived in our village, made an unannounced visit to our home to drop off my wages. What Sean had said to the joiner – if anything – I was uncertain, but the joiner's attitude towards me seemed to suggest that I was the in the wrong. I found this surprising because whilst working with him he too had expressed his dissatisfaction with Sean regarding certain matters. Some workers apparently accept that it is simply a fact that the employers they work for are entitled to treat them badly and at times will simply mutter the doleful refrain of "What can I do? He's the boss."

Having handed over my wages, the joiner then asked for the T-shirt given to me with the firm's name on. I said "hang on" and went back into the bungalow, returning with the item and, as I handed it to him, I said, "It was in the wash basket, but I managed to peel it off my underpants!"

Despite this hiccup, over the coming weeks we settled into things and Wendy was enjoying work in the local Spar shop, applying her experience whereby, at one point, she suggested to the owner that there should be better stock rotation to avoid wastage. On reflection, she recalls his horror at the thought of any wastage and over time she came to see him as an employer that definitely wanted his 'pound of flesh' from his employees.

We remained on the lookout for any prospective B&B's and went to visit two properties that were advertised as having the 'potential' of being turned into a B&B, but both proved unsatisfactory. One of the things that we noticed was that in the interim period between our Scottish holiday in 2003, some six months ago and now, was that the house prices had risen quite steadily.

When I began work with Corries, I learned that they were part of Tulloch Construction, which was a huge company spreading from Glasgow up and throughout the Highlands. They incorporated everything, including, plumbing, electrical, bricklaying, plastering, joinery and telecommunications, and it seemed to me that they had a stranglehold over building projects in the region. At the Corries interview, I had presented copies of my qualifications, but the manager at the time had told me that all new starters were placed on a reduced hourly rate for the first three months before then being placed on the relevant wage rate. I accepted this.

I was placed on a large hotel refurbishment building project in Aviemore and so the routine was that each morning we met in Inverness at Wilson's Plumbers Merchants at 7.00am. We would all then travel down to Aviemore in a minibus for the day's work. There were around twelve plumbers in all, with two or three new starters, such as myself. No bonus was paid, but I was pleased with how easily I picked most of the plumbing work back up.

One day, whilst we were in the *snap cabin,* one of the lads picked up on how I spoke, saying that I spoke 'like a teacher'. Years prior to this, I had realised myself that, having worked in a white-collar environment, the way I spoke had gradually changed. Social subcultures share a common language and we should not put someone down simply because they might come from a working-class background and have what might be referred to as a different language code. For, if we take them out of that environment and place them in a different one, their language code becomes more elaborate. The reverse can also be said. Work is work and, as the weeks went by, I remained content with Corries, knowing that eventually I would start my own plumbing business.

As for Wendy, the part-time work in the shop meant that for a number of hours she was on her feet and this was causing her some discomfort. Some ten years previously, following a visit to the GP over her joint problems, the doctor had told her she had what in 'lay person's' language was known as 'loose ligaments'. The medical term for this being generalised joint hypermobility. Indeed, this had been the reason for her shoulder to become easily dislocated many years previous.

After a number of visits to both our village GP and Raigmore Hospital in Inverness, she agreed to have steroid injections in the soles of both feet. In June 2004, Wendy was to celebrate her fiftieth birthday, so I carried out secret discussions with both Colin and Teresa and arranged for both of them, along with their partners, to stay in one of the local hotels for the weekend. Wendy was both surprised and delighted to see them and enjoy their company for the weekend.

Our pursuit for the right B&B was ongoing and we took frequent enjoyment in exploring the area around our home, and at the same time visiting and viewing prospective properties, but without success. Then one day we saw an advert for such a property in Glenmoriston. We went ahead and arranged a viewing and both of us immediately fell in love with the place and resolved that this was what we wanted.

The current owners were a retired English couple who intended to return to England. We submitted an offer, which they accepted, but part way through the deal we hit a couple of snags. To buy the property we needed a small mortgage of £30,000, but in due course, we were told by the bank that because the bungalow was a 'Dorran' build they would not lend on the property without a full structural survey.

'Dorran' properties were typical post-war system-built homes that were deemed as being non-traditional and very much like the pre-fab buildings that sprang up in the 1950s, meaning that essentially their construction was mainly of concrete panels. Our solicitor felt that the bank was being a little pedantic and said that, whilst there had previously been some problems with two storey Dorran homes, he was not aware of any such problem with any 'Dorran' bungalows. He went on to say that one can employ a builder to build an outer skin of bricks all around the bungalow, thus removing the status of it being a 'non-traditional' build. There was also a special paint on the market that, when applied to the external concrete panels, serves to protect against any possible deterioration. Anyway, we paid for the structural survey in order to secure the mortgage and the outcome of this satisfied the bank and they released the funds. We eventually moved into Briarbank in early August 2004.

Sitting on the edge of a forest, the bungalow was originally built as a forester's home, with the front garden being adjacent to the A82 roadway and on the other side of the road was the eastern shore of the stunning Loch Ness. Originally a two-bedroom property, a three-bedroom extension had been built on the side with an entrance door for two of the self-contained bedrooms. To enter the third bedroom, our front door was shared with guests and just off the hallway to the right was the third bedroom.

Two of the bedrooms were en-suite, whilst the third had to share our own bathroom. These three bedrooms all had electric wall heaters, as there was no central heating throughout the bungalow. The two front bedrooms had very good views of Loch Ness. Our living room had a coal/log fire, which also heated the hot water, and this was primarily used during the autumn and winter months, with the fire especially being enjoyed by Tetley the Jack Russell, as he would lay on the carpet right in front of it soaking up the heat.

To the right-hand front side of the property were a number of felled trees and we were told by the previous owners that we could cut these into logs for the fire and, in due course, I bought a chainsaw for this purpose. On the other side of the bungalow was a sizeable conservatory and to the rear there were a number of steps up the banked garden where it then levelled out. Sited at that point was an old caravan that was used for additional storage, along with a detached garage which was used to store the motorbike, garden tools and such like.

Briarbank was one of only four houses situated in the hamlet of Altsaigh, which had gained its name from the nearby fast-flowing river that ran into Loch Ness. Our nearest neighbours were Lillian and Dennis, a retired English couple who lived approximately 150 metres from us, and then some distance further on the other side of the river were Jeff and Connie. Jeff worked as a forest ranger whilst Connie was the post lady for the area. Close to them was the fourth house and this was a holiday home and, approximately two hundred yards south from us on the other side of the road and sitting on the loch shore, there was the Loch Ness Youth Hostel. All of these Altsaigh properties drew their water from the aforementioned fast-flowing river.

Travelling from the north, Briarbank was accessed on the right, just above the youth hostel, and as one turned off the road our drive was immediately on the right. On the left was a rough flat area, offering several car parking places for walkers and anyone staying at the hostel. Leading off in the opposite direction of our drive and away from the small carpark, there was a single-track road and, after around one hundred and fifty metres, Lillian and Dennis's cottage was on the right. A short distance further there was a large locked metal gate, making sure that the only traffic accessing any further up were forestry staff and ourselves. We had a key to the gate also because through it was our access to and from the garage.

Passing through the gate, and within eighty yards or so at the T junction, one would have to turn right, go up the hill a further eighty yards and then turn right, dropping down to our garage. Walkers of course access around the gate and, within a short distance, they would reach the aforementioned track, which formed part of what was then Scotland's newest walk, the Great Glen Way. If they turned left at this point, then they would head south towards the village of Invermoriston and, eventually, Fort William. Turning right then would take them to Drumnadrochit, and eventually Inverness.

The Great Glen Way was opened in 2002, with the walk beginning at Fort William in the southwest and continuing amidst some stunning scenery for 125 kilometres (70 plus miles) to Inverness in the north east. Standing with your back to the metal gate and by the T junction on the track, if you were to gaze right of the river and up on the wooded hillside, you would see a large wooden shed. That is where the water tank was situated for all of the Altsaigh residents, though a year or so later a bore hole was sunk on the loch shore to give the hostel their own water supply. How it all worked is hopefully best explained in the following paragraph.

On the river shore was a concrete bunker that held a submersible pump and, when the electronic ball valve in the hillside water tank senses that water is being drawn off due to the level in the tank dropping, it sends an electronic signal to the river-side pump, which in turn then pumps water from the river up to the tank until it is once more full. The electronic ball valve then in turn sends a message to the pump, which turns itself off. No doubt town and city folk might be aghast at homes having water direct from a river, but each year the Scottish Environment Protection Agency (SEPA) would visit and take samples from the river to assess its suitability for human consumption. We were all given a copy of the report, which always illustrated that everything was fine.

Being the only B&B in Altsaigh, we already had installed a couple of existing water safeguards. Firstly, as the water came into the building there was quite a large filter, which locals would say served to 'catch all of the prawns and shrimps'. The water would then pass through an ultraviolet filter with the aim of killing off any bacteria. All of the wastewater from the bungalow was collected in a septic tank buried in the ground adjacent to the bungalow and periodically we would have to arrange for this to be emptied. Though we felt that the B&B itself would benefit from some improvements, Wendy and I were delighted with our purchase in what we believed was a great location.

The A82 road begins in Glasgow and works its way up the western shores of Loch Lomond before passing through the desolate but exhilarating remoteness of Rannoch Moor. After that, it takes you through the stunning scenery of Glencoe, with its waterfalls and mountains on either side. Further on from that is Fort William, Spean Bridge and Invergarry, with yet more amazing scenery to delight the eye before you reached the pretty village of Fort Augustus, which straddled Loch Ness and the Caledonian Canal. There you would find Jacob's Ladder, a series of locks that would allow various sailing craft to travel both 'up or down hill', before then travelling on to their next destination.

If you continued north along the A82 a further six miles or so, you would cross the bridge that sits above the River Moriston. A short distance further is the small village of Invermoriston (inver meaning 'mouth of the river') and a further three miles north brings you to Altsaigh. North of that point, some seven miles further, is the village of Drumnadrochit, which in Gaelic means 'bridge by the hill'. Approximately another twenty miles and the A82 expires as it reaches Inverness, which acquired its city status at the turn of the millennium. The A82 road is hence one of the primary roads for tourists travelling through the Highlands.

One of the fantastic added bonuses of our location was that the bird feeders in our rear garden (of which there were a number) were visited almost on a daily basis by pine martins, a rare sight to see anywhere in Scotland, and we felt so privileged to see them so frequently. There was also a wide range of wild birds, such as greater spotted woodpeckers, tits and finches and every now and then we would catch a glimpse of a red squirrel.

That August we hit the ground running with the B&B, as it is one of the busiest months of the season, due to workers in many European countries taking their summer holidays. It was good to meet so many different people, not only from Europe, but indeed from all over the world. Speaking with many of them, although it is something of a cliché, proved that it is indeed the case that we have more in common than divides us.

Meanwhile, I was still working for Corries and would now travel the twenty odd miles each mid-week day into Inverness for 7.00am to meet up with the rest of the plumbers and then travel down to Aviemore, with us all in the minibus. Being local to the Highlands, the others may have been oblivious to the scenery that we passed during the journey to the site, but for me there appeared to be something different to see every day. Wild goats were commonly seen, and it seemed that it was only I who heard Andy remark one day that historically it was the Vikings who introduced goats to the Scottish countryside.

A chap named Jimmie was the project manager and, though we saw him each morning at the meeting point, he would then only visit the site several times a week. He always presented to me that he had the troubles of the world on his shoulders; he rarely smiled and often made short, snappy comments to individuals. Then one day another plumber told me a little of Jimmie's story.

Now a chap in his early to mid-forties, he had worked 'on the tools' for Corries for some time when, at some stage, they offered him promotion to the position of project manager. Over time, he was increasingly burdened with more and more work until he couldn't cope any longer and the poor man suffered a breakdown. After a suitable period of recuperation on sick leave, and being minded of his pending return to work, he asked the 'powers that be' in the office if, as and when he did return, he could go back 'on the tools'. A period of discussion ensued surrounding his motivation in seeking this request and he was assured that, when he *was* fit to resume work, if he agreed to retain his project manager's role, then things would be very different. He did, but as the storyteller went on, he explained that after a short period of time, he became a beast of burden once again.

I had become reasonably friendly with John and Andy, a couple of lads who started for Corries around the same time as I had. Prior to this, both had previously spent time working as pipe-fitters on the North Sea oil rigs.

John was a middle-aged chap and had moved up from Liverpool in the early 1970s to work on the rigs, whilst Andy – also middle aged – was a Highlander and, like John, he too lived at Nairn. The latter had trained as a plumber, but as with my friend John Light, he had veered into the mechanical pipe-fitting side and spent time working on the rigs.

Following the passage of time, I explained to them one day that our three months 'trial period' was now up and that we should ask to be placed on the relevant wage rate. They were rather reticent to 'rock the boat', probably due to the fact that they had previously been employed as mechanical pipe-fitters and not plumbers. So, one day I asked Jimmie about the matter and he said that he would speak to his manager back at 'the office' about it, which was in effect the chap who had initially interviewed me.

I waited a week or so and further mentioned it to him on a couple of occasions. Hearing nothing back, I decided to ring his manager direct one day. After some preliminary discussion, in which I pointed out that he had photocopies confirming that I had served a formal five years apprenticeship and that I was the holder of an Advanced Craft City & Guilds Certificate, he commented back with the startling, "Yeah I know, but yours is an old qualification."

I thought, 'well, how many times do you train and take the exam?' So, in reply I commented, "Mine was the traditional route, leaving school and becoming an apprentice for five years. What about Peter, one of your longstanding plumbers here on site? He is around the same age as me, but on the proper wage rate even though his apprenticeship route will have been the same as mine." Upon hearing this he edged around before I said, "Look, simply let me know what you intend to do and then I will know what I need to do."

I subsequently got the due wage rate, but perhaps having heard my difficulties in getting the promised increase, neither John nor Andy asked for their hourly rate to be lifted. Corries were finding it difficult to recruit plumbers simply because the supply just wasn't there, so they were using other ways.

A lad named Davy, who was in his late twenties and had spent some time in the Army, had been recruited as an apprentice. He thought I was having him on one day when, having overheard me respond to something by saying "aye", he remarked that I was learning the Scottish dialect. My response to this had been "Oh no, 'aye' is commonly used throughout Yorkshire", though he looked back at me, being unsure that this indeed was the case. Davy had at some stage been given the unfortunate nickname of 'Donkey' from the film Shrek because someone had decided that he supposedly had facial features similar to Donkey, one of the film's characters, proving that life on a building site can be cruel at times.

Another chap in his early thirties, married with a young family, had been taken on earlier that year, supposedly as an apprentice plumber, though he had previously worked in roofing for a number of years. I say 'supposedly' because he told me his story one day. Here he expressed his annoyance with what now appeared to him as the false promise of an apprenticeship because the September enrolment date for building college had come and gone with Corries never putting his name forward for the course. I didn't rub his nose in it, but clearly whilst he was carrying out certain plumbing tasks on site – at whatever low wage rate – he was merely a cheap pair of hands and I am sure that he himself felt this to be the case too.

I was talking to another plumber one day out on site when a joiner, having overheard me talking, approached me and in his Scottish accent said, "I know where you come from."

"Where?" I asked.

"Leeds."

"How did you get that"? I queried.

"I have family living in Sheffield."

This amused me and I said, "But the dialect in Sheffield, South Yorkshire, is very different to that of West Yorkshire and Leeds."

"Well, I knew you were from Leeds."

I thought trust me to bump into a Scottish joiner-cum-linguist.

As the hotel was reaching a conclusion, I was moved to some log cabin holiday homes close to the hotel that were being built. After a short time there, I was placed on a site on the edge of Inverness.

This site comprised of a number of three-storey office blocks that were being built and the site agent quickly pounced on me, complaining that it was about time that Corries had finally sent him a plumber because there was this, that and the other plumbing work holding things up. I got to work on what he had told me were his priorities, but after a few days of listening to his brusque manner whenever he spoke to me, I stood my ground. I suggested that he didn't speak to me that way and, if things weren't moving fast enough, then he should complain directly to Corries. He presented as yet another person who believed that along with promotion he must also take a number of 'nasty pills' each day because 'doggin' and bullying people is the best way to get results.

After several weeks on site, Jimmie sent two plumbers to help me. One was a young lad in his early twenties and the other an apprentice aged around eighteen. I was now in a position whereby, if there were any discussions to be had about the on-site plumbing, then the site agent came directly to me and, in addition to this, I was allocating work to the young plumber and apprentice, although with the latter I had to monitor his work and offer him guidance. In addition to this, I had to ensure that we had the necessary materials on site and so, in essence, these extra responsibilities were equivalent to the role of being a chargehand, so I approached Jimmie and asked for a supplementary amount to be added to my hourly rate. He simply laughed at what I had said, but promised to refer it on to his manager, adding that in his opinion I had no chance. The extra pay never materialised, which didn't surprise me.

One particular day, I was talking to the other two plumbers when the site agent showed and immediately started 'gobbing off' at me over something. Having listened briefly to his verbal onslaught, I met him head on, giving as much as I got. He stormed off and I remember that the two young lads had just stood there with their heads down to the ground, frozen throughout the verbal exchange, and I turned to them and said, "It's not that I've grown to be an awkward so and so as I've got old. When I was your age, I wouldn't let anyone talk to me like that."

They didn't seem convinced that you should stick up for yourself in such circumstances, and I remember speaking sometime earlier to two on-site joiners who lived at Wick, some one hundred miles north near John O Groats. These lads travelled down to Inverness at the start of each week and stayed in lodgings over the working week. They had complained to me one day about the site agent, wages and the job in general and, in return, I had said – somewhat naively in retrospect – move on and get another job. They responded by saying that there aren't any and that Tulloch's had a stranglehold on building work in the Highlands.

Corries were affiliated to the Scottish and Northern Ireland Plumbing Employers' Federation (SNIPEF), but that meant nothing to me for they were no different to many plumbing firms I had worked for down in England that had been affiliated to the JIB. I was recently talking to someone about some of my experiences over the years and the lad in question, who had neither worked in the building trade nor was in favour of trade unions, simply replied that "they won't be able to get away with things like that today."

I didn't respond, though; I simply thought, why not? It is just as easy today for a plumber, or indeed anyone, to start working for themselves for whatever reason, such as greater autonomy and the potential to earn more money by working for oneself. The problems begin to arise when that personal self-interest turns into obsessive greed and leads on to things such as the unscrupulous cutting of corners and/or over-charging. The sole trader starts to think bigger and wants more money and, as a result, starts to employ additional people, but the same greed and attitude not only prevails, but it grows. He/she now turns their attention to employees and begins to think of ways of exploiting them so as to further that greedy self-interest.

There is no effective regulatory framework for monitoring such unscrupulous behaviour and anyone complaining would no doubt simply get short shrift; as I had been bluntly told in the past, 'leave if you don't like it'. It then takes great bravery and determination to first invoke a formal complaint and then have both the strength and resolve to pursue things through an employment tribunal.

In a previous chapter, I mentioned the *Ragged Trousered Philanthropists* novel that was written by Robert Tressel, just after the turn of the twentieth century. The self and same relationships depicted in the book between employees, the chargehand, the foreman and the employer are just the same today as over one hundred years ago when Tressel wrote about his own experiences. Following the application that I had made to Inverness College in September of that year, I received a reply from them stating that I had been recruited as a supply lecturer for sociology and would be placed in their 'bank' of lecturers. It was also around this time that I decided to leave Corries and embark on building up my own plumbing business. Wendy developed some business cards for me and I began to circulate them around the area and, given that the B&B season had come to an end, she set about decorating the rooms.

Chapter 18

A Period of Establishment

One of the factors working in my favour was that in the Highlands tradesmen were in short supply and I soon began to steadily pick up a number of small plumbing jobs, whilst realising the benefits of the 'word of mouth' factor. Invermoriston is a small village comprising of the Glenmoriston Hotel, the post office-cum-general store, a craft shop and – another five hundred yards or so further on – there is a café. On the other side of the road from the post office was the village hall, a sizeable building where community events were held.

Towards the end of summer, Wendy had noticed that the village hall was to host lessons for Scottish country dancing and we agreed that this would be a good way to meet some of the local people who, as things turned out, owned a B&B like us. This did indeed prove to be an enjoyable way of getting to know other local folk and to have a *blether*, sharing experiences and allowing them to get to know their new local plumber.

One evening at the dance classes, a chap approached us and having overheard our Yorkshire accents he enquired where we had lived previously. "Leeds," we replied.

"Where abouts in Leeds?" he queried.

"Bramley," we replied.

"Me too. I used to have the fish and chip shop on the Fairfield estate." As it happens, this was less than a mile away from where we had lived. It is indeed a small world. With plumbers being rarer than 'hens' teeth' and work steadily growing, I now needed a van and, one autumn evening, I travelled over to Forres on the Moray Coast to view a Ford Escort van that was owned by a painter and decorator.

After giving it a 'coat of looking over' (no pun intended) we agreed a price and I bought it there and then. The trick now was to get it home so I ended up driving my car the forty to fifty miles home. The seller drove the van and his wife followed in their car in order to return home with her husband. A round trip for all of us of a hundred miles, but that's typical of how things work in the Highlands and you can't allow travelling distances to be an obstacle to general living. Be it work or shopping, if you aren't prepared to travel then living in the Highlands simply will not work for you.

I 'racked' the van out so that it would not only carry my tools but also hold a range of plumbing fittings in a tidy manner. As I went about doing work Cassie, our thirteen-year-old Jack Russell bitch, would be sat in the passenger seat, meaning that at lunchtime there was always a good place to walk her. Indeed, over time she became something of a novelty to folk across the area, accompanying me as I did my work. On the way home on an evening, I would often pull in by the Invermoriston village hall car park and take Cassie on a walk, which at one point would take us alongside the River Moriston and the waterfalls.

We were becoming accustomed to the more laid-back way of life. For example, shopping for many locals would always include having bit of a *blether* with the person on the cash till. And there was many a time when we were shopping in an Inverness supermarket and Wendy would comment as to how many women would leave their handbag hanging from the shopping trolley whilst they looked up and down the aisle perusing the items.

There was an implied trust with those around you, which stood in contrast to our previous experience of both living and shopping in a major city like Leeds. Such trust went much further and one day I received a phone call from someone, who I had never met, wanting a small job doing in Fort Augustus. The conversation went like this. "Yes, I can call Thursday around 9am, if that is okay," I commented.

"Yes. Okay, I won't be in, but that's not a problem."

"Oh, okay will you be leaving a key?"

"No," came the reply, "the door will be open."

"Okay, so what shall I do with the key when I have finished? Is there a place that you want me to leave it?"

And in a bemused reply the customer said "No, just shut the door".

I had another similar experience, also in Fort Augustus, when having completed several small jobs in the community rooms at the Kirk, the minister then took me around his manse to point out several small jobs that he wanted doing. He said several times that there was no rush and was at pains to stress upon me that the work could be done just when I "was passing".

Having shown me the work to be carried out in the manse, he then took me over to the detached garage saying, "Just in case we are out when you call, I will show you where the spare keys are."

Just around the corner of the door, he pointed to two sets of keys hanging on separate rusty nails and explained to me which keys were for the manse, with the others being for the community rooms. I subsequently made a point, though, of doing the work whilst the minister was at home.

In due course, I was asked to carry out a number of small jobs at the Glenmoriston Arms Hotel at Invermoriston. The hotel I learned was common in size to the hotels across the area, in that there were about ten to twelve rooms.

As one approaches Invermoriston from the south, at the centre of the village is a T junction with right leading on to Altsaigh and finally Inverness, whilst turning left would take you to the Kyle of Lochalsh, with the bridge leading over to the Isle of Skye. This particular road is known locally as 'the Skye road', and some thirty miles or so along this road is the remotely positioned Cluanie Inn.

Now, Wendy and I have fond memories of the inn because, a good number of years previously, we had stopped there on the BMW touring bike for some refreshments and, at one point, she had used the old phone box outside to ring home only to end up with a couple of inquisitive sheep hanging around the door outside which, being city folk, greatly amused us at the time.

I had quickly learned that in the Highlands plumbing outside of built-up areas such as Inverness, with its mains water and gas supplies, was very different and here at the Cluannie the cold water supply came from a nearby hillside on the other side of the road. Today, the Cluannie has significantly expanded and now incorporates a number of holiday homes and a petrol station. Travelling further along the Skye road brings you to the Kintail Lodge Hotel on the shores of Loch Duich and I spent some time here carrying out plumbing work as a number of guest rooms were being refurbished. My lunch times were spent walking Cassie down by the side of Loch Duich.

Just adjacent to the A82 was the fine Glengarry Castle Hotel set on the shores of Loch Oich, which lies between Loch Ness and Loch Lochy, and just like Briarbank, it is situated in the heart of the Great Glen. It was the 'word of mouth' factor that brought me to the hotel to carry out what turned out to be quite a number of plumbing jobs over a period of time.

On one such occasion, I was with a maintenance lad and we got talking about the gas fuelled *midgie eaters*. These seemed to be popular in the gardens of some hotels and B&B's so that guests could enjoy themselves without being bothered by the nuisance of the 'midge'. The best way to describe a *midgie eater* is that it presents itself as a vertical light with the gas bottle hidden away in a compartment at the base and at the top was a bag-like connection. Once turned on, the emissions attract the midgies and the poor things get zapped and are collected in the bag.

This said, I asked the lad if they actually worked and without saying a word he then walked over to a shed and returned with a plastic bag the size of a bag of sugar saying, "That is full of midgies." There is no doubt that many tourists that come to Scotland immensely dislike the midge, but there are ecological effects of reducing their numbers too significantly. For example, they are eaten by the native birds.

On one occasion, I was working in Fort Augustus doing a small job for an older lady and we were conversing when she explained that she had actually been born in the village. She went on to tell me of a time when, as a young girl, she had been playing with a number of friends when at one point on the surface of the loch they saw the head and neck of what they believed to be the Loch Ness Monster. Upon hearing this, I instinctively smiled, causing her to indignantly frown at me and she reiterated her point that she knew what she had seen, and I dutifully accepted her tale as fact.

One of the things that I hadn't been aware of was that, a short distance south of Invermoriston and positioned on the loch shore, there was a water treatment plant that provided fresh water for the village. I had been working in the village doing some tasks for an English couple and the chap told me that, on one occasion, when he was having a telephone conversation with a friend in Lincolnshire, who in turn had never visited Scotland. He had been explaining to his friend that the village water came from the loch. Now this conversation was taking place just several years following the widespread drought in parts of England – at one point water was transported in large tankers from the Kielder Reservoir in Northumberland down to areas of Yorkshire – and his friend, being mindful of this, asked what the villagers would do if the loch suffered from drought and dried up! We both had a laugh at this as the loch measures some thirty-seven kilometres in length with a depth of 227 metres!

I was working in Fort Augustus one day when I met a semi-retired Scotsman whom I had spoken to previously on several occasions. At one point he asked me outright if, being an Englishman, I had received much negativity from local folk for presenting as an 'incomer'. I inwardly knew that the village of Invermoriston was known by some folk in Fort Augustus as *'Little England'*, but in answer to his question I simply replied 'no'.

This completely threw him and he remarked, *"Well, I have and I'm a Scot!"*

However, he hailed from Glasgow and he believed the reason for such behaviour was due to him not being a Highlander. He commented further that some folk in Fort Augustus complain about 'the English' coming north. One apparent reason for this was down to the fact that many young locals find it impossible to get on 'the housing ladder'.

He said that one local Scot had been putting this argument to him one day and in reply he had said, "If you're selling your house and you end up with three bids, the highest one being from an Englishman, would you sell your house to him?"

The man in question gave no reply and so it was put to him, "It's because of people like you that the English are taking over the houses in place of young people!"

In response, I said that for many years down in England young people have faced similar problems, especially in rural and semi-rural areas. Owner occupiers all wish for their bricks and mortar investment to appreciate in value, but that brings with it consequences, especially when – for whatever reason – incomes nationally are being suppressed.

Positioned opposite the petrol station in Fort Augustus was the Scots kitchen café/restaurant and, in the early part of 2005, I completed for them the plumbing for a new toilet extension, along with other improvements both in the café and in the upstairs living quarters too. A lady called Sheila was the owner, but her son Hamish, along with his wife, tended to manage day-to-day matters. They were an exceptionally nice couple and, in particular, I got on with Hamish really well. Whereas Wendy and I had come to the Highlands for a more laid-back way of life, both Hamish and his wife enjoyed their holidays at Blackpool, along with its bright lights and hustle and bustle.

When it came to the time for Hamish to pay me for the work I had done, he also gave me an envelope offering a free Sunday lunch for two at the Inverlochy Castle Hotel near Fort William. As Hamish gave me the envelope, he went to great lengths to eagerly explain further that this hotel had in the past been used by some rich and famous persons, such as Sean Connery and King Hussein of Jordan. Indeed, Hamish said that for security purposes when the latter visited, the king and his entourage took over the entire hotel for the period that they were there. Given all this, Hamish went on to stress that we shouldn't simply just go, have the meal and leave, for on the contrary, he said that we should ask if we can see one of the rooms, along with taking the whole atmosphere in.

Neither Wendy or I are interested in the celebrity culture that has evolved over time but, having spoken to Wendy about the gift, we agreed that it would be a good idea to take advantage of the meal in June when it would be her birthday. As the time approached, I felt that given the fact that, because we were both busy and not able to get out on the bike as much as we would like, it would be a good idea to take a ride over to Inverlochy.

Given how Hamish had 'bigged' the place up, and being unsure of the reaction we would get if we turned up on the bike, I gave the hotel a ring to ask. I received a polite and rather diplomatic reply back saying, "That would be okay as long as you are smart and casual." That for us was a subjective attitude to adopt, so believing that our biker gear wouldn't fit the criteria, we decided to go in our old, but trusted Vauxhall Corsa.

When the day came and we drove into the grounds, we made our way to where we saw a concierge standing under a fancy canopy outside the main entrance. We stopped alongside him, announcing that we had a meal booked (and so we were not there to clean the windows) and he directed us to where the carpark was. Following us over, he opened the passenger door for Wendy and we then entered the hotel and were shown into the lounge, where we had an aperitif before being taken into the dining room.

A few moments had passed before Wendy began remarking on the expensive clothing worn by some of the other diners, whereas for me I hadn't a clue and I was ready for my dinner. Now, me being a Yorkshire lad, I must confess to feeling a little deflated at the quantity of food on the plate for the main meal, but overall the food was enjoyable and we left the dining room pleasantly full.

Whilst sitting back in the lounge, drinking tea and coffee and admiring our environment, I did as Hamish had urged me to and asked a member of staff if we could possibly see one of the rooms. A few minutes passed before a lady emerged and asked if we would like to follow her and we ascended the ornate staircase along the hall and, stopping at a room door that was unlocked, we were invited inside.

Overall, it was expectantly lavish, but one of the things that struck me most of all was not only the size of the bathroom, but the huge open fire that was no doubt lit as and when guests wished. We were given a leaflet and, looking at the room tariff rate, we saw that the cheapest room was a little over a staggering £500 per night!

As we left the hotel, the concierge bade us farewell saying, "We look forward to seeing you again." As we reached our car, Wendy and I both said to each other "Not a chance at those silly prices." We drove out of the grounds of the hotel and back into reality. Also, in the early part of 2005, I had begun work on a new house that was being built in Fort Augustus.

The potential owner, Fiona McLoughlan, was carrying out the work on a 'self-build' basis, and I was becoming aware that this was quite common in the Highlands. Effectively, this meant that she and others in the same position would open a 'self-build' account with the relevant builders and plumbers' merchants, in Inverness of course, and gain a preferential rate on items bought, akin to perhaps that of 'trade prices'.

Due to the shortage of tradesmen in the Highlands, I was becoming accustomed to hearing the occasional European accent and Fiona had recruited two German joiners to carry out the work on her house. After a couple of months or so, the wooden roof was ready to be tiled with the rest of the house almost half completed. Fiona explained to me one day that the workers and their families were invited on the Friday evening to an on-site barbecue.

The German joiners had explained to her that the tradition in their country when a house had reached the halfway mark with the fitting of the last roof beam was to hold a Richfest Ceremony, allowing the homeowners to celebrate the halfway stage of the build. In addition, the ceremony is intended to thank the people working on the house, with the homeowner having the opportunity to provide food and drinks for everyone in their honour.

The ceremony is not only a fun occasion, but is intended to bring luck and good spirits to the new home. On each of the two opposite apexes of the roof were hung a pair of boots with one symbolising the work being carried out by the workers and the other pair symbolic of the homeowners moving in. It was both an interesting and enjoyable occasion.

It was a little before the ceremony that one evening I received a telephone call from a builder named John Robertson in Applecross, Wester Ross, which is out on the west coast north of Kyle of Lochalsh. I was familiar with Applecross, and the fact that it was approximately ninety miles away, because in previous years, on several occasions, Wendy and I had camped there. His call demonstrated yet again the strength of the 'word of mouth' factor as he went on to say that he had got my name from Fiona in Fort Augustus. I was more than willing to consider the potential work, but I was also aware of the actual distance from our home.

Eventually, we agreed the following. I would be paid at my hourly wage rate for the travel time to and from Applecross. Because I did not want to neglect any local customers wanting plumbing work doing, and being mindful of the distance to Applecross, it was agreed that I would stay for three to four days at a time and lodge in a local B&B, the cost of which would be borne by the customer who we were working for. Along with that it was also agreed that I would get a packed lunch from the relevant B&B and have an evening meal in the Applecross Inn, all at the customer's expense. John was to ratify this with the customer, though he didn't envisage any problems. He would then set things up and get back to me with a start date.

Meanwhile, Wendy was busy finishing off decorating the B&B rooms and looking forward to the informal start of the new tourist season. As previously mentioned, we had the Great Glen Way directly behind us and the previous owners had explained that we would get people who were doing the walk wanting to stay overnight before setting off on their way the next morning.

We had also inherited an arrangement between Briarbank and Nick, the owner of the Glenmoriston Arms some three miles down the road in Invermoriston. Essentially, this meant that, with the emphasis on our walking guests, if they wanted a meal and a drink then I would take them down to the Arms and, later on in the evening, Nick would drive them back to the B&B. There was clear mutual benefit in such an arrangement.

Along with this, Wendy decided that she would also offer an evening meal to any guests wanting one, along with a possible packed lunch to take with them the following morning, enabling us to make a little extra cash. We soon realised that the walkers were reasonably well-organised, due to the fact they would use one of the sole trader car owners, who offered to transport their baggage (for a fee of course) from each evening's stay to the next, and so on and so forth. This meant that the walkers could enjoy some personal comforts for their evening, stay, and not have to carry lots of luggage along the walk.

We had also been made aware that during the season, when the youth hostel got busy and was full, staff would send people over to us for accommodation. For several hundred yards, both north and south on the A82, I had made a number of visible B&B signs and strategically placed them on the roadside so as to hopefully catch the attention of drivers before they passed our entrance. The front of the bungalow enjoyed good views of the loch and some evenings, when we had a full moon, the loch lit up and glistened in the moonlight. We learned too that, with the very soft water coming direct from the river, there was no need for hair or fabric conditioner.

Later that year, my sister and her husband came to visit and stayed with us for a week. After a few days, my sister Gill commented that Wendy ran the B&B in a very effective and efficient manner. But the time then came for me to begin the work over at Applecross.

The journey there, albeit long, took me through some fantastic scenery, not for the first time, as I travelled 'the Skye Road' at Invermoriston, past the Cluanie and Kintail Lodge Hotels, where from the latter one can clearly see the cluster of mountains known as The Five Sisters of Kintail. According to legend, the five sisters were the oldest of seven sisters, and the youngest two fell in love with two Irish princes who had been washed ashore during a storm. Their father would only allow these two younger daughters to marry once the older sisters had been married and so the two princes agreed to send back their five brothers once they had returned to Ireland. Although the five princes never appeared, the five sisters continued to wait until they eventually turned into mountains to extend their lonely vigil into and throughout eternity.

Onwards down the road to Dornie was the eye-catching picturesque Eilean Donan Castle, stretching out on the peninsula overlooking Loch Duich. The origin of the castle dates back to the thirteenth century and the reign of Alexander II. A few miles further and I take a right turn and follow the road that eventually leads to the village of Loch Carron, which sits along the shore of its namesake. Another ten to fifteen miles and I am at the foot of the Bealach na Ba, which is Gaelic for the pass of cattle. This very steep and winding road is predominantly single track and, until the mid-1970s, it was the only road linking Applecross to the rest of the country. Today, it is still regarded as one of Scotland's most notorious roads and climbing through some severe twists and turns eventually brings you to the summit, leading you to a maximum height of 626 metres or 2,054 feet above sea level.

About a quarter of a mile on from the summit you can pull in on the left and on a clear day look down and across admiring the breath-taking views of the stretch of water known as the Inner Sound and with it the Inner Hebridean Island of Raasay. Travelling on, I begin to move down the mountain until I pass the campsite and down to what is known as Shore Street (or simply the Street).

I turn left, past the general store-cum-post office and petrol pumps – said by locals to be the most expensive fuel in Britain due to distribution costs – then down the street. On my right lies the Applecross Bay and the Inner Sound and, in contrast, on my left are a row of houses with, in the midst of them, the Applecross Inn. The name Applecross applies to a number of small settlements in the area, such as Sand, Camusterrach and Camustiel, where I eventually found my 'digs'.

Having arrived at the B&B, I was greeted by Marjorie, the proprietor, a Scottish lady perhaps in her early seventies, who I found to be very pleasant. Once settled in, I went straight to the job to meet the builder, John, who was a local man living just two to three hundred yards down the road.

He explained that the manse was only about twelve years old, but due to a diminishing congregation, the Kirk had sold it and a Cumbrian chap by the name of Andy Collis was the new owner. John went on to express some irritation with Andy, who apparently kept badgering him about progress and a completion date. There was no broadband connection in the area and Andy kept faxing him for updates until he was told by John that the fax had run out of paper.

I was already familiar with the laid-back approach to most matters in the Highlands and, as I later observed, John was indeed a conscientious hard worker. Perhaps most English folk are not used to that approach, as opposed to the rush-rush stress and bother often associated with day-to-day work and living south of the border.

The Manse was a big house and would eventually offer four en-suite B&B rooms. The day progressed well and it was around 5.30pm when John shouted up the stairs to me that he was going and would see me in the morning. I went to the top of the stairs and said, "Okay, just leave me the key."

The reply came back, "Why do you want a key?"

"Well, you're going, aren't you? But with me being in 'digs', I'll stay until around 7.30pm."

"You won't need a key, Colin."

I went downstairs to where he was standing and he explained to me that, "When you go, simply pull the door shut and everything will be fine." I no doubt looked perplexed as my mind raced thinking about all of the materials in the house, along with some of the customer's personal belongings, not to mention my own tools.

John explained further, "The only time we lock our houses and car doors is in the tourist season; there is no crime in Applecross. If any local acted untoward, we would all simply drive them out of the village."

I was still looking bemused, but I said okay and bade him goodnight.

Over the next few weeks, I travelled back and forth to Applecross, staying at the same B&B. One morning at breakfast there was another B&B guest and, having engaged him in conversation, he told me that he was a joiner from Blairgowrie in Perthshire and he had just spent the previous day at another house in the village starting to fit a new kitchen.

We were both enjoying our cooked breakfast when he began chuckling to himself. When I queried this, he said that the chap where he was working in Applecross had said to him last night, "You won't see much of me tomorrow because I am nipping over to Inverness to do some shopping!" As the bemused joiner said, "It must be around a 200-mile round trip!" Yet that is just how it is.

The vet we used at Conan Bridge, near Dingwall, was about sixty miles round trip for us, but Marjorie had explained to me one day that they too used the same vet as ourselves, travelling some one hundred and sixty miles there and back!

On one occasion, whilst staying at the B&B, three other guests were present, a father and his two adult sons staying for a number of nights whilst they cleared timber debris and fallen trees on the nearby Applecross Estate. The three of them hailed from Aberdeenshire and had a dialect that I found very difficult to make out and understand so that I might converse fluently with them.

The hospitality of both Marjorie and her husband Ally was such that, on an evening, B&B guests had a sitting room to themselves and, on more than one evening, I felt quite embarrassed when trying to converse with these lads. After a while, when one or the other was talking to me, the other two would be smiling to themselves as if to say, 'he hasn't a clue what's being said to him'. For example, I remember the father talking to me on one occasion when he said in his strong dialect, "If where not careful we'll be toon pooches and gaping leather".

Noticing straight away my blank look, he asked if I knew what he meant. I shook my head so he explained "toon pooches" means empty pockets and "gaping leather" meant ripped trousers.

One of the highlights of such evenings was that around 9.00pm Marjorie would enter with a large pot of tea supplemented with lots of home-baking. This was shortly followed by Ally coming in with a bottle of single malt with generous tots all round. Very nice people indeed, and their son, Donnie, also lived close by, working full-time for the Highland Council whilst also being one of the local volunteer firemen. There was a small fire station in the village and, occasionally, I would see Donnie and several others in their service uniforms in the Applecross Inn following a training session.

One morning following breakfast, the Aberdeenshire lads left before me and Marjorie exclaimed, "Eee there are times when I don't know what them boys are saying."

I said, "Thank God for that, Marjorie, and you're Scottish. I thought it was just me." She went on to point out that the lads spoke in the ancient Doric dialect, which is specific to the North Eastern Scots.

A number of weeks passed by and work at the Manse was progressing well. Andy Collis and his wife had a couple of rooms set aside in the Manse and decided to come up from Cumbria and just stay for weekends, primarily to satisfy themselves about the progress. They were a pleasant couple, with the usual tale of having previously visited the area leading them to fall in love with it, something which I could wholly relate to.

Meanwhile, back home the B&B season was beginning to take off. Along with the redecoration, Wendy had also purchased new bedding and a number of accessories for the three B&B rooms. Along with family visits from Gill and Bernard, we also enjoyed separate ones from our daughter Teresa and Simon, her partner, along with one from Colin, his wife (Sara) and our granddaughters, Lauren (aged six) and Abbie (aged three).

Teresa and Simon only stayed for the weekend, though we did manage a little sightseeing with an afternoon tea at Glengarry Castle Hotel. For the later visit of Colin and his family we hired a minibus and, like with our other family guests, we took pleasure in showing them some sights and local attractions, such as a visit to Eilean Donan Castle, a boat trip on Loch Ness and a meal at the Scots Kitchen.

On the evening before Colin and his family were due to travel back, we both got stuck into a bottle of malt whiskey and the next day after breakfast, it was Sara who had to take the wheel and drive the family back home. One of the measures we had taken early in the year to generate business was to send a number of flyers to the Squires Café Bar near Sherburn in Elmete and, to some extent, this move did pay off, but in a small way.

We had a group booking for five people over a summer weekend and this just nicely filled our three rooms. Their visit was an interesting one. They arrived on three motorcycles and, as we greeted them, they began enthusing over the journey and were buzzing about certain aspects of it. I went to get refreshments for them whilst they sat by the tables in the garden.

There were three guys and two women and one of the lads explained that they were all police officers, whether that included the women, I didn't pry. In due course, I showed them to their rooms and then later in the evening I made two car journeys down to the Glenmoriston Arms for them to enjoy a drink and a meal. They were duly introduced to Nick, the owner, who would return them to Briarbank later that evening.

At breakfast that morning, they entered the dining room and in the kitchen Wendy and I could hear their uproarious laughter. I entered the dining room enquiring if they had had a good evening, which brought about even more thronging laughter. One lad said that it had been a great night topped off by the fact that Nick, who owned a VW Golf car, had crammed all of them in, with one of the lads getting into the boot! Like most people on holiday they were simply letting their hair down and out for a good time.

With today being Sunday, they had planned to have a ride over to Applecross, but after breakfast I did slightly dent things by pointing out that one of their bikes had a rear tyre that had no tread and was quite bald. I made several phone calls on their behalf to motorcycle shops in Inverness but to no avail; it was after all Sunday. They decided to go out for a ride locally and I left them to enjoy their last day in the Highlands.

It was about a week or so later that I bumped into Nick from the Arms and asked him if he recalled the episode of filling his car with the five individuals. "I do," he grinned back.

To which I replied, "Did you know that they were all police officers?"

He recoiled, looking quite pale, and said in a panic, "You're joking!"

I laughed and bringing him back down to earth said, "They thought it was hilarious and had a right laugh over it." A number of weeks later one of the 'police' couples booked in with us again for the weekend.

Eventually, the work in Applecross was completed and I knew from comments that had been made to us over the course of the project that everyone was happy with the range of plumbing and heating undertaken by myself. Indeed, John had introduced me to another Applecross builder named Duncan, who asked me if I would be prepared to carry out full plumbing and central heating on an old cottage that he had just begun work on. Duncan explained that it would be on the same remuneration terms that I had just received, and I duly agreed.

I was unaware of the actual age of the cottage that was now being completely refurbished, with the new roof already having been raised in height. The owners were a young English couple, perhaps in their early thirties, and they too had recently moved up from England.

Tim had worked down south as a mental health nurse and went on to explain that he was filling his working days carrying out some labouring and other things such as painting. In England, his wife had also worked in the health field and was now driving across the region fulfilling the duties of the community nurse. They were a nice couple and, similarly to English people moving to the Highlands, they simply wanted to get away from the day-to-day grind of town and city life.

When I commenced work on the cottage, I was able to take our Jack Russell, Cassie, as previously dogs were not allowed in the B&B of Marjorie's. Being some fourteen years old, she was happy to stay curled up in the passenger seat of my van and have a walk first thing in the morning, at lunchtimes and then in the evening before bed. Duncan's partner had a B&B that allowed dogs to stay and, at times and whilst working at Tim's, I also stayed at the Applecross Inn where they had several rooms that they let to workmen and walkers.

As the work progressed, I noted the oldie world feel of the fixtures and fittings that were going into the place. The new roof was of corrugated sheet metal, the huge Rayburn solid fuel stove was claimed by Tim after a hotel up the west coast had undergone a refurbishment; all of the light switches were round brown bakelite, which I recalled from my childhood back in the 1950s. The radiators had been sourced from Edinburgh and were of the really old school type that had undergone a respray in order to be sold on. Incidentally, I was informed by Tim that his friend's van that was used to transport these seven very heavy individual radiators from Edinburgh had struggled to get up the Bealoch na Ba and subsequently broken down – somewhat luckily – at the top of the pass.

When the used cast-iron bath was brought into the property for fitting, Tim explained that it had been found close to the sea-shore, complete with taps and waste, and the used kitchen Belfast sink when it arrived had its ceramic glazed finish completely crazed. All of this was explained by Tim on more than one occasion as the 'traditional' look and finish that he and his wife wanted for their new cottage. As a local lad himself, Duncan explained to me that he had spoken to his father about the 'traditional style' that was being sought, who in return had said that back in the day folk couldn't afford anything different and it was often 'make do and mend'.

For some time now, having worked in the area for several months and taken an evening meal in the Applecross Inn, me and Cassie had become reasonably well known. Whilst I was enjoying my meal, she too would be having her biscuits. Sometimes working behind the bar were a middle-aged (husband and wife) English couple. John Robertson had told me that the guy had worked as a headteacher down in England and went on to say that personally he didn't have a lot of time for him.

This couple had a cottage close to the Manse and one day this chap had mentioned some work that they wanted doing and could I call and give them an estimate. As requested, one day I called and I must confess that I found his manner somewhat rude. For example, after seeing the work that they wanted doing, I commented that I would work up a written estimate, to which he retorted, "Well, I don't want any silly prices!"

Now, whether this was his general demeanour, or whether it was saved for manual workers in overalls, I don't know, but I had a bad feeling and never bothered giving him the written estimate. As the work on the cottage was nearing its conclusion, Tim was talking with Duncan and he turned to me and asked when I thought the water would be turned on in order to test everything out. I replied and he came back enquiring, "Will there be any leaks?"

I answered accordingly, saying, "There are hundreds of man-made joints here. For example, just one tee piece has three and, when tightening any joints, one can over or under tighten nuts. I can honestly say that, on that basis, I don't get many, if any leaks at all." And then looking at Duncan, I asked, "Duncan, have you ever nailed a pipe?"

Replying instinctively and with a wry smile, he said, "Yes I have."

A week or so after the water had been turned on and things tested out, I received a phone call from Tim saying that there had been a leak and when a floorboard was lifted it was found that Duncan had put a nail through a water pipe! He went on to explain that Jimmie, the recently retired local plumber, had carried out the necessary repair. Generally speaking, one gets the utterly erroneous impression, especially from anecdotal comments, that the only people who make mistakes are tradesmen and other blue-collar workers.

Back at Briarbank, business was good and Wendy had prepared a number of evening meals for walkers. As the season progressed, she resolved that, whilst the extra cash from such meals was handy the added preparation, cooking and clearing up afterwards added significantly to her working day. I recall that we had a German family stay with us for several days and one morning, as Wendy cooked each breakfast and I was about to take it through to the dining room, she advised which one of our guests it was for. Each time I went in with breakfasts, the young girl, aged about twelve, would look expectantly, seemingly wishing it to be hers.

By accident it turned out that she was going to be the last to be served. As Wendy had almost finished cooking her breakfast, I got a plate and placed about four of five baked beans on it and held it quite high as I went into the dining room. I was met once more with the expectant look of someone hungrily waiting for breakfast and as I lowered the plate her face turned to anguish at what was on it. Spontaneously, the rest of the family observed matters and broke out in laughter at the prank. Having enjoyed this brief moment of hilarity, I then served her with a full cooked breakfast.

When the season was in full swing, we did indeed receive people sent over to us from the youth hostel, and on occasion we too were full and unfortunately were unable to accommodate them. Early one evening, we had a knock on the door and were met by two chaps in their twenties, who had been sent over to us by the hostel staff. We explained that we were full, but having a tent and camping equipment with them, they asked if they could camp in our rear garden, which we allowed for free. With the dining room full the next morning, Wendy cooked them two breakfasts (for a nominal charge), which they ate in the kitchen with us.

In early autumn, we had a return visitor named Peter. He had stayed with us for a week the previous year and indeed had been to Briarbank on a number of prior occasions. The previous owners had informed us about him and the one-week's stay with us was respite for him because he was a carer for his wife, who suffered from multiple sclerosis. The previous year, he had not stayed for the full week; we had then believed that he had been anxious about his wife in his absence. This year he did stay for the full term and, on his last day with us, he proudly showed Wendy and I a stag's skull with small antlers, saying that he had bought it for his wife "because she loves animals". We found this somewhat ironic that a lover of animals would want the skull of an animal that had been shot. As autumn crept in, and the B&B season fizzled out for another year, we decided to have a few days down in Leeds, staying with Wendy's mum and visiting family.

The journey from Briarbank to Leeds was a little over four hundred miles, taking several hours. Wendy's mum, Iris, lived on the Seacroft Estate in Easdale Mount. She had been an army wife for twenty-five years or so, travelling all over the world, and during that time she had given birth to ten children, three boys and seven girls. Her husband, Frank, had now been deceased for several years and, after years of being at the centre of a really busy household, she was now living alone.

Iris had been born in Leeds and, when Frank left the Army, she had been instrumental in wanting to return to the city, and in particular Cross Green, where her own parents were still living. Her house in Seacroft was a three-bedroom semi-detached council house that, like thousands of others, had been built in the immediate post-war period and was of concrete panel (or 'systems built' type) construction.

Over the next couple of days, we visited Teresa and her partner, Simon, at their home in Armley, and also Colin and his family who had moved from their home in Pudsey and were now living in the village of Ackworth, near Pontefract. With an enjoyable short break behind us, we set off on the long journey back to the Highlands.

Along the way, Wendy started to feel increasingly unwell and became cold and shivering. The next morning, we arranged a visit at the doctors' surgery in Fort Augustus and, after seeing Wendy, Doctor Skeogh wanted to call an ambulance there and then to take her to Raigmore Hospital in Inverness. Wendy refused and we went home, collected some of her things and then left for the hospital, where she was admitted and eventually diagnosed as suffering from 'an infection'. She spent two weeks in hospital and was treated with intravenous antibiotics, though the origin of the infection was never discovered.

Unfortunately, the hospital antibiotic given to her was Amoxicillan, and this can give the severe and unwanted side effect of joint pain. Given her longstanding problem of 'loose ligaments' (that effects ten percent of the population), much of her joint pain returned and sometime later, following several visits to the doctor's, she was referred to the Belford Hospital Fort William, where she received a steroid injection in her left hip.

Still in the winter period, and within a couple of months, Wendy was readmitted back into Raigmore Hospital, again feeling really unwell. Once more, we were informed that it was another infection, but this one proved more devastating than the previous one. After a four-week hospital stay, Wendy was discharged with chronic kidney failure.

The consequence of her condition was that she was left feeling constantly fatigued and tired. Almost at the same time as her hospital discharge, I began experiencing a swelling and pain in my right knee. Having spoken to my sister Gill and making her aware of this, she came up from Leeds to stay and help out with household tasks.

With the swelling and pain in my knee not improving, one day the three of us visited Raigmore A&E, where the doctor I saw explained to me two options. Firstly, I could elect to be admitted and the following day I would have minor surgery on my knee in order to drain what was described as a bursitis. Alternatively, his second proposal was that, here and now, he could make a small incision in my knee and attempt to squeeze out the excess fluid. I elected for the latter option and left with the knee strapped and the instruction to take one month off work and also to attend the doctors' surgery twice a week to have the knee monitored and re-bandaged.

On one occasion whilst at the surgery, Doctor Skeogh spoke to me about the stoicism displayed by Wendy and, in response, I commented that whilst she was indeed stoic she would often resist receiving help when she really knew that it was needed. Meanwhile, Gill had initially come to stay for one week, but made it an extended stay of two weeks. It was a selfless undertaking for at the time, Steven, her husband's youngest brother, was terminally ill with cancer.

As winter passed and we moved into spring, we began to get a trickle of B&B guests and Wendy struggled. Whilst cooking breakfasts she would have to leave the kitchen to be physically sick. After some discussion, we both agreed that the B&B was no longer tenable. Generally speaking, we moved to Scotland both acknowledging that, to become established and have feelings of being settled with our new way of life, it would take several years. Now a little over two years since our move, I myself had been getting homesick and, due to these feelings, I now suggested that we should sell up and return back to England.

However, Wendy wanted to stay and spoke of a bungalow for sale in Fort Augustus, suggesting that we go to see it with the potential of moving there. However, my mind was made up and, before we moved to Scotland, we had both agreed that if one of us wanted to return at any time then that is what we would do. Over time, it was a decision which has caused me much regret, but one that I have had to learn to live with.

The decision was taken and Briarbank was put on the market for sale. After the tranquil setting of Altsaigh, neither of us wanted to go back to living in the vast concrete jungle of a city, with all that it entails, so we decided to look at the potential of buying a property somewhere around the Ackworth area, where our Colin was living with his family. We wanted a bungalow property and prices in this area were around £10,000 cheaper than Leeds.

One weekend we travelled down from home to view several potential properties and, driving around the areas concerned, there was more than one occasion that we both glanced at each other implicitly thinking 'this is so different to what we have back home'. There was no snobbery intended, but it was the stark contrast to what we had become accustomed to at Briarbank and what was on offer with our contemplated move. Yes, the area was semi-rural, but still a very different setting, with a greater populous, along with much, much more bricks, mortar and concrete, as opposed to open spaces, trees and other greenery.

Having viewed a bungalow in Upton, once we arrived back home, we made an offer, which was accepted. I had begun work on a new build house in Applecross, but I had to inform the owner of the reasons why I would not be able to continue with the work. Locally, having mentioned to some people that we intended moving back 'down the road', we found that the same word of mouth that had quickly brought me plumbing work some two years earlier was now having the opposite effect, with work gradually drying up.

With the sale of Briarbank going through, we had made enough in order to pay the small mortgage off, buy the bungalow in Upton outright and still have a few quid left over after moving costs. We recruited the services of a small sole trader removal company at Tore (near Muir of Ord) and it was agreed that he would also carry the motorbike and attach a trailer in order to bring my plumbing van to what was to be our new home in Upton.

The evening before the day we were scheduled to move, Wendy went to attend a knock on our front door. After some conversation she came back into the living room and explained that it had been Doctor Skeogh. She had been passing down the road and stopped in order to speak with Wendy and wish her the best of luck. What a nice gesture, though I knew she had an admiration for Wendy.

Chapter 19

As One Door Opens, Another Slams in your Face!

On 6 August 2006, we bade farewell to Briarbank and the Scottish Highlands and began our journey back 'down the road' to what was going to be our new home in the ex-mining village of Upton. Because of Wendy's more or less constant fatigue due to her condition, Colin and his wife Sara kindly offered to help us unload the removal van and then sort things out into some initial kind of order in the bungalow.

The detached bungalow was built around 1990 and is situated in a quiet cul de sac, offering two bedrooms, a kitchen, living room, bathroom and full central heating. The outdoor garage was handy for storing my motorbike, plumbing materials, tools and the other usual stuff that one finds in garages. Upton is a former mining community, with the mine opening in 1926 and closing in November 1964, due to an assessment of it being unsafe. There is a large council estate that is commonly referred to as 'the pit estate', as many former miners and their families were housed there.

The village is situated in the south eastern corner of West Yorkshire and, at one time, due to past changes in electoral boundaries, it had previously formed part of the county of South Yorkshire. In the 2001 census, it had a population of 3,542 people. Before leaving Briarbank, we had booked a two week holiday in the Southdown Hotel at Filey. The hotel was then (it is now holiday apartments) positioned overlooking the beautiful Filey Bay, and after a week or so of settling into our new home, we headed off for our holiday.

We had with us our Jack Russell bitch, Cassie, who was now fifteen years old. Poor Tetley had suffered a stroke within a couple of days of us moving to Scotland and had slowly deteriorated over the following two years. He had sadly undergone euthanasia whilst Wendy was in hospital and I still recall the long forty-five-minute drive to the vets at Conan Bridge. Once there, the vet, who had been aware of the dog's slow deterioration, commented politely that we had perhaps kept him longer than we should have done. Tetley was the second dog over a number of years that I had the sad task of carrying out the final act by taking him for euthanasia.

With some difficult times of late behind us, Wendy and I were now looking forward to our seaside break before fully settling down to living in Upton. Filey is a place that Wendy and I have never tired of over the years, with its beautiful large sandy bay, with the very rocky Filey Brigg to the left, whilst on the right one can catch a glimpse of the seaside resorts of Primrose Valley, Reighton Gap and Flamborough Lighthouse in the far distance. Many years ago, I heard that Filey folklore will have it that the rocky Brigg that stretches out far into the sea is actually the fossilised remains of a dragon that was slain by a local butcher who went by the name of *Billy Biter*.

Within a couple of days of being in the hotel, it soon began to resemble the 1970s comedy sitcom *Fawlty Towers*. The owners were a middle-aged couple and, whilst 'Sybil' was always polite and diplomatic her husband, 'Basil', was the complete opposite.

Due to the number of guests in the hotel, there were two breakfast sittings, and upon their arrival, people were given an allotted time for them to enter the dining room. One morning, heads turned in feverish expectation as 'Basil' strode quickly through the room like a man on a mission, before stopping at a table where he brusquely told the family sitting there that it was not yet their time to have breakfast!

On another occasion, I lifted a cereal dish only to startle a silverfish insect which went scurrying about in the dish below. As we were leaving our room one morning, we noticed water coming through the ceiling and 'Sybil', somewhat pointing out the obvious, said that the water was coming from the room above and that they had probably overfilled the bath. She promised to sort things out before we returned to the hotel.

All of the guests that we spoke to had arrived at the same 'Fawlty Towers' analogy as we had, especially when in the early hours of one morning we were all awoken by the noise of the fire alarm sounding. 'Basil' and 'Sybil' ushered guests outside of the hotel whilst they went back inside to investigate matters. Many of us standing there began to giggle, perhaps inappropriately given the circumstances, but we simply saw this as one of a number of continuing farcical events taking place in what presented itself as a surreal sitcom, with ourselves as the willing actors. Fortunately, it had been a false alarm and we were told that we could re-enter the hotel and go back to our beds. The two weeks came to an end and the fun and frolics were over and it was back to our new home.

With the plan being that I would work for myself as a plumber, I placed an ongoing advert in the local newspaper, organised some business cards, placing them in a number of local shops in Upton and the adjacent villages of South Kirkby and South Elmsall. Added to this, having selected certain localities, I tramped the streets, posting cards through people's letter boxes. As a result of my collective efforts, work began to come in and things looked promising.

In the autumn, Wendy joined a twice-per-week keep-fit class at the nearby village hall and, though it was for the over-60s she was allowed into the group. She found the people there very friendly and inviting, but looking back over the years, and perhaps due to her gregarious nature, she has always got on well with folk.

Once again, she was reconnected with routine scheduled appointments at the Renal Outpatients Clinic, St. James Hospital in Leeds. Very early in 2007, I was becoming concerned that her health was deteriorating, but as usual she shrugged things off, saying that she was okay. Fortunately, in early February 2007 she had an outpatient's appointment and the consultant, seeing that she was clearly presenting as unwell, strongly urged her to be admitted into hospital there and then. Following some resistance, she reluctantly agreed.

During her first week in hospital, we were told that the cause of the problem was an infection, though they were unsure about the actual cause, but as was the case in Raigmore Hospital, she was given intravenous antibiotics. Matters deteriorated around the end of that first week and, one evening when I visited, she had been moved down the ward into a single isolation room, due to the fact that she had now been diagnosed as having the added and worrying problem of clostridium difficile (commonly referred to as C-Diff, one of several hospital 'super bugs' that are highly contagious and life threatening).

C-Diff was the cause of death of the older lady who had previously occupied that room. One of the symptoms is severe diarrhoea and thorough cleanliness and hygiene are essential. At one point, Wendy reported a staff nurse for not washing his hands both before and after he had entered her room in order to treat her.

During her first week in hospital, I was given a floral gift to take into her from the ladies at the keep-fit class, along with a gift of some flowers that a neighbour had bought for her. Both gifts were extremely kind gestures. My daily routine amounted to working, coming home in a timely fashion, taking Cassie out for a walk, feeding her and then driving the twenty-five miles or so into Leeds for visiting time at 6.00pm. I was arriving home around 9.00pm and, after ringing family and close friends to offer an update, at around 10.00pm I had an hour or so to myself before going to bed.

Ten days in to Wendy's admission to hospital, my sister Gill enquired how I was coping and invited me to go to her home in Leeds prior to visiting at the hospital, so that I could have a cooked meal with her and Bernard. After two to three weeks, Wendy was still in the isolation room when early one morning I received a telephone call from one of the nurses at the hospital.

She explained that Wendy was extremely upset and wanted to come home immediately. She handed the phone to Wendy, whom I have never known to be so distraught. When I had finally managed to calm her down, I said that I would come down to St. James's straight away.

I had a job arranged and I rang to rearrange it, but the chap wasn't amenable to that and gave me some grief saying that if I didn't turn up at the previously agreed time – because "this is business" then I should not bother at all. I promptly made my way to Leeds and arrived there around 9.30am.

When I arrived, Wendy and I had a chat in which she shared with me some of her concerns. Later, around lunchtime, I spoke to the doctor when she came around. I explained to her that Wendy was unable to lie in bed due to extreme discomfort and hence the chair that she was now sat in also had to double up as a bed and, in addition to that, through the night time staff were not giving her any relief for breakthrough pain.

Throughout, Wendy simply sat there saying not a word, and I spoke to the doctor saying, "She is now withdrawn and being non-communicative because no one has been listening to her." That afternoon, Wendy was taken to a treatment room and underwent a procedure to drain excess fluid from her lungs and the doctor said that she had left a message for night staff to provide her with medication for breakthrough pain.

That evening, as 8.00pm arrived signalling the end of visiting time, she didn't want me to leave and uttered that she wanted to come home. Staff allowed me to stay an extra thirty minutes, but when the time came it was very upsetting having to finally leave her. The very next day she was moved into the High Dependency Unit (HD Unit) and informed that she would have to begin haemodialysis, where she would be hooked up to a dialysis machine in order to have her blood cleaned and the excess fluid removed from her body, due to the fact that her kidneys were no longer functioning. In essence, this was now the beginning of her requiring dialysis three times per week.

Following a stay in the HD Unit, she improved to the extent that she was once again placed on the general renal ward, but yet again there were problems leading to a deterioration in her health, and she went back into the HD Unit for more intensive care. After a period of time, she improved once more, and I remember a visit of mine coincided with that of the consultant, who said among other things that during her stay in hospital there had been times when they thought that they might lose her.

Once more, she went back onto the general ward and, together with her regular dialysis sessions, she began to improve to the point that she was ready to begin eating properly, but the problem for her now was – according to her – the ghastly hospital food on offer. So, to overcome this and following discussions with Gill, the 'meals on wheels service' was effectively launched.

Now this worked as follows. Gill and Bernard always had a cooked meal around 5.00pm and a meal was now also 'plated up' for Wendy, which was then sealed as appropriate and wrapped in towels and such for insulation. As I finished my meal, I then set off straight away for the hospital to coincide with the start of visiting. Indeed, on a couple of occasions when I delivered the food to Wendy, she found it too hot! This went on for a couple of weeks or so and on the weekends I prepared a meal for her at home, placed it in one of the panniers on the motorbike and took it into Leeds.

The hospital never did find the cause of the 'infection', though because she also has polycystic liver, with several large cysts, they suggested that one may have bled for some reason, thus causing the infection. Following a visit to the Liver Unit, she was informed that to surgically remove any of these large cysts could be problematic and, at this moment it time, it would be best to leave things as they are.

Over the period that she was in hospital, several things still stay in my mind. Firstly, one evening upon my return from visiting, I noticed that someone had mowed the front garden and luckily days later I was told which neighbour it had been, thus enabling me to thank him. Secondly there were times when I wished that my Mam and Dad were still around for me to talk to which was perhaps, on reflection, an indication of how low mentally I was feeling. Still, at home I had our dog Cassie for company and I recall on one occasion sitting on the settee feeling very low. Cassie clearly sensed my mood and came up to where I was sat, wagging her tail and nuzzling me with her nose. It is really true that dogs are fantastic companions.

However, the poor dog fell ill around this time and, following a visit to the vet, I was told that she most likely had a benign lump in her bladder, causing her to frequently feel the need to wee. Oral antibiotics were prescribed and, whilst they worked, periodically there was a showing of blood in her urine causing her to need a further visit to the vet for further antibiotics to combat any infection.

Following ten weeks in hospital, Wendy was finally discharged, but now there was an ongoing need for her to attend St. James's Dialysis Unit three times per week, to undergo four hourly sessions of dialysis. This was a temporary arrangement as eventually she was to attend the Dialysis Unit at Clayton Hospital, Wakefield, due to it being closer to home.

To facilitate the dialysis process she had what was referred to as a Tesio line surgically placed in her neck, and this had two plastic tubes for connecting up to the machine. Again, this was a temporary measure as routinely haemodialysis patients would use a fistula, which necessitated another surgical procedure (usually in the arm), linking a vein to an artery. In place of tubes, once at the dialysis unit needles were inserted into the fistula.

Because of her hospitalisation with a serious illness, Wendy was told that it would be twelve months before her body had fully recovered and only then would she be placed on the transplant waiting list. Moreover, to allow room for any potential future transplant, she would have to undergo elective surgery to have one of her enlarged polycystic kidneys removed. Once she had been transferred to Clayton Hospital, she began by undergoing dialysis every Monday, Wednesday and Saturday mornings, starting at 8.00am and finishing at noon. Upon her return home, she would lay on the settee for a couple of hours or so to recover.

Because the ambulance transport service could arrive anytime between 7.00 and 8.00am, Wendy rose around 6.30am. Other dialysis patients were collected either before her or alternatively on the way to hospital. Over time, she became stressed with this arrangement, as sometimes the ambulance would call around 7.00am and at other times it was just before 8.00am, causing her a degree of anxiety and, on multiple occasions, she would ring the dialysis unit to see if she was being collected.

Other matters added to her anxiety too. However, before discussing these, let me explain that dialysis not only removes toxins from one's blood, but also excess fluid, because having no kidney function leaves one unable to pass urine. Wendy sought advice from the hospital nutritionist and broadly adopted a 'renal diet'. So foods such as bananas, which have a lot of potassium, were not eaten and potatoes were brought to the boil, the water along with its potassium content emptied out, fresh water added and then brought back to the boil and served. As a dialysis patient, one is only allowed one litre of fluid a day, and this includes not only tea/coffee, but also items such as gravy, mashed potato and in effect anything else that will reduce itself to liquid in one's body.

Initially, there were times when Wendy would come home following dialysis absolutely tired and 'washed out'. She was advised that this was because of her blood pressure being so low and this was down to the dialysis machine being erroneously set to remove more fluid from her body than was necessary. This happened on quite a number of occasions, though when she became aware of the reasons for her low blood pressure – and gauging the amount of fluid she needed to have removed – she would ask the nursing staff to set the machine accordingly. There were a number of occasions when she had to really assert herself because some staff felt that they knew best and, on occasions when they had not listened to her, she came home completely washed out with low blood pressure. Some years later at an outpatients' clinic, the consultant sat before us made the point to a medical student, that was also present, that renal patients have a very good knowledge and understanding of their medical condition and, as such, can manage their condition well.

Another matter that concerned her was the routine way in which some dialysis staff would tell her and other patients how much a medical procedure that was being given to them was costing the National Health Service (NHS). As Wendy and I would agree, no one chooses to be ill, nor do they wish to be treated as a charity case tugging their forelock in gratitude for the treatment given to them. It made me mindful of the words of Oscar Wilde when he said, "Today we know the cost of everything, but the value of nothing."

In order to eliminate the risk of infection, The Ambulance Transport on offer was dedicated to carrying dialysis patients only. However, on a number of occasions when Wendy and her dialysis colleagues were being collected at lunchtime, the driver had previously picked up a general hospital patient in order to drop them off at *their* home along the way. This concerned patients and Wendy in particular as, on more than one occasion that year (2007), she was hospitalised for a short period due to an infection, and having the Tesio line in her neck placed her at a greater risk of infection than a fistula would.

We are both similar in ways and Wendy too likes to know relevant matters so that she can both understand and exert as much control over things that affect her. Within the first couple of months of her hospital discharge, I was still feeling really low, so I made a teatime appointment to see our GP.

I began to explain to him what had been happening and how I was feeling when, after a while, I noticed him glance a number of times at the clock on the back wall above me, so I said, "We'll leave it at that then, you must be busy." I began to rise out of my seat.

"No, no, it's okay," he replied.

"No, it doesn't matter," I said. "You keep looking at the clock on the wall." I did stay, but only for the time it took him to write out a prescription for medication to treat my depression. I was disappointed because I felt that a GP was the one person I could share my feelings with and get a professional response from due to the adoption of a genuine interest. Again, I was reminded of this false social illusion that work roles can be simply defined as either professional or non-professional.

As people do, Wendy and I continued on with life as best we could and, later in the summer of 2007, due to the restrictions on our ability to have any meaningful holidays, we decided to look at buying a static caravan on the east coast, around Scarborough or Filey. For some bizarre reason, around this time we received a 'flyer' in the post advertising a camp site the other side of Hull and, having discovered that Scarborough Hospital had no dialysis unit, we ended up buying a static caravan approximately forty-five minutes east of Hull at a small village called Kilnsea.

Kilnsea sits at the top of Spurn Point, which is at the mouth of the Humber Estuary. The site itself had been a military base until the late 1950s, when it was sold and became a caravan and holiday site. Indeed, there were then and still are some remaining concrete fortifications that rest on the beach. This coast, as we would eventually find out, is the worst coastal area in Europe for erosion. Local leaflets tell the stories of past villages that were taken by the sea. The reason that, in the nineteenth century, the new Withernsea Lighthouse was built set back from the coastline and in the centre of the town due to the knowledge then about the devastating effects of coastal erosion.

The purchase of the static caravan gave us both a psychological lift and Wendy eventually was able to change her dialysis days to Mondays, Wednesdays and Fridays, thus allowing us, as and when, to go to the caravan Friday evening and come back on Sunday. The fact that the site was not overly commercialised was to our liking, along with the fact that there was easy access onto the beach.

Early in 2008, Wendy elected to go into hospital to have one of her enlarged kidneys removed. Prior to this happening, the dialysis unit at Clayton had acknowledged the serious nature of the surgery and the discomfort Wendy would have to endure travelling to Wakefield three times a week in an ambulance minibus, so they assured her that on dialysis days she would be collected by an ambulance car. However, following her hospital discharge, the day after she was due for dialysis, instead of being collected by car, it was the ambulance minibus that turned up. Over the next few days, both Wendy and I spoke to dialysis staff, but to no avail and she was left with a lot of anxiety, further compounded by the ongoing issues, comments from staff regarding costs of treatments, general hospital patients sharing the transport, and the ever-present risks of infection.

Once fully recovered, she was eventually placed on the transplant waiting list, offering some glimmer of hope for the future. Following our attendance at an annual general meeting of the St. James's Kidney Patient Association (KPA), I became involved with their efforts at monitoring and promoting renal patient services via periodic meetings between Yorkshire ambulance service managers and renal managers meetings. The KPA members were an interesting mix of individuals on dialysis, transplant patients and carers, such as I, and through my involvement I gained further insight and awareness of relevant matters.

At the end of the year, we attended the KPA Christmas party, held in the Thackray Museum, St. James' Hospital, and then in January of the following year we went with them as a group to see the pantomime at the Alahambra Theatre in Bradford, where the star of the show was the Yorkshire comedian Billy Pearce. It was a real joy to see Wendy laughing and thoroughly enjoying herself, and I later mentioned this to our Teresa, who subsequently contacted Billy relating this to him. He sent a photo of himself along with a really kind message.

As 2007 came to an end, we both reflected on the purchase of the static caravan and duly agreed that it had proved to be a really good purchase, enabling us to get away and have some brief, but welcome respite. In the early part of 2008, Angela, Wendy's youngest sister, then living at Amble, Northumberland, explained to her that there was a new litter of Jack Russell puppies in Hadston, a nearby village, and asked if we be interested.

We made the journey to view the puppies, selected one and several weeks later Bobby became a new addition to the household. Cassie was now getting older and one day when I was walking her Ross, the young lad who lived over the road from us, came across to us and, being an inquisitive twelve-year-old, said, "How old is Cassie now?"

"Seventeen," I replied.

He queried further, "So what's that in human years?"

Using the formula of one dog year equating to seven human years, I carried out the calculation and replied, "A hundred and nineteen years old."

Clearly having lost his train of thought he excitedly exclaimed, "*A hundred and nineteen years old, who's had her all that time?*"

I explained to him his error, bade him farewell and walked on chuckling to myself. Several months later, Cassie who was now also taking medication to prevent her from fitting, refused to eat anything, despite trying to tempt her with all manner of tasty food and, after a discussion with the vet, it was agreed that she would have to be euthanised. For a number of months before this, she had slept in her basket at my side of our bed because through the night she would need to go outside for a wee. With her gone, I hadn't realised how lightly I had slept listening for her to stir through the night so I could take her out and into the garden.

I had managed to build a plumbing business up and, if work ever went slack, I simply went out tramping the streets in nearby villages posting business cards, and this appeared to work quite well. I was able to contact the relevant City and Guild authorities and they sent me a number of large stickers that I placed on my van. My City and Guilds Certificate also enabled me to become a member of the Chartered Institute of Plumbers and Heating Engineers and again I was sent a number of their stickers to place on my van. I was able also to use their logo on my business stationery, along with that of the City and Guilds.

Through the KPA, Wendy and I became aware that dialysis patients could have, given the available facilities, dialysis away from home, thus allowing for us to have the potential of a prolonged holiday. After some initial difficulties in achieving this, we managed to get two weeks holiday at the caravan, though this would mean Wendy having to travel back into Hull for her dialysis at Hull Royal Infirmary each Monday, Wednesday and Friday.

I drove her from the caravan into Hull for the first session and waited in the car for her, sometimes going for a walk before we both drove back to the caravan. Following two sessions, she decided that she would not seek dialysis away from home again because for her it wasn't like having the normal holidays that, prior to her condition, we had previously enjoyed. Therefore, never again did we seek to arrange dialysis away from home.

Somewhat disconcerting to us at least was the fact that the private company that had won the hospital contract for running the dialysis service was being openly criticised by its NHS renal staff for using inferior equipment. And so, for the rest of the year, we used the caravan when possible from Friday evening until Sunday. In any event, Wendy often remarked that come Sunday she knew that she needed dialysis the following day. On occasion, our Colin's two daughters, Lauren, the eldest, and Abbie, would spend the weekend with us and Gill and Bernard would make use of it also on weekends when we ourselves were not going. The year passed by and we moved into 2009 with still no sign of a transplant for Wendy.

At times, she would get anxious and frustrated over the dialysis transport being late, being told the cost of treatments such as a periodic iron injection and so on. The fact is that Wendy is wholly independent and does not like to rely or be beholding to anyone, and that is a fundamental part of her inner strength and self-discipline. It was perhaps around this point that I rang the dialysis unit and spoke to a staff nurse to explain that Wendy was feeling quite down, and I felt that they should know.

In fact, we were both quite low and I myself visited the GP once again and was prescribed more medication for depression. We pressed on and I spent some time moving the kitchen from the front of the bungalow into the small second bedroom at the back, because that is where we get the sunshine, not only in summer but also over good days in winter.

We had French doors fitted in the new kitchen also. I fitted a new combination boiler, all new radiators and eventually moved the living room also from the front to the rear of the bungalow, with the bedroom now moved to the front. Around August 2009, Wendy's sister, Angela, rang again to say that there was another litter of Jack Russell puppies at the same address in Hadston village, so again we journeyed up there and, as before, we selected this time a black and white bitch, collecting our newly named Suzie several weeks later. Once again, we now had two Jack Russell dogs in our home, creating puppy mischief and giving us both pleasure.

Since commencing dialysis, Wendy had undergone at least two surgical procedures in order to introduce a fistula to her arm, thus enabling the infection-prone Tesio line to be removed. Ideally, a working fistula provides a higher blood flow in the radial artery, but due to her having small veins, these had in a short space of time broken down and, on one occasion, she experienced intense pain during one of these procedures.

Sometime in late 2009, Wendy and I began to have conversations about the possibility of me donating one of my kidneys to her. We were both aware that early in the year one dialysis patient in her mid-forties had received a donated kidney from her husband, but within a matter of hours a blood clot had resulted in it killing off the kidney. The lady had subsequently spoken to Wendy expressing their devastation and that both she and her husband were now not only both clinically depressed, but having to recover from major surgery knowing full well that the intended outcome had not been achieved. We were also aware of a middle-aged chap whose kidneys had for some reason failed when he was eleven years old. Over the years he had undergone four failed transplants, one of which had been from his brother. Alongside the negatives such as these, there were also positives in that we had met one man at the outpatients' clinic who received his transplant in the early 1970s and another lady who was approaching the twenty-fifth anniversary of her transplant.

The fact of the matter is that a donated kidney – be it from a live or deceased person – is only seen medically as another form of dialysis with no 'forever' guarantee attached to it. We decided to press ahead and approached the Transplant Co-ordinators Office at St. James's Hospital. The first test was to do with compatibility and this we passed.

Over the early months of 2010, there were a number of further tests, which we passed. One such test concerned checking both of our hearts and in the unit where this was carried out the clinician I was with complained to me that managers were taking their time to appoint a new receptionist, and as a consequence medical staff like him had been placed on a rota to carry out reception duties. I wasn't too surprised by this because as part of the drive for efficiency savings managers either delay or don't bother recruiting new staff who might leave. Around this period Wendy finally underwent a successful surgical procedure to have a fistula created in her right arm. However, one has to wait a period of time for the fistula to strengthen prior to its use. The penultimate piece in the testing jigsaw puzzle was a joint meeting with us, a renal consultant, renal surgeon and a transplant co-ordinator.

Most lay people think of the need for compatibility and when we asked about the solidity of ours his answer was, "Well, when people ask this question, I use the analogy of cars and, for you, well you're not the Rolls Royce and you're not the Mercedes, but you are the Mondeo compatibility level, which we deem good enough to proceed with."

One further question was in relation to the work that I do and, following surgery, how long I was likely to be off work. He explained that whilst the surgery would be keyhole, to retrieve the kidney they would have to make an incision of about two to three inches in my stomach muscle. The stomach muscle would be stitched, but he explained that for manual workers, such as myself, resuming work too soon could result in a hernia caused by the stitching tearing open. To prevent this occurring, most manual workers needed to be off work between three and six months.

The final piece in the jigsaw was a visit to a designated counsellor, whose role in the transplant process was in relation to the Human Tissue Act. One Saturday morning we travelled to York to see a chap who turned out to be both a church minister and an anaesthetist. Wendy met with him individually first and then it was my turn, but at the end of our meeting, he politely determined that I was not fully aware of the seriousness regarding some of the implications brought about by undergoing such surgery. He said that he would ring me sometime during the following week and once again ask me certain questions and, if my response was judged again as being insufficient, then he may stop the transplant operation going ahead.

When I informed Wendy, we were both panicked by this and, as I went to work on the Monday morning, she rang the transplant co-ordinator at the hospital. She rang me later that morning to say that later that day a meeting had been arranged for us at the hospital to discuss matters with a renal surgeon. When we met the surgeon and discussed the questions that had been put to me two days earlier, I took the opportunity to write down the response from the surgeon.

We offered our grateful thanks and left waiting now for the counsellor to, as and when, call me later in the week. It was about two days later that, whilst working, I received the dreaded telephone call. I asked him if he would hold for a moment whilst I went to my van, not revealing that in there I had the renal surgeon's response written down on a piece of paper. The questions were asked and this time he was happy with the answers that I gave him. With the formal side of matters now concluded, it was arranged that, following our discharge from hospital, I would initially stay with Gill and Bernard. Wendy's sister, Angela, along with her niece, Elaine, would look after the dogs and be there for when Wendy was discharged. Moreover, because neither of us was to lift anything heavy – a kettle included – they kindly agreed to stay until we both had recovered, which would be approximately six weeks. In due course, the day arrived, and we finally got our date for admission.

Chapter 20

'From me to you, to you to me'

On Thursday 9 May 2010, we were both admitted into the Renal High Dependency Unit at St. James's Hospital in Leeds and underwent preliminary measures pending the surgery that was to take place early the following morning. The following day saw an early-morning visit from our daughter, Teresa, and Wendy's sister, Pamela, before it was time for me to head off first for surgery, in advance of Wendy.

The transplant was a success, with the consultant telling me later that Wendy now had a better kidney function than myself. The strangest thing for her was having been self-disciplined over the past three years plus in trying to keep to only one litre of fluid a day, she was now being told to drink copious amounts of water in order to get her new kidney to function properly.

Whilst I was getting over the effects of the morphine, I kept hearing her talking to both unit staff and family and friends on the phone, saying how well she was now feeling – and she certainly sounded good. The following Monday, I was discharged and, as planned, I went to stay with Gill and Bernard, who looked after me for a couple of days, though once I heard that Wendy had been discharged I returned home, where once again we were grateful for the support and care of both Angela and Elaine.

With Wendy now able to pass urine, much to her delight she returned once more to a frequent mug of tea in place of the stringent cup and saucer. I was unable to drive for the first six weeks and so Angela, for the first week or so, drove Wendy and I to St. James's in order for her medication to be monitored and balanced out – especially the immune-suppressants. These visits into Leeds gradually tailed off accordingly, until the renal doctors were satisfied that they had got the right balance, because too high a dosage could be just as bad as one too low, meaning that the kidney would irretrievably be damaged.

Though the transplant was a success, Wendy was advised of certain dos and don'ts and, being Wendy, she dutifully became self-disciplined, not wanting to jeopardize her new kidney. For example, she must eat eggs bought via a shop or supermarket, rather than free range eggs from any other source such as a farm. No natural yoghurts, because of the internal bacteria, bagged salad should also be avoided, unless thoroughly washed prior to serving, because it is full of chlorine from the manufacturing process. Most of us enjoy the sunshine, but she must stay fully covered and preferably wear a sun hat because, due to her suppressed immune system, she is more at risk of getting skin cancer.

At the beginning of my second week at home, I noticed that one of my legs was becoming swollen and grew worse as the week progressed. So, at the Friday teatime, Angela took me down to see my GP and he advised that I go to the A & E Department at Pontefract Hospital, due to what he believed was a suspected thrombosis. This I did and, in the early hours of Saturday morning, I was placed on a ward and then, the following day, I was told that it could be the middle of the following week or later before I would be able to have a scan to confirm the existence or not of any thrombosis.

In the interim, I was given a blood thinners injection in my stomach and was told that I should attend the hospital each day prior to receiving the scan for the injection to be repeated. I must confess to feeling really vulnerable and uneasy with this position. The following day, Angela and Wendy accompanied me to the hospital for me to receive the injection. Once there, and having waited a short while, I received my injection and the nurse then decided that the dressing over the incision made in my stomach required replacing. Though she replaced the dressing, she admitted to being concerned by the look of the site and called a doctor.

The doctor declared that I had cellulites, an infection, and then asked, "Where did you have the surgery carried out?"

"St. James's Hospital, Leeds," I replied.

"Did they say that you could return if you had any problems?" she enquired.

"Yes," I said, feeling somehow relieved that I would be going to St. James's. Hearing all this outside the cubicle, Wendy had been on the telephone, spoken to the Renal Unit in Leeds and they had said that, rather than go into the A & E Unit, I should go straight to the High Dependency Unit, where a bed would be waiting for me. Wendy and I were greatly relieved as we had both felt a lack of confidence with what I had just experienced.

This doctor only served to reinforce my view that so called white collar professionals are no different to other workers, Whilst I am full of support and admiration for the NHS – indeed, it is both a socialist principle and policy to have free health care for all it is my socialist conviction that anyone who does not earn a living from some form of capital, but instead has to work for a wage or salary in order to live, is a member of the working class. This will no doubt bemuse a lot of people and many will shudder at the thought, but that is the reality and, within every sphere of working life, there are good and bad workers and at times all workers make mistakes. I digress, but nevertheless I felt the point needed to be made. Having arrived at the High Dependency Unit, I was given a bed and within an hour or so a renal surgeon called in to see me.

He looked firstly at the dressing and asked if it had been me that had fitted it. When I explained that it was done at Pontefract Hospital, he made no comment and having removed the item he declared that the problem wasn't cellulitis, as we had just been told, but in fact he said that I had an abscess just under the healing incision. He explained to me what he was going to do and, with his fingers, he burst the abscess so that puss was emitted from the wound. Then, having satisfied himself that he had extracted all of the puss, the wound area was given a thorough clean with the proper fitting of a new sterile dressing.

I was then placed on the general renal ward with the explanation that the following morning (Monday) I was to have a scan on my swollen leg. This did indeed occur early the following day. Later in the morning, when the doctor made his rounds, he explained that the results of the scan had shown that there was no thrombosis at all, and he went on to explain that on occasions some patients that undergo surgery can experience this kind of swelling. I was discharged and sent home.

Over the next few weeks, Wendy continued to make progress and moreover she was so hugely relieved not to be going three times per week for dialysis. At the end of six weeks, Angela and Elaine were still with us and I had been sent two appointments in the post, one at the Job Centre Plus in Wakefield and the other with ATOS, a private company engaged by the government to monitor and assess those claiming some form of sickness or incapacity benefit.

I was able to claim employment and support allowance, due to my situation, and at my point of hospital discharge I had been given a three month sick note. Wendy accompanied me to the ATOS interview and, though there were a number of questions, other than being asked to routinely bend my arms, there was no physical test.

We left thinking no more of it and a number of days later, as required, I attended the appointment with the Job Centre Plus. I went into the building naively not knowing why they wanted to see me, but this was soon rectified when I was interviewed with a view to them finding me some kind of work! I was both annoyed and dismayed and went on to explain my situation; I had just donated a kidney to my wife and, when medically judged fit and well, I fully intended resuming my work duties with my plumbing business.

Having heard this, the woman seemed embarrassed that I was there at all and politely went on to advise me that I may have my benefit stopped, but that I could appeal against this. I left the building believing that it had all been a mistake. Following a further week or so, we bade farewell to both Angela and Elaine and remain ever grateful for their selfless care and support. Just prior to my three months sick note expiring, I received a telephone call one morning from a chap at Barnsley Job Centre Plus.

He went on to explain that it was "a courtesy call" and did I know that my benefit had been stopped? I was gob-smacked and explained that I wasn't aware. He remarked about my recent meeting at ATOS and asked if I had received a copy – as I apparently should have done – of their assessment. I answered no and he went on to explain that, after the three months hospital sick note had expired then, according to ATOS, I would be again fit for work.

We went on to have a conversation and he was very sympathetic and took time out to explain in detail how I should appeal and that, in the next few day, he would send me the relevant papers. The role of ATOS, as ascribed by the austerity driven Tory/Liberal Democrat coalition government – dealing with the 2008/09 banking crisis – was to essentially get as many people off sickness and other related disability benefits and, as such, they were then and still are paid by their performance/results.

At the 2012 London Paralympic Games, ironically sponsored by ATOS, I read an article accompanied by a photo in one of the national newspapers. The photo showed a crowd of disabled people, some in wheelchairs, protesting outside the ATOS offices in London and, at one point, the article stated that in March of 2012 a terminally ill woman with cancer was declared fit for work by ATOS and she had subsequently died. Someone locally has since ironically said to me that these days "if you can lick a stamp, then you're fit for work."

Following the above phone conversation, I went to see my GP and he declared that, given I was still feeling twinges around the site of the surgery, then I was not fit to return to my manual job and consequently gave me another four-week sick note. At the same time, I received the benefit appeal application and comprehensively completed it and returned the forms in the post. What a load of hassle and, as far as I was concerned, simply unnecessary aggravation.

After the end of the further four weeks on sick, I resolved to go back to work. Given Wendy's 'new lease of life', we were able to fully enjoy the caravan much more, along with our two young Jacks; things were finally looking up. However, following two to three months back at work, I noticed a sizeable lump over the site of my scar and ensuing visits to the GP and hospital confirmed that it was indeed a hernia and the hospital scheduled me for further surgery.

In March 2011, I was admitted into St. James's Hospital again, but this time for the hernia repair and, following a stay of around five days, I was discharged. Several weeks later, I had a repeat of the same hassle again, with a scheduled visit to see ATOS. Though the hospital issued me with an initial three month sick note, again the ATOS 'assessment' was that once the sick note expired, I would be fully fit to resume work.

It was about a year or so later that I had occasion to speak with a customer of mine, an experienced nurse who had worked at the NHS

Walk-in Centre in the Leeds city centre. As part of the wider coalition government's austerity programme, and the drive for more what are euphemistically called NHS 'efficiency savings', like so many others around the country, the centre – initially set up to provide a more local resource and ease pressure on hospital A&E departments – had been shut down and, in due course, she had taken up employment with ATOS.

She went on to explain that this turned out to be only for a short while because the overriding emphasis was to throw people off sickness and other related incapacity benefits at any cost. As a consequence of this aim, her manager had constantly spoken to her about not refusing a greater amount of cases for benefit, but in response she had told him that, as an experienced nurse, she felt that she knew those individuals who were and were not shamming. She became disillusioned and left.

Well, for myself, I duly went back to work after the three months on sick and, although I was mindful as a manual worker of being cautious, yet again after a couple of months I found another lump over the site of the scar. After yet more investigations, this proved to be yet another hernia.

Wendy and I subsequently attended an appointment at the Renal Unit and, after speaking with the consultant and another doctor, they removed themselves from us to discuss matters, but Wendy overheard the consultant saying that he was constantly saying to renal doctors that they need to use more mesh when carrying out such procedures. The consultant reappeared and said that he was going to refer me to a surgeon at the Leeds General Infirmary because this chap repaired hernias quite differently to his own doctors.

After a couple of visits to the Leeds General Infirmary to see the surgeon, I was once more scheduled for surgery and, on the day itself, I had to arrive at 7.30am at St. James's, where I was directed to a waiting area. There a number of people were all awaiting surgery of some sort or another, all from different doctors. After some preliminary matters and a brief meeting with the registrar, I went to the operating theatre and, whilst waiting to be taken in, I listened to the complaints of one staff member concerning the problem of staff bullying within the hospital.

After that, the next thing that I noticed was intense pain as I was apparently being moved from a trolley on to a hospital bed. Being only partly successful with this manoeuvre, one nurse went around the other side of the bed, grabbed my hands, placed them on the bed rail and then urged me to pull myself across the bed and, in doing so, I felt another bout of pain. In response to my cries, one nurse asked another what surgery I had undergone, and the glib reply came back, "Just keyhole."

Up until that point, I had been completely out of it, no doubt still being under the influence of the anaesthetic. When I finally came around, the ward I was in had ten beds, five at each side, and within the first hour or so

I overheard more than one patient uttering concern about this, that and the other relating to the care being afforded to them.

The following morning, a nurse helped me to sit at the side of my bed and I attempted to wash myself. I felt so weak when standing and was unable to walk to the toilet in the corridor outside of the ward. Seeing the difficulties that I was having she commented that I wouldn't be going home that today.

Later in the morning, a doctor came and told me that I would be going home today and her comments caused me a degree of alarm and distress because I simply didn't feel well enough. A little after lunch another doctor came and, from the foot of my bed, announced that he had been part of the operating theatre surgical team and, having explained to him how I felt and the contradictory remarks about going and not going home, he told me that I *definitely* would not be going home today.

By now, I simply wasn't sure what was happening, and I was feeling increasingly vulnerable and anxious. And then a woman came from the hospital pharmacy to explain what medication I was being prescribed in readiness for my discharge today. The level of staff communication had been horrendous, with seemingly the left hand not knowing what the right hand was doing, and thankfully there were no more visits from hospital staff telling me that I was or was not going home.

There appeared to be no concept from anyone what the impact of this might be for the poor patient lying in the hospital bed. To my relief, I did indeed stay in hospital for another night, but later that afternoon I was to be at the centre of more chaos, which began when a student nurse brought me a jug of water with a beaker and said that they needed to check that my bladder was working okay. Therefore, could I drink three beakers of water and, when I was then ready to go to the toilet, could I notify her as she would then bring a machine to check that my bladder was indeed emptying itself.

This made sense to me because when the hernia had previously been repaired, I had undergone the same test, along with ensuring that my bowels were opening. At that time, I was told that the tests were a formality to ensure things were okay before being discharged.

In due course, I announced to the nurse that it was my intention to go to the loo, but when I came out she said that the machine was on another ward therefore I would have to repeat the procedure and drink three more beakers of water. Time passed on and again I said to her that I was about to go to the loo to pass water.

When I came out the nurse and the ward sister were stood in the corridor by the nurses' station and the former again announced that she couldn't find the machine and, before anyone could say a word, the sister turned to me and somewhat abruptly said, "You haven't undergone a urological procedure so you don't need to have your bladder checked."

I went back to my bed feeling completely confused. Now hospital wards being what they are you can almost hear a pin drop and early that evening I overheard the chap who was directly opposite being told that he would be going home early the following morning. He explained that was fine because, at the moment, there was currently sickness in his household at home. A short while later, the nurse approached him and said, "Actually you're going home this evening." I could see the look of incredulity on his face.

His adult son appeared a short while later and, walking down the ward before reaching his father, he inquisitively asked his father if he had told ward staff about the sickness at home. He replied that he had and in a loud voice he then said, "All they're bothered about is the bed."

As you do when in hospital, you enter into a level of conversation with patients close to you and the chap to the left of me had earlier explained that he had some sort of blood disorder. Well, imagine my surprise when the same student nurse who had earlier asked me to drink copious amounts of water approached him and said that she was going to check his bladder function with a machine and proceeded to pull the curtains around his bed. Minutes later, when she had finished, I asked him if he had undergone any "urological procedure"?

He answered "no", as I expected him to, and clarified with me once more that he had a blood disorder.

I replied saying, "It looks like you've just had my scan then".

Early the next morning, I was told by the ward sister that I would be going home later that morning. Angela had once again travelled down from Northumberland to help Wendy, so I rang for her and Angela to collect me. A short while later, the ward sister said that because they needed the bed immediately, could I now wait in a waiting room for my family to arrive. There was no convivial farewell and I took a place in the waiting room, feeling something of a hindrance.

Finally, they came and I remember feeling a little shaky and had some shivers as I got into the car, but it passed and I felt no more of it. Home at last and the following day Angela headed back up north. Wendy didn't have the confidence to drive all the way into Leeds and that was one of the reasons for Angela coming to help. A couple of days out of hospital and I went to bed around lunchtime due to feeling unwell.

I began to experience the same shivers and shaking as I had at the point of my discharge, so Wendy rang the GP for advice and he asked if we could possibly come to the surgery. She drove me down to Ackworth and, upon getting out of the car, I could barely place one foot in front of the other. The GP thought that I was possibly suffering from pneumonia and suggested a visit straight away to the A&E Department at St. James's Hospital.

Not being confident herself about the pending drive, she rang our Gill and Bernard in Leeds and they came over and collected us both from home and took us to the A&E. Once there, and following some tests, it was decided that I had some sort of infection and was given some antibiotics. Upon reaching home, as we were dropped off, we gratefully thanked my sister and Bernard.

Over the next few days, I gradually recovered from the infection. Over the years, Wendy and I have occasionally reflected on our ups and downs due to ill health and, in doing so, we have been both mindful and grateful that we were able to carry out and achieve what we did largely due to the support of family, very much in the same way as others do on a day-to-day basis up and down the country.

Collectivism has always been, and still is a far superior social value to individualism. As a couple, when necessary and the need arises, I am there to help Wendy and in turn she is there to help me. In a light-hearted way, it's what the Chuckle Brothers would describe as 'from me to you, to you to me'. For some unexplainable reason, I escaped the clutches of ATOS and finally went back to work after three months on sick.

Overall, over the past three years, I had spent a total of ten months on sick leave and, perhaps if following the transplant operation I had been allowed to fully recover before returning to work, and not have my benefit stopped, it would have saved both time money for the NHS. Of course having 'earned' the Employment and Support Allowance benefit over these ten months I was duly sent proof of these 'earnings' for me to give to my accountant so that I could pay the due income tax!

The negative psychological scars of my last experience were still strong and, shortly following my discharge, I lodged via email a complaint with the relevant hospital matron, though she took some time to respond and initially appeared to be ignoring me.

Given this, I wrote offering a deadline for her to reply and an offer of a date for us to meet, failing this I would contact my member of parliament. It did the trick. For me, the purpose of a meeting was not only to share my very poor experience, but also to bring to her attention certain matters – naively believing that she would be unaware of what other patients appeared to be enduring on a daily basis.

When the meeting was convened, Wendy accompanied me and, sat alongside the matron in the room, were the ward sister and someone taking notes, which I had asked for. From the outset, the point that they had initially raised and kept returning to was the fact that the purpose of setting up that particular ward was to speedily get people off the waiting list, which was no doubt linked to the overall performance of the department and the hospital itself. The fact that they had targets to meet was frequently stated by them. Whenever I hear of the pre-eminent nature of 'targets' as the driving force for public services, I am often reminded that the plain truth is that organisations do not have targets, only people do. Alongside our personal concerns about patient compassion and care, these two hospital managers – as is often the case – talked about 'targets' as though they had been handed down from the heavens above and therefore must not only be blindly followed, but also take precedence over the very essence of good nursing care and best practice.

In the context of this, one wonders if 'robotic' professionals such as these ever question what they are asked to do or simply get on and strive to reach crudely determined targets, stopping only on occasion – if at all – to realise that they might compromise the core interests of patients. The matron went on to comment that, following my complaint, she had initiated a system whereby all patients whilst on the ward were now given a short questionnaire about the care being offered to them whilst in hospital. Wendy immediately seized on this saying "And do you think that these will be completed in an open and honest way? Don't forget patients are being invited to potentially criticise staff who *still* have ongoing responsibility for their care."

They looked bemused and this possibility appeared not to have crossed their target-orientated minds.

Having shared our concerns we left them with their targets and, shortly afterwards, I eventually returned to work mindful that the surgeon had said that he had put plenty of mesh around my hernia, but still I was nevertheless cautious. Due to the three months of being off work, to help generate jobs to carry out, there was the customary tramping of the streets in the surrounding areas to put business cards through letter boxes. I had previously carried out work for quite a number of schools across the area, though this had appeared to dry up probably, I thought, due to the 2008/09 global banking crisis.

Chapter 21

Explaining Another Crisis of Capital

Life throughout the 1980s for us as a family was blighted by periodic unemployment, financial insecurity and poverty, and indeed this was the case for millions of other Britons. I have continued my reading in order to understand history and how, as a society, we have arrived at where we are today, and this ongoing self-educating journey has found me constantly asking "why?" By doing this I have become not only a critical thinker, but also an iconoclast.

The very first economic crisis of British capitalism resulting in a recession occurred in 1827 and approximately every ten years after that the inherent contradictions of capitalism (such as the overproduction causing a saturation of markets and decimating demand) meant that Britain has been plunged into periodic recessions, causing untold social hardship, an increase in poverty and social misery as people – if they had one – lost jobs, incomes and even their homes. Unable to sell their labour power – a precondition for the working class in capitalist society – in order to achieve the basic necessities of life, hardships over the years have not only been utterly huge, but also a social outrage. Still, pro-capitalist politicians and economists firmly believed that the only way to run the economy was through a laissez fairre approach, which simply means 'leave well alone', because markets know best and, as such, they will always self-regulate.

That was until the Depression came about in the 1930s and laissez fairre economics failed abysmally to offer any answers. This period contributed greatly to the thinking of William Beveridge, who as a liberal wanted to abolish what he saw as the five 'giant evils', which were want, squalor, idleness, ignorance and disease. By the start of the Second World War, he had set out a blueprint for welfare changes that he believed would begin to eradicate these 'evils'.

Around the same period, an economist named John Maynard Keynes, another liberal, had developed a new macroeconomic theory that was to change the thinking and policies of governments all over the world in the post-war period. In the mid-1920s, Keynes had criticised what he saw as the hugely damaging reparations that had been exacted on Germany following their defeat to the Allies at the end of the First World War. Arguably, the severe damage caused by these reparations to the German economy, along with the widespread social misery, contributed to its political destabilisation and the emergence of a breed of politics never seen before – fascism.

Keynes believed that laissez fairre economics was deeply flawed and had run its course. It simply hadn't the structural ability to respond not only to the economic Depression, but also to the periodic recessions in the economy. Simply put, Keynes advocated that governments should have a greater role in their economies and, to begin with, key industries should be nationalised, thus bringing about 'mixed economies'. In addition, government funding of public works and the country's infrastructure would initially create tens of thousands of jobs and, in doing so, people would spend and consume innumerable goods, thus creating more jobs and more money to circulate in the economy. He believed that 'full employment' – given the period this was a concept that was solely about men – could be achieved and a by-product of this would be a sustained increase in government tax receipts that would enable the Beveridge welfare blueprint to become a reality.

His theory went on to expand on the ability of governments to use certain fiscal levers, such as tax and interest rates, in order to manage their economies and this he argued would serve not only to maintain 'full employment', but also avoid the historic pre-war recessions, referred commonly today in benign terms such as 'booms and slumps', the trade cycle, the economic cycle or economic downturn. The post-war period and thereafter is often referred to as a time of 'consensus politics' and a time of collectivism, though the right wing maintained their outright opposition towards what had been the development of greater welfare and social democracy

This term 'collectivism' refers to the state taking responsibility for the expansion of social democratic policies, such as free healthcare, welfare benefits, sickness benefits, local authority personal social services and subsidised rented council housing. To reduce social discrimination the introduction of progressive tax policies would be key, though the extent to which these were indeed introduced in any meaningful way is open to debate and, with it the true extent of Britain's post-war social democracy.

In America, the pro-Keynesian economist John Kenneth Galbraith advised post-war governments in their efforts at introducing and advancing social democratic policies. In the early 1950s, a delegation from the American Health Association (AHM) visited Britain to view and consider the new National Health Service offering free health for all, but upon their return to America they spent millions of dollars in propaganda attacking any form of socialised health care.

Then in the 1970s, this key role of the nation state was surpassed and undermined by the growth of both monopoly capitalism and globalisation. Large businesses and corporations gained even greater economic and political power, which was often monopolistic. With the ascendancy of right-wing politics throughout the 1970s, culminating with the election here of Margaret Thatcher in 1979, the Neo-Liberals quickly set about dismantling the framework of Keynesianism economics and succeeded in revamping laissez fairre economics by re-branding it as 'market forces' or 'free market economics'.

Gradually, governments internationally drew back from any significant role in their economies and in America 'free market economics' returned with the election of the new President Ronald Reagan (1981–1989) and his period in office became known as 'Reaganomics'. Here in Britain, industries were being denationalised and, where possible, there was the gradual introduction of private business ownership over public services, possibly with a view to bringing about total privatisation.

A key cornerstone for the advocates of 'free market economics' is that governments should exercise what is frequently and euphemistically referred to as 'prudent' public spending. Indeed, earlier this year (2020) in March, after the chancellor had declared his budget, the former prime minister, now a back-bench MP, Teresa May stood up in Parliament stating that a cornerstone of Conservative governments was always to exercise "prudent" spending on public services.

In 1988, the British Government brought into being the Financial Deregulation Act, thus paving the way for banks and financiers to pursue their fanatical greed for further profits via global financial markets. Now government intervention in the operations of markets was widely viewed as anathema, though notwithstanding this there was a recession in 1990/91. However, the Neo-Liberals still pressed on and indeed, seeing that Keynesianism was dead, the Labour Party too adopted 'free market' economics and, under their leader Tony Blair, re-branded itself as 'New Labour'.

In response to the 2008/09 financial crisis, the government – as a number of economists at the time noted – adopted a part socialist approach in order to deal with the crisis, as they used billions of pounds of taxpayers' money to carry out the huge bail out of the private banking debt. A socialist response in part because, though the gigantic debt was socialised and absorbed by the people, any profits that the banks made remained in private ownership.

With the New Labour government having bailed out the banks, the new coalition government of 2010 decided that, though ordinary people across the country had paid for the bailout, this wasn't enough and they should also endure additional burdens to regain *their* monies given by the government to bail out the banks. So, an economic programme of austerity was introduced, which ten years later still exists today.

Local authority budgets have been cut, affecting the vulnerable, such as those reliant on social care services, public sector wage increases frozen for ten years, hospital services cut – the St. James's Renal High

Dependency Unit closed just months following our transplant – to the extent that it is now socially accepted as 'normal' and a common expectation that A&E Units will be fully stretched, with some at crisis point over the winter period.

The introduction of Universal Credit, followed by the announcement in November 2015 by Chancellor George Osborne that he intended to cut the benefit by one billion pounds, has – along with the sheer bureaucracy facing applicants – resulted not only in misery for claimants, but also with instances of both para-suicide and actual suicide. We have also witnessed the introduction from North America of food banks for people – including many in work – who don't have enough money to buy the basic necessities for life.

Casual labour was done away with in the mid-1960s, thus ending the insecurity of employment and income for those workers and their families affected by it. However, it has now been re-introduced and euphemistically labelled as 'zero-hours contracts'. It is impossible here to deal with the devastating social impact caused by the financial crisis and the ensuing austerity measures that are still happening today due to the political choice to introduce a punitive programme of austerity.

I say it was a political choice because, given that the Tories and other free marketers want to keep public expenditure to a minimum, many would argue that ten years after the banking crisis they continue to use this as an excuse for public consumption in order to stifle public services of funds. Let us not forget, though, the mantra recently proclaimed by Theresa May that Tory governments always seek to be prudent with public spending.

Private corporations and global enterprises are like vultures and will invest in those countries that offer the greatest benefits to them, that is cheap labour and low taxes. These enterprises are stateless and will quickly move somewhere else if greater profits can be had and governments know this, and they therefore tacitly offer themselves as helpless captives, often competing to offer the greatest incentives for the least return.

There is merit in considering the inherent contradictions of capitalism which consequently causes social inequality, poverty, low pay and hardship. In order to actually maintain a country that tolerates social discrimination and poverty, it is unbelievably the case that the government spends tens of billions of pounds of tax payers' money each year on a host of supposed support schemes, such as a raft of welfare benefits, tax credits for the low paid, education support grants, free school meals, the Pupil Premium and Pension Credits and health spending on health conditions related to poverty.

In the 1980s, to further the drive for 'free market rented' housing, one of the measures taken by the government was to abolish the Fair Rent legislation that offered protection to tenants against exploitation from rogue landlords. Since then, 'free market' rents have soared to the extent that the government has placed a cap on the amount of housing benefit to be paid in relation to such bloated rents, thus leaving countless tenants to somehow meet the financial shortfall.

The very first meaningful English poverty survey was carried out in the East End of London in 1883 by Charles Booth, concerning the London Borough of Tower Hamlets. For those who see no value in history and from the top of their head suggest that things are far better than they used to be, it is worth looking at Tower Hamlets today. A measure of the progress since the time of Booth's research reveals that today Tower Hamlets has the highest poverty rate across all local authorities in England and Wales, along with the highest rate of child poverty in the country. And yet politicians and other commentators frequently talk about the need to reduce poverty, along with the doomed efforts that they are making because such efforts are essentially through the structure of a capitalist economic system. Such platitudes are a mere sop and an illusionary attempt to show that firstly capitalism isn't the cause of poverty and hence, secondly, something can be done about it.

Capitalism is the cause of poverty and not the remedy. As Hegel, the 19th century philosopher, correctly pointed out, the one thing that we learn from history is that we don't learn one thing from history. And to paraphrase Marx, whilst we think that we make our own history, we do not do so under the conditions of our own choosing. That is because there are certain social forces, factors and influences affecting the way that we live. We are social products of the culture within which we live, yet a great many of us are completely unaware of these social forces, factors and influences, and their impact upon our daily lives.

We tend to individualise the personal troubles that we encounter and fail to see them as social issues, often shared by others that are part of the social structure in which we live. As such, there are times when the social structure requires modification, or if the social issues are so great a complete overhaul of the entire society may be necessary in order to address these personal troubles and social issues.

Up to 1980, I had prided myself on the fact that I had never been made unemployed and, whilst I had had a number of jobs, I had always been successful in moving for increased wages. Then in 1980 for the first time, I was staring redundancy in the face. Why was this and what were the reasons? From this simple social base point, I began striving to question and understand my employment situation and how it was likely to impact on me and my family. From having done this, I have come to question so many things and, in doing so, strive always to find the truth.

Over the years, I have heard so many people grumble in a general way about so many different social situations, but then simply declare that "ah well, we can't change anything. Who are we? There's always been one rule for them and one rule for us, it's always been like this and always will be." This should not however be viewed as a tautological situation that will never change, because history tells that if one thing is certain it is that constant change is here to stay. The following is a brief overview of past society and events and, for the reader, this digression is best explained as follows...

Firstly, let me make the point that when the rich and powerful in England began to set their sights on even more land and riches, the first peoples that they had to subjugate were the English. The emergence of petty kingdoms brought with it the emergence of strong and brutal leaders and out of this emerged the present-day royalty, through a web of intrigue, conspiracy, inter-marrying to strengthen alliances, and downright brutality. Feudalism was little more than slavery for the bonded serf and his family, and when the lord wanted soldiers to fight then serfs had no alternative but to obey.

The earth was firstly inhabited by primitive peoples who hunted and gathered for the basic necessities of life. They lived in a communal way, sharing the fruits of their labour, and this is what Marx called 'primitive communism'. Hitherto, all societies have been divided on a class basis, and it is class action that has been the driver of history. The master and slave societies saw the latter dependent on the former for their basic necessities and, whilst the dissolution of such societies did away with slavery, private property remained.

In England in the eleventh century, King William of Normandy introduced the feudal system, which also became a common feature of Europe and Latin America, although in the latter the centre of the system was the hacienda and not, as in England, the manor house, abbey or castle. The feudal system existed for approximately seven hundred years. The lord of the manor had at his disposal serfs and their families – who were to all intent and purposes slaves – bonded to him by feudal law and these worked the land, tending first to those lands of the lord before managing their own strip from which they eked out the basic necessities and made small crafts.

At harvest time, again the lord's harvest was gathered in first and, after he had consumed all that he could, any surplus would be sold at markets and often bought by merchants who also dealt in crafts, cloth and all manner of things. Many of these historic market towns are still with us today. For example, around the beginning of the twelfth century, the North Yorkshire town of Knaresborough began to grow as it provided a market and attracted traders to service the needs of the manor, which happened to be in this instance not an abbey or manor house, but the castle.

The lot of the serf and his family, as peasants or 'commoners', was a miserable one and, over the course of time, there were uprisings, for example, Wat Tyler in 1381, Jack Cade and the men of Kent in 1450, and Robert Kett and the uprising in Norfolk in 1549. By the early part of the fifteenth century, innovative developments in the use of land slowly led to social changes and we began to see the breaking up of feudal retainers and the expropriation of peasants from the land, causing them to wander the land and, in order to gain food, many became beggars, robbers and vagabonds.

Across Western Europe and here in Britain, the authorities responded to this vagabondage with harsh legislation. Old beggars unable to work were granted a beggar's licence, but sturdy ones were tied to a cart tail and whipped until blood streamed from their bodies and they then had to swear an oath to return to their birthplace or where they had lived for the past three years and to give an undertaking that they would work. Such an ironic and cruel punishment, given that they had been forced off the land and had been driven by the urge to secure the basic necessities of life. However, if a second offence occurred then they received another whipping along with the removal of half an ear. A third offence of vagrancy would result in execution for being a common criminal.

If anyone refused to work, then they were condemned as a slave to the person who had initially denounced them for not working and being an idler. The slave's master could feed and treat the slave as they saw fit, and they had the sole right to force them to do any form of work, no matter how disgusting. However, if the slave failed to work for two weeks, then they were condemned to slavery for life and branded with a red-hot iron, either on their forehead or back, with a letter S. The master could hire him out to others and, ultimately, if the slave ran away three times, then the master could execute him as a felon. For someone labelled as a vagabond, then if he failed to work for three days he was taken to his birthplace and with a red-hot iron the letter V was branded on his breast.

The families of these poor creatures were treated also as slaves, with children being compelled often to become 'apprentices' who, if their master so wished, could also be whipped and put into chains. I wonder today how much - if at all – the true history of the English working classes is ever taught to our children in schools? Although there were uprisings as a class, the peasants were not as significant as the merchant class, who over the centuries grew in both their economic and political power. This reached its zenith in 1647, when the merchants who had persistently been refused changes in the law to further benefit their trading interests, decided that enough was enough and took up arms against the feudal King Charles I.

Led by Oliver Cromwell, the merchants embarked on a social revolution that has been widely distorted by historians as no more than a civil war between the king's Cavaliers and Cromwell's Roundheads. The king was defeated and executed in 1651, thus paving the way for capitalism to develop. No doubt over the seven hundred years of feudalism many merchants would have said the same as members of the working classes do today, "We can't change anything, who are we? There's always been one rule for them and one rule for us, and it's always been like this and always will be."

Over these centuries, the inherent contradictions of the feudal system evolved to the point whereby the merchant class increasingly realised its own self-interest and slowly became 'a class in itself' and, by taking up arms in 1647, they became a 'class for itself'. The same applies to what Engels saw as a flawed economic system in that, as capitalism evolves, it continues to 'dig its own grave'. Marx saw that gradually – as with the merchant class – the working class will come to see itself as 'a class in itself, for itself' and overthrow capitalism, thus taking society to the higher level of existence that is democratic socialism.

I believe it to be the case that, when the time comes, society will have to build museums to demonstrate what poverty was like with the devastating impact that it had on people's lives. Hence my belief is that the corrupt, exploitative and wasteful system that capitalism is will reach an advanced stage, a pinnacle, and then be swept aside, consigned to the dustbin of history. Several months ago, I had occasion to speak with an affable sort of chap who I had met and conversed with a number of times previously.

We were both 'putting the world to rights' and, at some point, I said to him that I was a socialist. His reply went something like this: "Well, socialism's awright, but I bet if yer got all the money in't country and divided it up equally amongst everybody, then in six months' time we'd be back where we started." Feeling confident that within these few misplaced words he had demolished the idea of socialism for good effect, he reiterated the same crass comment again.

This argument I had heard before and his comments left me in no doubt that it was clear he had no idea about socialism. I then went on to wonder if he had any clearer idea what capitalism was, given that he, along with his family and friends, were living their lives in such a society. In any event, I offered no response to his comments and, at times such as these, I can't help but feel a little despondent at the lack of awareness and understanding that people have of the world around them.

In a similar vein folk over the years have also said to me something such as "if yer think socialism is okay then read Animal Farm by George Orwell". Such comments are wholly erroneous because in reality the book is a satirical view of both authoritarian and totalitarian societies. As a democratic socialist Orwell distanced himself from what was happening in Stalin's Soviet Union, and also as was the case with many thousands of left thinking British in the late 1930s, he went over to fight in Spain against Franco's fascists and was seriously wounded. Moreover he was also witnessing the rise of fascism in Germany

For me it was also unusual to openly comment that I was a socialist because, unless I knew anyone well, it was a declaration rarely made.

When we lived in the Highlands, one day I got into a conversation with a left wing musician regarding the likes of Billy Bragg, Phil Ochs, Pete Seeger and Ewan McColl, and he suggested to me not to openly declare my political views because I might lose customers because of them. Added to the above skewed comprehension of socialism from my affable chap and others are the distorted views and comments that people have, which equate to the former Soviet Union and socialism. Like so many I grew up hearing negative news reports and comments about the poor quality of life for people living within the so-called communist/socialist Soviet Union.

Whilst one can understand the Russian people wanting to rid themselves of the Czarist tyranny, the pre-existing conditions for the October 1917 Revolution were not right. Writing in the 19th century, the evolutionary analysis of Marx was that when capitalism reaches its *advanced* stage, and when the working class as a whole fully realises its own interests and potential, then at this point capitalism will fall and international socialism will be the victor.

As an industrial country, Russia in 1917 lagged behind most of its European partners, so much so that not only was capitalism still emerging, but Russia was still predominantly an agrarian society with a significant peasant population. Moreover, following the failed revolution of 1906, Lenin developed the idea of bringing about a 'vanguard party' that would form a dictatorship over the proletariat. At the time, revolutionary socialists such as Rosa Luxemburg criticised Lenin's new mode of thought because, amongst other things, his concept of bringing about a vanguard party was undemocratic and would exclude great swathes of the Russian working class from numerous forms of decision-making, following the success of any future revolution.

Because these two key factors, along with other preconditions, were not present at the point of the 1917 Revolution, the foundations of the Soviet Union were built very much on sandy ground. By the mid-to-late 1930s, news was coming out of Russia regarding the deadly purges of Stalin and, three years following his death in 1956, the Soviet leader Khrushchev heavily criticised the leadership of Stalin.

One of the key aims for the success of socialism was to take from capitalism control over the means of the production, distribution and exchange of goods for the ownership and benefit of the people. By the 1980s, it was clear that through the Soviet Communist Party, whilst there was worker control over the means of production, there was inequality concerning both the distribution and exchange of goods along similar lines to that of capitalism.

The Soviet Union came to be regarded by many as a 'transitional society', in that it could slide either into full-blown socialism or alternatively into capitalism. History shows that it has slid into the latter in spite of the overarching ideology of being a Marxist/Leninist state. Similarly, the overarching ideology for those of us living in Britain and other western countries is that of a parliamentary democracy, in that we have a democratic vote once every five years to elect a government which carries out the peoples' will. The word 'democracy' is a derivative of two Greek words, 'demos' meaning the people and 'kratia' meaning rule by. Arguably the rise of populist politicians and parties – Trump in America and Farage and Boris Johnson here – over the past ten years or longer is due to the dissatisfaction by voters that the 'system' isn't working for them.

Like so many people, I despair at the constant unwillingness of politicians from all parties to offer clear and unambiguous comments and answers to straightforward questions. That for me is wholly undemocratic and completely at odds with democracy. I agree with the view of many on the left who state clearly that because all politicians are democratically elected then they should in turn be always accountable, recallable at any given time, to those who elect them and, if necessary, face de-selection. This is not a new concept for, at the time of the 1848 Paris Commune, that is exactly what happened in relation to those elected to positions of authority, and it is more akin to the ideals of democracy than what we have to currently endure today. Several years ago, one Conservative politician was the subject of a piece of investigative journalism that probed into his alleged dubious business dealings and, over a time, he consistently denied any wrongdoing until the evidence against him was so compelling and irrefutable that his final response on the matter was to say, "I have over-exaggerated my denial. Jabberwockian and vacuous talk from mealy-mouthed politicians represents the kind of democracy that is on offer today.

Chapter 22

Attempts at Leading a 'Normal' Life

The word 'normal' as we know it is a problematic concept because what is 'normal' to one is different for another. Being on dialysis is better than not having such a valuable service available (as in some countries), but for Wendy, and to a lesser extent myself, it was not 'normal' for either of us. When we had the two weeks' holiday at the caravan, Wendy still had to travel to Hull three times a week for dialysis and then return to recover, yet when we returned home and she resumed dialysis at Clayton Hospital, some staff were saying how lucky she had been to get away and go on holiday. For her it wasn't a 'normal' holiday. However, we were now able to enjoy life without the constraints of dialysis.

We bought another caravan and had it positioned at the front of the site overlooking the beach and sea and our Colin's girls, Lauren and Abbie, regularly came with us. Our Teresa, husband Simon and their children, Olly and George, also spent a week at the caravan. Young George would have been around two years old at the time and he had been named after his great grandad George Potter, which pleased me greatly.

Wendy has never taken the transplant for granted and it was some twelve months following the surgery that her lingering worries were diagnosed by her GP as anxiety requiring medication, which along with the other pills she still takes today. In 2012, Wendy was hospitalised on three occasions over the course of a matter of months due to recurring water infections and, as a consequence of this, she was on each occasion given intravenous antibiotics. The difficulty was that, shortly after hospital discharge, the infection quickly reoccurred, so it was decided, in order to combat this, to give her three prescriptions of differing strength oral antibiotic tablets, to be taken on alternate months. She also had at least two worrying experiences over these hospital stays.

Each occasion that she was admitted into hospital she made sure to take her medication too. Now, at one point whilst on the ward a nurse brought Wendy's medication for her to take, but seeing that one of her anti-rejection pills was wrong, Wendy immediately pointed this out to the nurse, who replied that these were the pills that the doctor had set aside for her to take. Knowing the potential implications of following such false instructions, Wendy assertively told the nurse that the doctor was incorrect and, if she would check the medication that she had brought with her into hospital, the nurse would see the error. The nurse brought the correct tablet and the matter was resolved.

On the third occasion that she was admitted, over the weekend she was given some medication by a junior doctor, which caused her to have some problems. The connection between the medication and symptoms was not apparent to the doctor at that time and she ended up in an isolation room, due to the belief that she was suffering with the hospital super bug C. Diff.

With no consultants on duty over the weekends, when one did come around on the Monday and saw Wendy in the isolation room, he demanded to know who had prescribed this wrong medication and she was immediately taken off it, allowing the symptoms to dissipate. Just more mistakes by some workers, though in a hospital environment when carried out in relation to vulnerable patients, they are potentially unsafe and serious. Wendy has been through so much over the years and will rarely complain, and I am often reminded of her 'stoicism' that Doctor Skeogh – our GP in Fort Augustus – often spoke about. Prior to her illness that had led to three plus years on dialysis, we had regularly enjoyed holidaying in so many different places. Yes, Scotland figured a lot, but still we holidayed in different places. We would often recall particular events and occasions concerning this or that holiday with very fond memories.

I remember very well the both of us being on the annual BMW bike rally at Blair Atholl in the early 1990s and camped at the side of our tent was an older chap from Wales. One day, we got into a conversation about touring in Scotland and he had a map spread out on the ground and spent some time pointing to places and enthusing over the visits that he had hugely enjoyed and then, at one point, in a light-hearted manner, he declared that upon dying, "I want to come back as a Scot."

This conversation stayed with me for several days as it had the effect on me of wanting to see much more of Scotland, and especially the Highlands. Wendy and I had never holidayed apart, and it was about a week later that I tentatively began talking to her about me taking a solo journey up to Scotland. She agreed and asked me which places that I intended to see and, having an itinerary in my head, I reeled of my list only for her then to exclaim, "How long do yer think yer going for?"

I replied, "One week?"

She rejoined with, "One week? You'll be away for one week?"

It was agreed with no bother and the first occasion that I ventured to Scotland alone was in the mid-1990s and this was on the BMW K100, which had a 1,000cc engine and was ideal for touring and easily carried my tent and other camping equipment. I remember especially in the Highlands simply going around bend after bend and seeing some fantastic vistas. The small town of Inverary was going to be my last night's camping and, having arrived early at the site and erected the tent, I went into the town for a look around.

There are two old prisons that are now tourist attractions and I went into the one that still had the old court all mocked up with the judge, the person in the dock and other lifelike characters. Before entering the courtroom, one passes through a gallery illustrating a number of artifacts, along with some background stories of folk back then and short details of their misdemeanours that had caused them to be brought before the judge.

I vividly remember the case of a young man in his early twenties who had been warned on a number of occasions about riding his horse 'at great speed' down the main street before his luck had run out. I couldn't help but make the analogy with some young people today that drive cars, and ride mopeds motorbikes at speed because quite often they feel little or no fear and, in such situations, they seem to present themselves as invincible.

That evening, I went into the club that was on the site and, given that it was Friday evening, it was full of Glaswegians who had made the journey to stay in their caravans on the site. Most of my time was spent listening to conversations, which I found it difficult to understand due to the dialect.

The following morning, it was pouring with heavy rain so, with no sign of any let-up, I packed everything away on the bike and then, before setting off, I visited the toilets and tried to dry my bike gloves under the hand dryer. Despite the rain, my trip was spectacular, taking in some fantastic scenery and places such as John O Groats and down the North West Coast, Scourie, Ullapool and Applecross.

The following year, Wendy and I, along with Tetley and Cassie, our two Jack Russells, journeyed north in our Ford Fiesta, broadly taking in the same itinerary that I had done the year before. This turned out to be an exceptionally hot summer, with the aforementioned droughts in some parts of England. On the way down the North West Coast, we took in a trip across to Cape Wrath, which is located in the very far North West. This began when, along with the two Jack Russells and about a dozen or so people, we clambered aboard a small boat/ferry that took us across a loch and then at the other side we left the boat behind and continued our journey in a small minibus along a dirt track road that in places bounced us and the expectant group of sight-seers from side to side.

The land itself belonged to the Ministry of Defence and Wendy and I noticed that it was quite desolate, devoid of any trees or bushes. After ten to fifteen minutes, as we approached the lighthouse, an American tourist shouted to the driver, "Are there any toilets here?"

"Oh yeah," came the reply back, "they're up there by the McDonalds!" He quickly followed up with, "Kid, you'll be lucky to find a bush!" He was right, though having got off the bus and having a meander around, we noticed that the coastal views were truly spectacular.

A day or so later, we were camped at Ullapool on the shores of Loch Broom, listening to the water gently lapping as we chilled out with a few cans in the water to cool the drink down. Several days later, we were camping at the bottom of Glencoe when, one morning, the heat in the tent was so strong that, at around 7.00am, it caused us both to become uncomfortably hot, so we dressed and sat outside our tent.

Whilst we were sitting outside having breakfast, the temperature steadily increased and at one point we both gazed up at the snow-covered tops of the mountains as we sat below in our summer clothes. It seemed so surreal and, shortly after this, we saw a yellow Highland Council wagon pass slowly on the nearby road and the big letters on the side of it said *GRITTING*. Another surreal moment, until we later heard on the car radio that, due to the intensity of the heat, many road surfaces were breaking up during the course of the day and hence extra grit was being applied to the surfaces.

My second trip prior to moving to the Highlands was around the turn of the millennium and this was also on the BMW. That trip also proved memorable in more ways than one. My first stop was on the edge of the small town of Dunkeld in Perthshire and, having pitched my tent on the site, it began to rain that evening and, indeed, continued to do so the following day, which was Saturday.

Dunkeld sits on the River Tay and my tent was pitched on a flat piece of ground several metres away from a tributary that ran into the Tay. From here, the ground gradually rose up to a fence and, on the other side of this, was an old wooden chalet and at some point on the Saturday, having seen the water level slowly rising on the tributary, I got talking to the chap staying in the chalet. He was about my age and, as I spoke to him and shared my concerns about the incessant rain and the slowly rising water in the tributary, he commented that since being a child in the late-1950s he had stayed in what had been his mum and dad's chalet many times and not once over all that time had the tributary broke its bank.

I was the only biker on site so I was feeling confident that things would be okay following the reassurance from my knowledgeable neighbour. I took the short walk into Dunkeld to get a bit of something to eat. Later that evening, when walking back to the site, I was some one hundred metres from the entrance when a large 4x4 car came out of the site down the road and stopped as it reached me, no doubt noticing my bike jacket.

The window was lowered and someone asked, "Are you Colin Potter?"

I said yes and then I was told that both the bike and my tent had had to be moved due to the tributary breaking its banks. Back at the site my tent had been un-pegged and dragged away from the banking and my bike had been manually lifted to drier ground.

My first thoughts were for the bike, as I had secured it with a large 'D' lock through the front forks, but it was okay. Where my tent had been, there was now the flooded tributary making its fast-flowing journey into the River Tay. The chap from the chalet appeared and offered me a place to sleep for the night, but first I packed my things up as best I could and gratefully placed the tent in the site boiler room so that it could dry out.

The chap in the chalet offered me a beer and we had a brief natter before I turned in for bed. The next morning, I managed to see the weather forecast on his telly and, on the strength of this, I headed for Findhorn Bay, situated about five to ten miles east of Nairn on the Moray Coast. The rest of the trip passed by uneventfully.

There were two occasions following the transplant when I ventured up to Scotland by myself on the motorbike. The first was a several day break on the Yamaha FJR 1300 sports tourer, and on this occasion I rode to Ballachulish near Glencoe, staying in a B&B. On the second occasion, I decided to stay in youth hostels for cost reasons and my first stop was at New Lanark, just south of Glasgow. The hostel there was in the setting of the factory that had been owned by the nineteenth century textile manufacturer and philanthropist Robert Owen.

Compared to being in a car, there is a terrific sense of freedom that riding a motorbike gives one. However, by this time Wendy had absorbed a number of news stories over several years pertaining to motorcycle accidents, which had the effect of significantly reducing her interest in riding.

Having spent one night at New Lanark, I headed for a one-night stay at the hostel in Ullapool, and this is pleasingly situated on the main street overlooking the harbour. My intention was to take the ferry from Ullapool over to the Isle of Lewis and Harris and stay a couple of nights at the community run Ravenspoint hostel. I had purposely booked my ferry crossing for Monday morning due to the fact that I was aware that on the Hebridean Isles – for religious reasons – pretty much everything closes on a Sunday, and I have heard comments that 'everything' can mean that in children's playgrounds the swings are chained to the frame, hence rendering them unable to be used.

Monday morning came and, once on board the ferry, we began what was to be a journey of approximately two and half hours. As we sailed away from Loch Broom, we slowly passed the Summer Isles positioned to the left and I was reminded of the time when Wendy and I, along with a number of other tourists, had taken a boat trip to the Isles.

I remembered that as we had disembarked by one of the isles, we were told to have a wander around, but to be careful of nesting birds. The views were indeed beautiful, but there was more than one occasion when we were dive-bombed by birds who were completely averse to human intruders encroaching on their land and too close to their nests. This left Wendy and I feeling more than a little uncomfortable about the trip. Luckily for me today, the weather for the ferry trip was good and at times one could see porpoises swimming close by and then we reached

Stornaway and, down below deck, I unsecured my bike and made my way through the town and travelled south to the hostel.

When I reached the place, I found that there was only one other hostel resident and, shortly afterwards, I found out that he was from Inverness and had come across to enjoy some walking. Given that it was still May, it didn't surprise me too much that, other than myself, there was only one other person.

The second day I had taken a ride to the south of Harris and, upon my return to the hostel, I noticed damage to the other chap's Nissan Micra car that was perhaps only several years old. I say damage when in fact it was quite significant because every panel on the passenger side of the car – front wing, front passenger and rear passenger doors and the rear wing – had been severely dented in. When I saw him, I queried what had happened and he explained that a couple of days previous, on the Saturday, he had parked up in a remote spot having predetermined a walk that he was to undertake. Sometime later, upon his return, he discovered the damaged car and initially thought that some lads had driven past and, for some unknown reason, caused the damage.

Upon arriving back at the hostel, he rang to police up at Stornaway and the officer whom he spoke to asked if he would bring the car up to the police station there. This he did and, having gone into the station, the officer went outside into the car park to see the damage and, according to the chap, the officer offered his explanation. The officer said that this had happened before and that the damage had been caused by a ram!

He went on to expand on this by saying that Saturday had been a sunny day and, whilst the car had been parked up, a ram must have happened by close to the car and, upon seeing it's reflection in the paintwork, thought that he had a rival. So having headbutted the car and stepped back the reflection was seen again and hence there was another headbutt to the car, and this must have been repeated a number of times, perhaps until the ram felt confident that he had seen his rival off!

Having related this to me, the chap asked the officer if he would write him a letter for his insurance company in order for him to make a claim and, as he commented to me, "My insurance company is in Swindon and, without the letter from the police, can you imagine their response if I was myself to offer them the explanation about the ram?"

What a bizarre tale indeed, and I meekly asked him if he would mind if I took photos of the damage as folk back home would also look at me in disbelief without the photographic evidence. Once back home I was able to tell the story and the photos proved valuable because, as I thought, some people thought it was a bit of a tall story.

On one camping holiday, Wendy and I were staying for several days on a site that was on the edge of the village of Glenluce, near Stranraer in South West Scotland. This was a pretty village and one evening we were in the local pub on the main street and I went up to the bar for more drinks and, stood at the side of me, were two lads in their early to mid-twenties.

As one of them began ordering, it was clear from their accents that they were from the South of England, and he began explaining to the barman that they had seen the advert back home for Irn Bru. He went on to ask if they sold it and whether he had any more details about the drink. Well, the barman, being a bit of a lad with a dry sense humour, saw his opportunity and pronounced to wind the two lads up with some brief details about Irn Bru, before ending by saying "and it's made with real girders." The two lads appeared to accept this as indeed being the case because the advert they had seen on the telly had now been confirmed to them by a knowledgeable local Scot.

Whilst staying in Glenluce, we decided to journey up to Ardrossan on the east coast in order to get the ferry over to the Isle of Arran. Wendy was battling her trepidation of going on the ferry for the forty-five-minute crossing and, with it being a glorious sunny day, the sea was reasonably calm. We went down below to the dining area, but she was completely reluctant to sit near a window and take in the views.

A couple of years ago, whilst camping near Dumfries, we decided to take the car down the coast and once more visit Glenluce, but once there we were both saddened to see that the main street as it looked simply run down and we surmised that the possible reason for this was the banking crisis and ten years of austerity. There were occasions, both at home and at the caravan, when we shared with each other our memories of such holidays and it slowly became the case that we were getting rather tired of the restricted nature of the caravan. What with the site fees and the insurance, we didn't feel financially that we could have a week or so holidaying anywhere else, so we decided to sell the caravan in 2015. Within a short space of time, we had bought an air beam tent –along with camping equipment – big enough for us both and the two dogs.

Our Teresa had suggested an air beam tent due to the fact that, once the four beams were blown up, all one had to do was simply peg the tent out. That year we had holidays in the secluded village of Dent in Dentdale, Cumbria, as well as Scarborough. I was still having the occasional ride out on the motorbike, though since moving to Upton, and given all of the 'ups and downs', I often thought about selling it. The last time Wendy had been on the back of it was when we lived in Scotland, however, I must confess that when I was out riding I really enjoyed the buzz and freedom that it offered.

At the end of 2015 it was my sixty-fifth birthday, though rather than retire I decided to keep on working. The following year saw us looking forward to summer, when we could once again go off camping. Wendy had, for the past twenty-five years or so, been plagued with back and hip problems, which she had been told was the result of being run over by a motorcycle at the age of eleven. The problem was becoming significantly worse and, in the early part of that year, her mobility had become so poor that at the most she could only walk for approximately five hundred yards before being in severe discomfort.

Her GP referred her to the pain clinic in Doncaster, but rather than undergo a further streroid injection into her hip, which she had had on a number of previous occasions, it was suggested that she join a water-borne exercise class at a swimming baths specifically for those with joint and muscle problems. This she did and we both enrolled for weekly classes at both Pontefract and Normanton Swimming Baths. After a period of time and evaluation, she felt that there was, if anything, only slight benefit from the classes, so another visit to the GP was made.

I had been looking on the internet at the possible benefits from acupuncture and, when the doctor said that all he could suggest was increasing pain killers or a return to the pain clinic. I queried acupuncture with him. He was ambivalent about the benefits and Wendy agreed with his suggestion that he refer her back to the pain clinic. At a later date, the visit to the clinic failed to prove useful and they were unable to offer any more than a further steroid injection.

With such poor mobility and discomfort, Wendy decided to pursue the acupuncture option and began paying privately, visiting one that was in a nearby village. Amazingly enough, after four sessions, she was feeling appreciably better because the discomfort was no longer constant or as severe and her mobility had significantly improved. There are occasions still when her back or hip trouble her, but not to the extent that it did.

Shortly after the transplant operation, we decided to move to a different GP surgery, as we had both become dissatisfied with the treatment that we had at times experienced. Since 2007, I had been treated by my doctor due to suffering with depression and now at the new surgery I had seen the same GP on a number of occasions because of my problems with anxiety, and I was happy with his overall approach.

A couple of years following these visits, I had an appointment regarding a review of my medication and saw a different GP who upon my arrival introduced me to a student whom he explained was present – if I didn't mind – to observe matters as part of her training. After a short while of talking to him, I saw him repeatedly take a number of quick looks at the clock on the wall behind me. I said nothing at the time, though as I left, I thought to myself how unprofessional and especially when he had a student present who is meant to be observing the right way to carry out a consultation. Moreover, I had been a patient sat before him talking about my mental health and he couldn't extend me the courtesy of letting me speak while he listened. The anxiety in my head was working overtime at being treated that way, as though I were a non-person, and I found it difficult to overcome my anxiety.

A couple of weeks later, I was having stomach problems and, having rang the surgery, I was given an appointment with the same doctor who, after examining me, said that he would arrange for me to have an ultrasound test. As I was leaving, he made a flippant and what I considered to be a wholly erroneous remark about the NHS, which I seized on and, in an effort to prove my worth as an individual, I gave him an anxiety led lecture about the NHS.

The time came and, after having the ultrasound, I was told to make an appointment for the results, so I decided to go back to the first GP, whom I had previously seen concerning my mental health. When the appointment time came, I remember it was a Thursday afternoon and, from entering his room, I felt that he proceeded to give me 'short shrift'. For example, he had a piece of paper in front of him on his desk and, at some point, he pushed this across to me saying "that's the results of your ultrasound scan." He never bothered to discuss them with me. He appeared disengaged throughout, though he said that he would arrange an appointment for me to have an x-ray the following morning at Pontefract Hospital.

I got the impression from him that I was wasting his time. When I had seen him previously we had always got on okay, but this occasion was very different. I concluded that the other doctor had put something on my file and now this doctor was acting both subjectively and negatively on whatever had been written about me. Once again, I left the surgery feeling extremely anxious and spoke to Wendy about it when I reached home.

That evening we had a 'muscle and joint' exercise class at Pontefract Baths and, all the way through the session my anxiety had taken over and my mind was constantly dwelling on the interaction with the doctor and the fact that he had viewed me in such a negative way. With such thoughts racing away in my head, Wendy could see the frame of mind that I was in so, as we left the baths, she agreed that I might drive the short distance to the hospital with a view to cancelling tomorrow's x-ray appointment.

When I reached the reception and began explaining to the receptionist there was also a radiographer present and, rather than cancel the appointment, he convinced me to have the x-ray done there and then. This I did and, approximately a week or so later, I returned to the surgery for the results and booked an appointment with the same GP. The results were fine, but I also politely explained to him how I had left his surgery recently feeling quite low and that same evening had gone to the hospital to cancel the x-ray appointment for the following day. I went on to explain the earlier consultation that I had with his colleague – though, I did not name him – and how at one point he had glanced at the wall clock repeatedly, and this when he had a patient in front of him who was discussing his personal mental health difficulties. I added also that a student had been present and that 'clock watching' was unprofessional on a number of levels.

He concurred with this comment via a nod of his head and I added, "I decided to see you again after that because, having met with you on a number of times previously, you have never proved to be a 'clock watcher'", to which he nodded again in agreement. I also commented that, when I returned to see the 'clock watcher', when I picked him up on what I saw as an erroneous comment about the NHS, the 'lecture' I gave in response was to demonstrate to him that I wasn't a non-person, but like everybody else I had value.

Since explaining matters to the GP, I have had reason to visit him on several occasions and we have established a good rapport, and he even seems to enjoy my 'doctor' jokes. Anxiety is something everyone experiences at time, but feelings of anxiety can be constant, disproportionate to the actual events and so overwhelming. For me, anxiety has meant that at times there are sleepless nights along with an urgency to get whatever it is that is causing my anxiety resolved as soon as possible – in other words, I must dot the i's and cross the t's – but at times, some things are not easy to resolve and regrettably linger on.

Retirement has helped because when I was working there were times when the night before I would get anxious about the following day's work. This even happened though these imminent jobs I had undertaken many times before.

Since the transplant, Wendy too has anxiety problems and, along with her medication, she has taken to playing the card game *patience* on her mobile and she says this helps her anxiety. Putting mental health problems to one side, we both like to see the back end of winter and, at Easter time in 2015, young George had a long weekend with us at Scarborough and then, in the school summer holidays, he came with us to Hadston in Northumberland, the home of Angela and her wife Nikki.

By now, we had made a number of visits to their home and we really enjoy the surrounding area, and the fact that it is only a few minutes' drive to the beach. The fifth anniversary of our kidney transplant was in May 2015, and we spent this with them and, upon our arrival, we were greeted with a specially made transplant anniversary 'kidney' cake.

Later in that summer, when George accompanied us with Angela and Nikki on holiday, we were looking after their two dogs along with our own. However, we still managed to enjoy some days out. On one such day, we took George to see Bamburgh Castle, with its stunning physical presence overlooking the North Sea.

There were lots of artifacts of interest, but George especially wanted to see the dungeons and, as we entered the gaol area, behind one set of bars were several skeletons with arms above their heads manacled to the wall. George was staring at them and, with my dry sense of humour, I said to him, "Do you know how they died?" He shook his head, so I replied, "Every time the jailer came in he said to them, 'Hands up if you don't want any food'!"

As usually happens with our grandchildren and my jokes, he simply looked at me, just like the time I said to him "I think I'll live forever because at the moment I'm not doing too badly." The following year, we decided to put the bungalow on the market with a view to moving back into Leeds to be close to Teresa and her family. The for-sale sign went up in early spring, but as we went through the summer, we only had several visits from people wanting to view it.

Then in late summer another estate agent suggested dropping the price to a level that would mean a reduction of around £15,000 from the original price that it was listed for. Wendy and I later discussed what to do and decided to stay where we were and use our savings to buy a motorhome, which is something that we had spoken about on and off for the past twenty years or more. For both Wendy and I, a motorhome evokes that feeling of being able to have a degree of spontaneity and simply pick up and go where and when you want to.

Having carried out the usual search on the pages of the internet, we did indeed buy a motorhome in September 2017 and managed to have one long weekend in it at Boroughbridge before the end of that year. Two months later, on 15th November – the same birthday as our Colin – Teresa gave birth to a baby girl who was purposely named Evelyn after my mother. As with the naming of George, this again pleased me greatly.

Christmas came and went and, around February in the New Year, I began noticing that, when I was out walking the dogs, I was becoming short of breath. On occasion, I had to stop for a moment.

A visit to the GP showed that the ECG test was fine, so he decided to refer me to the Hospital Cardiology Unit. Several days later, I developed a pain below my armpit on the left side of my body and the following day, late in the afternoon, I suddenly had immense debilitating pain and at this Wendy dialled immediately for an ambulance. A first responder came and, after some initial tests, he then rang for an ambulance, which took me to Pinderfields Hospital at Wakefield. Wendy followed down with our Colin and I was kept in overnight, being placed on a Respiratory Ward.

The following morning the consultant made his ward rounds with a number of junior doctors and, though I was feeling ill, at some point, I said to him, "I'm wearing the wrong T-shirt, aren't I?" and pointed to the large writing which said, 'AGED TO PERFECTION'. Though most of the junior doctors sniggered, the consultant appeared to ignore my comment. Though I was ill, I still had something of a sense of humour.

Later that day, I was told that I had blood clots and pneumonia on both lungs and, consequently, I remained in the ward for around five days. Some tests were carried out in hospital to establish the cause of my illness, but these were inconclusive, so when I was discharged I was prescribed blood-thinning tablets, pending further outpatient visits for more tests, which later took place over a period of several months. These subsequently offered no reason for the blood clots and pneumonia, so I continue taking the blood-thinning tablets.

It was a little after my discharge from hospital that I was talking to several kids in our street about my being ill and I said to them, "Yeah, Wendy rang 999 and four ambulance men raced me to hospital – I came third."

During my recovery, and after giving the matter some thought and discussing it with Wendy, I decided at the age of sixty-seven to retire. Having worked for fifty-two years, this was initially a strange feeling, but unlike some people at the point of retiring, I felt no loss of purpose or meaning and for me it was good not to have my days determined and slavishly driven by the clock. Just as it was in the 1980s, when I was unemployed, I have always found things to do.

When the Easter holidays came, Wendy and I took young George away in the motorhome to Ravenglass on the West Lakeland District coast. In fact, it is the only coastal town in the Lake District National Park. The weather wasn't too good, but nevertheless, we had a good time and both Wendy and I were becoming more familiar with camping in a motorhome.

The holiday was rather eventful because one day George and I were outdoors playing a 'monster' game – as all sixty seven year olds do – with each of us having to hide in turn, and the game also involved a lot of running about. At some point, I was running, but had pulled up suddenly, having severe pain in the back of my left calf, so I ended up hobbling back to the motorhome.

Once inside, I was sat down, George, who was seven years old then, looked at me and acknowledging my injured leg said, "It's because you're old, Grandad." I looked back and replied in a matter of fact tone, "No, it's not that at all, I'm only sixty years older than you, George."

He stared back and a few seconds later replied, "That's a lot, Grandad."

The day following our return home was a Sunday and I went to the A&E Department at Pinderfields Hospital and was given a pair of crutches and an appointment for the Physiotherapy Department several days hence. With regular visits to the Physiotherapy Department, the injury took about two months to come right. In the summer of that year, Wendy and I spent about five weeks up in the Scottish Highlands, predominantly wild camping in the motorhome.

There are no trespass laws in Scotland, so having ensured that we had plenty of food and water, we simply stopped wherever we wished. Some of our stops saw us at the side of roads, where a few steps from the motorhome meant that we were on the beach. In fact, knowing the Highlands as we do, we were able to stop at remote locations and walk on beaches that had no other footprints but our own. Out on the North West Coast, and just above Kinlochbervie, Oldshoremore is one such place, with its beautiful isolated and stunning beach.

On occasion, since we moved back from Scotland, Wendy has been curious about wanting to see what Briarbank, our old home, was like now. At one point, we made the journey there and parked in the small car park at the bottom of the driveway and proceeded to walk around the dirt road to the back of the property. There we saw a sign advertising 'tea & coffee', so we made our way down to the back of the bungalow.

After an initial greeting, we were shown to the front garden and once seated we enjoyed our drinks. Towards the end, Wendy announced to the lady that we used to live there, and this resulted in us getting a guided tour of the place. We eventually said our goodbyes and Wendy said to me that she now felt contented that she had paid Briarbank one last visit.

Both Wendy and I often say that we could quite easily live in the motorhome and it has surely proved to be one of the best things that we have ever purchased. Last year (2019) saw us again spend around five weeks up in the Highlands, along with trips elsewhere either side of the Scottish visit.

Wendy's sister Jenny had travelled over from Canada on a number of occasions over the last ten to fifteen years, staying with us of late, and in September last year Wendy went on a planned three-week trip to visit Jenny in Canada. Her one previous trip on an aeroplane was approximately twenty years ago, when she had gone on holiday to Fuerteventura with Teresa, so she was a little daunted this time around.

On the day of her flight we drove down to Manchester Airport and, by all accounts, going through the airport procedures and flying wasn't too daunting after all for her. Three weeks later, she arrived back having had a great time; Jenny had drawn up a terrific itinerary of things to do and sights to see, such as Niagara Falls.

Following our experiences during the 1980s, we have both taken an active interest in national party politics and the effects that they have on the lives of others as well as our own. Since the middle of 2017, national politics have been dominated by Britain's referendum decision to leave the European Union (EU). For the right-wing ideologue members of the Tory European Research Group (ERG) this was the ultimate opportunity for the country to become nigh on a totally free market economy by getting rid of the collective regulatory framework of the twenty-seven members of the EU.

It was claimed that Britain will be able to trade openly and freely under the rules of the World Trade Organisation (WTO). Without entering into the full ramifications of the benefits that we were told would be available to the British people, the Vote Leave campaign bus had blazoned on the side of it that leaving would mean an extra £350 million extra each week for the NHS. Moreover, we would be able to strike our own trade deals with other nations and, in short, as has happened throughout time, the British people were once more fed a giant helping of *pie in the sky* (the term was coined in the early twentieth century by Joe Hill, member of the Industrial Workers of the World Trade Union – fondly known as the Wobblies) followed by a massive dessert of *jam tomorrow*. Sadly, once again they fell for it. Given that Britain is the fifth richest economy in the world, what these great 'new opportunities' and individual benefits people can expect from leaving the EU is beyond me and I have yet to meet an individual who can explain the ramifications to me.

On the run up to the referendum held on 23 June 2016, I happened to call into the local barber's shop in the village. I took a seat as there were three or four lads before me. They were having a discussion about the pros and cons of being in or out of the EU and, having sat for some time listening to the discussion, Paul the barber said to me, "What do you think, Colin?"

In response, I said, "Well, we're told that leaving will allow the country to make our own laws, but we already have the power to do that. Like you, I have seen financial cuts to the NHS, adult social care and all manner of public services, even down to the fact that some local authorities have had to close public toilets.

We are already the fifth richest country in the world, so economically what does coming out of the EU mean? Are we going to overtake Japan, China and America in our future economic performance? The only benefit for working people is that our employment rights are enshrined in EU law. The benefits of coming out are for big business only and not for the likes of us." No one replied back.

Over the past ten years or so the UK economy hasn't performed too well and before the 12 December 2019 December, general election predictions were that Britain was on the verge of a recession and that, internationally, we were on the edge of a global economic recession. Both Wendy and I were hoping for the election of a progressive Labour government that would reverse the ten years of cuts to the NHS and other public services. Disappointingly, the electorate voted for the pro-Brexit Tory Party and more of the same.

Chapter 23

Me and Old Age

Prior to becoming a university undergraduate in 1986 at the age of thirty-five, I never really thought about the ageing process and, if pressed on the matter, then my thoughts and opinions would have fallen into the negative stereotypical view of ageing. That is to say, growing old means that we simply reach a stage where we will have 'had our day' and become 'past it'. To put things more broadly, that 'stage' is where older age means there is an inevitable decline and degenerative process in both our physiological and biological powers and hence, to some extent, we become a burden on society.

However, as with so many other areas of life, studying Social Policy and especially Sociology in both a conscientious and meaningful way has enabled me to step outside of my day-to-day world, with its pre-existing views and opinions, in order to look at the world anew.

As mentioned earlier in my final year of studies, I elected for a course that considered old age in a modern society and the topic for my dissertation looked at the way pensioner groups reacted to aspects of ageism. I came to the conclusion then – and believe even more so today – that old age, as with so many realities of life, is socially constructed and is a process of multi-dimensional inequality, which has its roots in life history and the context of social political and economic policy.

As someone who is now approaching his seventieth birthday, it is my experience that amongst older individuals there is an immense variability in the process of ageing, which means that whilst physical ageing is inevitable, physical disability or dependency is not. For example, as a keen motorcyclist, over the years I have met and heard of a number of bikers who were in their seventies. The oldest one that I have met was a very fit-looking eighty-three-year-old who was dressed in his one-piece leathers and riding a very 'meaty' sports bike.

To ride such bikes at speed requires both physical and mental capabilities. Whilst ageing can cause the slowing down of mental processes, for some older individuals the stimulus of life experiences can improve psychological functioning. As a point of reference, chronological age is used quite extensively, often to assist bureaucracy and administration, but often in a simplistic and arbitrary way.

The government uses chronological age to determine when both men and women can retire from work and receive a state pension. From the mid-1930s onwards men were able to retire at the age of sixty-five – though it wasn't until 1948 that they became entitled to a state pension. As I grew up in the fifties and sixties, I remember hearing promises from politicians that, for both men and women, as the economy thrives with the introduction of new technology and Britain becomes more wealthy – as was inevitable, or so it sounded – then the age of retirement will gradually come down, so that retired workers may enjoy the fruits of their labour and more leisure time. This emphasis on more leisure time was meant to be a move away from the situation whereby folk retired from toil only to die a few years later. Indeed, for many years with women's retirement age at sixty, again I remember yet more false promises that it was only a matter of time before the retirement age for men would be reduced to match that of women.

However, as with all social policy within capitalist societies, it is highly tenuous and, regarding retirement and pension entitlement following the banking crisis of 2008, two years later in 2010 the chancellor of the Exchequer decided to raise the retirement age for women to that of men, that is sixty-five. With further increases, the current retirement ages are women sixty-six and men sixty-seven, with plans for further age increases in the offing. One can be forgiven for thinking that it is little wonder that there is currently an issue of obesity when, over the years, successive governments have fed the people on huge amounts of pie in the sky followed by even larger helpings of jam tomorrow.

Put simply, the government's argument appears at first sight to be plausible – "people are now living longer and hence there is a bigger *burden* on the rest of the working population". Again, it is the use of such loaded wording – especially in the midst of a period of austerity – which is designed to enter the consciousness of the electorate and serve to divide opinion thus – "why should we work to pay for them to retire at sixty-five and get a state pension when we're still slogging our guts out?"

Firstly, as I have said, it is a fact of life that all social policy areas are tenuous under capitalist economies, hence the broken promises as with pensions, along with the *'never ending story'* with present and historic governments' efforts to deal with poverty.

Secondly, market economics has no interest in social justice, as profit and more profit is their sole goal, and therefore they will always look to invest where it will financially benefit them, that is in countries with a low tax regime and low wages. Lifting the retirement age is but one of many measures designed to reduce the amount of taxation required for ongoing pensions and other public services.

Thirdly, the way in which the government presented its argument implies that for some unexplained reason all of a sudden it has come about that people are in fact living longer and this in itself is a huge and unexpected surprise that no one has been able to foresee. In effect demographic changes impacting on people's longevity have been occurring, certainly throughout the twentieth century, and indeed William Beveridge in the 1930s took such changes into account when drafting his blueprint for welfare changes. In 1954 the Conservative government set up the Phillips Commission to consider purely and simply the demography of older people in relation to the future costs of financial expenditure on government coffers. This they did and were successful in more or less predicting the correct number of retired people right up to 1979. In the late 1950s Richard Titmus, the British social scientist, expressed his concern about the constant use of the term 'burden of an ageing population'. The problem is that all governments adopt a short-term view and seem only to be concerned with the period in which they are in office – hopefully, at the end of this successfully getting re-elected. Since the late 1970s we have had an adversarial political system whose foundations are diametrically opposed class interests with ongoing antagonisms and, along with the uncertainties of a boom and bust economic system, these factors do not facilitate long-term rational planning. A single party true representative democracy would be significantly more effective.

Fourthly, there can be no doubt that some workers may want to continue working rather than retire, but at times of economic recession, older workers historically have been encouraged to give up work – no doubt with the tacit view and acceptance by them that they have 'had their day' – in order to allow jobs to be offered to younger people. Juxtaposed with this, since the 1980s, when firms have been euphemistically 'downsizing' or seeking to make 'efficiency savings' older workers have often been discarded largely because they are on higher pay grades than others, and this has often been deemed as 'acceptable' because these newly unemployed workers can slip into retirement. Successive governments have adopted an arbitrary and restricted view of chronological retirement, with older people viewed as a homogenous mass when in effect, as with the rest of society, they are marked by diversity of class, gender, ethnicity and mobility and overall factors of functional age.

Functional age is problematic and difficult to measure, due to the differing occupations that people have had over the course of their lifetime, for example, manual work as opposed to a job demanding less physical strain on the body. Many look forward to the cessation of full-time burdensome work, whilst others look more positively towards pursuing activities that had previously been restricted to them. On the other hand, retirement can be a disaster to those who were devoted to work, have few or no other interests, and have inadequate income.

Some eight years ago as Bernard (my sister's husband) approached the age of sixty-five and retirement, he made a poignant comment to me that several of his peers had passed away shortly after they had retired from work. Frankly, at the age of sixty-seven, when I personally chose to retire,

I had worked for fifty-two years since leaving school at the age of fifteen. I had had enough of manual work and, in fact, I was pleased to finish altogether. No doubt like many others I don't want to see yet again the lengthening of retirement whereby the number of years following the cessation of work to death become squeezed into a mere few.

Since my last hernia surgery, I constantly used a hernia support belt when working and today I put up with frequent discomfort due to wear and tear in my neck, 'trigger finger', arthritis in my right wrist and weakness in my arms and shoulders. One of the things that I certainly do not miss is having my life dictated by clocks and the slavish concept of time itself. Over the years, I have worked on building sites where the builders' own employees have had to 'clock in' by use of a 'clocking in machine', but the resistance to this would often lead to some recalcitrant worker putting building sand into the inner workings of them as a crude form of industrial sabotage.

Now that I am retired, I take our two Jack Russells for longer exercise enjoying the semi-rural environment and the many different walks, stopping on occasion to listen to nothing else but the cacophony of bird song or the wind rushing through the trees. I now have the time to admire nature and marvel at the number of 'wild' flowers, so labelled and consequently often discounted as being of no note. On occasion, I stop and take a photograph of a flower or one that might be lending itself to a butterfly or a bee, both busying about searching for pollen. Time just to simply enjoy looking at my surroundings, including the different types of grass.

Having been urged over the years to save for our retirement by successive governments, due to the banking crisis and the ensuing austerity measures, like many other older persons, we were then and still are, ten years later, affected by the significantly low interest rates impacting upon our meagre savings. Whilst this is bad enough, it is small beer compared to the fact that over the years many workers have been mis-sold private pensions by unscrupulous and greedy predators and so their retirement plans have had to be significantly adjusted.

One of the myths surrounding the rigid concept of retirement is that older people have ceased to be productive. The concept of retirement is perhaps a counterproductive one, in that it does nothing to lift the stature of older people and only serves to perpetuate negative myths and stereotypes. For example, we don't say that we have retired from school. A more and suitable term would indicate some form of transitional third phase in life, which is seen and viewed not in any ageist way. Sadly, our society is geared to this narrow notion of production attached to that of formal work and, as a concept, retirement lends itself to this myth of older people being unproductive; having now wound down, they simply want to 'potter around the garden'.

Of course, older people reduce their formal production when they cease work yet, on the other hand, many remain immensely productive in the absolute wider sense of the word. For example, some older people may want to continue in formal employment whilst others can be found in innumerable volunteer capacities working – and being productive – in multiple kinds of working environments. As Wendy and I have frequently visited several hospitals over the years, older people are visibly around, from staffing formal enquiry desks to running internal cafes. With affordable children's daycare being yet another perennial social policy issue, many grandparents constantly undertake informal caring roles concerning grandchildren, enabling the parents to go out to work and be productive, and thus saving the state countless sums of money in childcare. There are also those who care for sick and disabled relatives, yet again easing the financial strain on the public purse.

Around nine years ago, Wendy's mum, Iris, began to experience problems with her memory so on several occasions we travelled to Seacroft in Leeds where she lived by herself and, following visits to see a memory nurse, we were eventually advised that she had vascular dementia.

This being the early stages, she was able to remain at home, though the medication given to slow down the progress of the condition caused her to have side effects such as dizziness and it was withdrawn. The next-door neighbour to Iris was a young woman called Trish and she had three young children of her own. Trish would regularly take a meal around to Iris and also keep an eye on her and telephone Wendy with frequent updates, though we ourselves did drive into Leeds in order to visit her quite regularly.

Certain aids and adaptations were fitted to the home to enable Iris to hopefully move around safely but, following a number of months and the deterioration of Iris's condition, it had become clear that she needed more formal care input. A family meeting was convened at her home, hosted by someone from the Social Services Department. This culminated in this person saying that Iris qualified for additional care, but it would have to be given by a private agency.

I was aware that, from the 1980s onwards, there had been the gradual out sourcing and privatisation of both community home help services and care homes and, when I queried why the local authority could not use its own home help service, the reply came back that her manager would not be pleased with her if the work was not outsourced to the private sector. She seemed to pick up on my concern and, almost in defence of her decision, went on to say that whilst some private agencies were not particularly good, the one she was thinking of was, and in fact they were caring for her own mother. In hindsight, one can only imagine whether that was true or not.

The daily visits would be for a half-hour duration and a record of the events were to be documented in a log that was left with Iris. Following the introduction of the service, Wendy was soon receiving calls from Trish that the worker was frequently staying with Iris much less than the half hour and, upon visiting Iris herself and reading the log, we became unsure what was being done. For example, the daily log would often read "Asked Iris if she had had dinner and she said that she had." Well, most people are aware that dementia sufferers lose their short-term memory first, and our own experience with Iris was that if asked she was unable to recall what she had eaten for dinner. We became increasingly concerned when one day Trish rang and told Wendy that the carer had turned up and, whilst she went in to see Iris, her assumed boyfriend stayed in the car, holding on his knee what was presumably their dog.

After five minutes or so, the young woman came out and they drove off. The young worker was about eighteen years old and, whilst we did not want to be ageist, Wendy and I discussed the young woman's level of experience in looking after people suffering with dementia. Never had she once prepared a meal or even a sandwich for Iris and, along with a number of concerns that had come to our attention over several months, we decided to complain. In the interim, Trish maintained a watchful eye over Iris, frequently taking her meals in.

Following the prescribed complaints procedure, I wrote to the company head office and, in due course, I gained a response that Wendy and I remained wholly unhappy with. Given this, I wrote to Iris's member of parliament who, as a former leader of Leeds City Council, in turn contacted senior management at the Social Services Department. Following a suitable period of time, we received a response that not only upheld our initial complaint, but found a number of other issues; most notably, there was the fact that none of the agency's staff had ever received any training regarding the care of people with dementia!

The 'home care service' was withdrawn and initial reaction might be to criticise the young worker, but it is quite common to hear of such agencies, both in the community and in care homes, to let staff work with little or no training, which would be an added-on cost for the company. Given the woefully low social status of older people throughout our society, it is relatively easy for such firms to operate and attempt to maximise their profit margins whilst allegedly caring for our older citizens. Many of these workers are earning only the minimum wage, and this includes those who do have some qualification, leading many to resort to using food banks. Some months ago I recall someone from the National Care Association – the co-ordinating body for care homes – being interviewed about the future introduction of the proposed new living wage and he commented on the financially ruinous nature for all care homes from any increase in staff wages.

Following the judgement on our complaint, Wendy's mum soon had to enter a residential care home that had previously been visited by Wendy and one of her sisters. At the time of visiting this new facility, Wendy later told me that her sister, noticing the relative new building, had commented to her that "This really looks to be a nice place."

Wendy had replied that, "Just because it is new doesn't mean to say that it is good."

However, with the commitment from the home that they were well equipped to care for dementia patients, Iris formally moved in. Initially, things seemed fine, as when we visited Iris was in the lounge area, along with other older folks, and at this stage she was able to wash, dress and eat her meals herself. However, following several months she deteriorated suddenly and was confined to her bedroom by the staff. When we visited, she would be sat in a chair facing the small television with the subtitles on with her back to the only window. As Wendy commented to me, dementia patients are unable to make any sense of television subtitles.

Iris still knew when she needed to go to the toilet and, after several weeks, on one visit Wendy went looking for a staff member because her mum needed the toilet. The residential care home manager brusquely told her that Iris now had an incontinence pad on and when that was soiled then a staff member would place her on the bed and change it.

Alarm bells were now starting to ring and, not long after this, when Wendy and her sister Mandy made a mid-week visit, their concern was heightened further when Mandy went looking for a member of staff. Upon finding one, she recounted that the sad woman had simply broke down into tears, stating that she was the only member of staff caring for all of the residents on that floor.

She then said to Mandy, "But if you come on a weekend there will be lots more staff on duty, and do you know why?"

Mandy still shaken by the woman's initial reaction shook her head.

The woman said, "Because that's when most people visit! We are simply unable to carrying out the work properly that we have been trained to do."

Upon hearing this, almost immediately, Wendy began making enquiries with other care homes, especially when the manager carried out a massive U-turn, telling her that they could not offer the level of support required for dementia residents like Iris, despite declaring some months earlier at the point of admission that they could! Arguably the profit motive for such homes is to fill any vacant places in order to ensure ongoing funding from the authority. Not too long after this, Iris moved into a nursing home on Barwick Road in Leeds.

Within a week, the plastic toddler's drinking cup with its plastic teat had been discarded and she was back drinking her tea out of a 'proper' mug and, when visiting with Wendy, I willingly became the 'tea boy'. She still remained medication-free for her dementia, due to side effects, but when we visited she was always in the lounge area and, on occasion, had her hair done by the visiting hairdresser, or she was listening to the various entertainers that visited the home.

She was visibly much happier, and it was clear that there was more interaction with individual residents. Dementia patients especially need stimulation. However her steady decline continued, and she passed away in the home where she had been well looked after.

Iris was another woman who, along with people like my mam and millions of others, participated in the Second World War effort and, added to this, she must have undergone untold worry when Frank, her husband, had been taken as a prisoner of war by the Nazis. He himself gave twenty-five years of his life to his country through serving in the armed services. How extremely sad that, like so many others, come retirement and their eventual need for help from the nation's formal care services, it should pathetically amount to that as outlined above.

Paralleled with this reality of older people's lives, the hypocrisy of our country is such that periodically it briefly immerses itself in the glorification of war. Such commemorative events are led by the so-called 'great and the good', who vow at these events that "we shall remember them" and "lest we forget". During the 1980s the concept of 'community care' became the new and frequently used term, but the promise never materialised as local authority services, such as the home help service, began to charge those vulnerable older people wanting help. Following on from the dismal service provision of the 1980s, there has been a significant growth in private residential and nursing homes, making care for the older and elderly person increasingly institutionalised.

Older people value their independence and should be afforded community services to enable them to reside in their own homes for as long as possible. Throughout all of the formal care services, the fact that older people are seen as isolated recipients of such services can underpin what is often an unequal power relationship. Alongside this, one can argue that, when older people themselves submit to dominant stereotype notions of old age, it serves to both promote and legitimise infantilising and wider aspects of discrimination that are in effect ageist and possibly abusive.

Over the past number of years, I have noted a degree of further anecdotal evidence about the way older people are treated. A number of years ago, I carried out a small plumbing job for an older man whose wife had recently died and, in a therapeutic sort of way, he was at pains to tell me some of the instances when he had visited her in a local hospital and witnessed the lack of dignity afforded to her. Her hair was often in disarray and, on one occasion when he visited, she had been placed in the chair at the side of her bed with her nightie up around her waist displaying her private parts. I can still see the sadness in his face as he spoke and the anguish when he solemnly confessed to me how much he regrets failing to speak to staff on her behalf.

Another local lady, who is a dog walker that I occasionally bump into, told me that a couple of years ago her elderly mum was admitted into a local hospital because of a broken hip incurred due to a fall in her own home. Whilst in there, she had occasion to be taken to the toilet by a member of staff and, being left there for some time, she had fallen and broken her other hip. This lady went on to say that, because her mum was incontinent, one evening that she visited she had taken a pad. She changed her mum herself only to find that when she visited the following evening – twenty-four hours later – her mum was still wearing the same incontinence pad!

I was told by another person that, upon visiting an older relative, he found that the hospital ward itself stank of urine. Other local people have told me of loved ones going into care homes only to be taken out and placed elsewhere due to the dissatisfaction of family members at how the homes were being run and the impact on their loved ones.

Any historical overview of the welfare state will reveal that, from its very inception, both the state pension and local authority personal services for the elderly have frequently been criticised for being under-funded by the Exchequer. In contrast with this, the post-war period saw a boom in private occupational pensions that have been hugely subsidised by the Exchequer with tax handouts. The people who benefited most were those on high incomes, who had signed up for what became known as 'top hat' schemes.

During the 2017 general election campaign Teresa May, the Tory prime minister, openly declared that adult social care in Britain needed reform. This followed on from the supposed sudden revelation that older people in Britain were all of a sudden living longer, therefore this was yet another 'eureka' moment for the Tories. After ten years of austerity, affecting year on year the ability of local authorities up and down the country to adequately meet the social care needs of adults, as always the Tory response is "What, me guv? No no. I didn't do anything, guv. We have just found out about it."

Again, it was the classic Tory stealth approach to a public service, de-fund and allow it to not work as it should, wait for complaints to come in and then privatise it. Well, much of it is privatised and supported by taxpayers' money, so Teresa May announced her great idea. In care homes, those people that own a home are compelled to sell it with the proceeds going towards the ongoing cost of their care. Well, it was now being proposed that if any vulnerable older person should need community adult social care, and they own their own home, the ongoing costs would be added up and then, when they died, their home would be sold to pay back the cost of their social care. Great, not only do older people have to endure – at times indifferent and shambolic – privatised care services, but now they can pay for the privilege also.

The plain truth is that, across class, ethnicity, gender and sexual orientation, we all have the potential to grow old and therefore, collectively, at least we should be concerned that services are appropriate and well delivered. Imagine the outcry if children's nursery provision was run in the same indifferent manner as those for older people. More importantly, when one talks about social discrimination, where is the overall moral conscience?

Quite recently I was watching the television when I both saw and heard a senior Tory politician deem it necessary to declare emphatically that he was a Christian. Indeed, at times over the course of any particular year, the media sees fit to enlighten their audiences with images of prime ministers and such like either going in or out of some church or another – especially at Christmas – implicitly illustrating their Christian credentials. Few would doubt the fact that morality underpins so many Christian beliefs. It is often said that the test of any modern society is how it looks after its sick, disabled and vulnerable people. If one was to posit this to those that are both self-styled capitalists and self-styled Christians, one can only imagine that they would say.

"Yes, of course we are indeed Christians and we care deeply about the plight of the sick, disabled and vulnerable. We only wish that the economic system would allow us to do much more for those in need, but frustrating as it is for us too, it won't."

Then, having responded and pointed out to the worthy brethren the ongoing gross inequalities in health, incomes and the ownership of wealth, they would no doubt respond saying, "Again you are right to say that it is something around 7% of the population who own the vast majority of wealth in Britain, but nothing can be done to change that because those in that 7% are the *wealth creators* and without them there would be no investment and jobs, so there is no other way but the current system."

Jesus himself was an ordinary workman, a joiner or carpenter and, presumably, if he walked anonymously in our midst today, lost his job and applied for Universal Credit, then he too would have to wait five weeks for any monies and somehow pay his rent and feed himself in the meantime And if he fell afoul of the benefit system, like countless others have done, then he would have his benefit sanctioned. As the Son of God, after visiting the food bank for some basic necessities of life, if he stopped in the street on his way home and asked the gathered self-styled worthy capitalist and Christian brethren why so many men, women and children do not have the basic necessaries of life and go hungry given the development of modern civilisation over the last 2,000 years, he would be told, "We are sorry, but it is impossible for *the system* to be structured in any other way to what it is." As if to imply that it is God-given and *not* socially constructed.

In December 2019 it was announced that the Chinese city of Wuhan, the capital of the central province of Hubei, was witnessing the emergence of a previously unknown and highly virulent disease named Coronavirus (Covid 19). This is a disease that essentially attacks the lungs along with other organs, such as kidneys. As it quickly began to cross international borders, countries began to introduce their own 'lockdown', along with measures to deal with the virus and the World Health Organisation (WHO) declared it as a world pandemic. In turn, the United Kingdom announced a 'lockdown' on 23 March 2020, and this has meant the closure of schools, businesses (apart from food outlets) and many workers are off work, having been what is termed furloughed. People have been asked to self-isolate in their own homes, go out and exercise once a day, 'but maintain social distancing' by staying at least two metres apart from each other.

People that fall into a vulnerable group – those aged seventy and over – category must stay indoors. Others with conditions such as asthma and diabetes fall into the vulnerable category, and here Wendy is included because she takes immuno-suppressant medication.

Though the government has tried to put a *gloss* on its efforts to deal with the pandemic from the very outset, with the passage of time a number of criticisms have emerged, especially some concerning the welfare of older people. From the beginning of the pandemic, the daily update of deaths by the government has related to only those people that had died in hospital, though from the start of April onwards reports began filtering through about the growing number of deaths of both older people and staff in care homes. At the start of the pandemic Britain had the least hospital beds per capita than most European countries. Because of this shortage of hospital beds at the start of the lockdown, over 25,000 vulnerable older people were discharged from hospital wards and into care homes up and down the country. The vast majority of these people were not tested for Covid 19 prior to their hospital discharge and as a consequence many were infected and took the disease with them, ultimately contributing to the deaths of over 20,000 care home residents and staff. Moreover some months later it was reported that many of these older people had also left hospital with DO NOT RESUSCITATE attached to their notes though such drastic measures had never been discussed with either the patients or their relatives

Over the past several months, many people have recognised the interconnected way in which their lives depend on other workers for a multiple range of services. Ironically, many of those standing outside their homes applauding the NHS workers each week will have voted at the recent general election for a Tory government believing that the last ten years and, in particular, the NHS cuts, including very lengthy freezing of public sector wages, was necessary. The question is will these same people – who now have some awareness of the inter-related way in which their lives and their families are collectively dependent on these key workers – continue to offer their support as and when public sector cuts are introduced by the government? Will they be happy for NHS workers to suffer again a pay freeze for several years? And given the recent heightened public awareness that the vast majority of care workers are paid no more than the minimum wage, will they support any efforts to get this derisory pay increased to that of the living wage? Or will this recent stirring of a collective consciousness give way to the return of the individualism with its silo mentality that largely prevailed before the pandemic crisis? For the government, they will attempt to claim that all economic and political ills are firmly down to the experience of Covid 19 and it will be another case of 'errors have been made, others will be blamed'.

The current period and what the future brings will be perused over and considered by the historians, but what and how that is presented for public consumption will be open to conjecture. Whilst such public issues are discussed and debated in the context of a capitalist political, economic and social cul de sac, it is worth reiterating my earlier point that social issues are often shared within a community and change *may* be made with structural modifications. However, if this isn't possible, then at that point it must be acknowledged that positive and lasting structural change requires the renewal of the whole social system. Though, in response to this, some may ask, why? Just like many others, my vision is of things that never were and I say why not? As I approach my seventieth birthday later this year I feel that, although I have lived much of my life, I still have a life to live, and I trust that I have demonstrated that you can only understand the history of an individual by understanding the history of the society in which they have lived.

The End

Ingram Content Group UK Ltd.
Milton Keynes UK
UKHW021222210523
422036UK00011B/119